RELEVANCE REGAINED

From Top-Down Control to Bottom-Up Empowerment

H. Thomas Johnson

THE FREE PRESS
A Division of Macmillan, Inc.
New York

Maxwell Macmillan Canada
Toronto

Maxwell Macmillan International
New York Oxford Singapore Sydney

THE FREE PRESS
A Division of Simon & Schuster
1230 Avenue of the Americas
New York, NY 10020

THE FREE PRESS and colophon are trademarks
of Simon & Schuster Inc.

Manufactured in the United States of America

10 9 8 7 6 5 4 3 2 1

Library of Congress Cataloging-In-Publication Data

Johnson, H. Thomas
        Relevance regained : from top-down control to bottom-up
Empowerment / H. Thomas Johnson.
        p.   cm.
Includes bibliographical references and index.
ISBN: 0-7432-3627-0
1. Industrial management.   2. Industrial management—Data
processing.   3. Management information systems.   4. Customer
relations—Data processing.   5. Total quality management—Data
processing.   6. Suggestion systems.   7. Managerial accounting.
8. Competition.   I. Title.
HD31.J555   1992
65—dc20   92-6762
                                                               CIP

For information regarding special discounts for bulk purchases, please contact Simon &
Schuster Special Sales at 1-800-456-6798 or business@simonandschuster.com

For Elaine and Thom
with love

Aim therefore at no less than all the world,
Aim at the highest . . .
—Milton, *Paradise Regained*

CONTENTS

Contents

PREFACE

Everyone in the business world today realizes that the key to long-run competitiveness is total customer satisfaction. But few companies seem to understand how radically their customary ways of doing business must change for them to profitably compete in today's global economy. Most seem to view the change as an evolutionary progression from the present, not a revolutionary overhaul of the way they do business. To profitably satisfy its customers in the long run, a company must be run as though the customer were in charge.

Impeding the revolutionary changes companies must make to be totally customer driven is management information. Specifically, the performance measures most companies use to control behavior encourage employees to subordinate customer satisfaction to accounting results. Accounting-based performance measures drive employees to manipulate processes and cajole customers in order to achieve cost and revenue targets. Inevitably, this practice diminishes competitiveness and impairs long-run profitability.

The pathway to long-run competitiveness requires companies to develop performance measures that drive employees to keep statistical control over processes that satisfy customer expectations. Part I of this book explains how American businesses after the 1950s, by using top-down accounting results to control behavior, impaired their ability to run flexible processes capable of adapting to and satisfying customers' expectations. Part II proceeds tentatively to explain how process-level information can enable employees to achieve the flexibility and responsiveness companies require to compete on a global basis.

Considering the demands companies must meet to compete in the global economy, I believe that accounting has no place controlling how people work in today's business enterprise. Control is the major theme of what companies practice and universities teach under the name of management accounting. Accounting information should not, I think, be used to control business operations. Accounting goals should not be used to direct and control workers or managers. Ac-

Figure P–2
The Top-Down Control Cycle

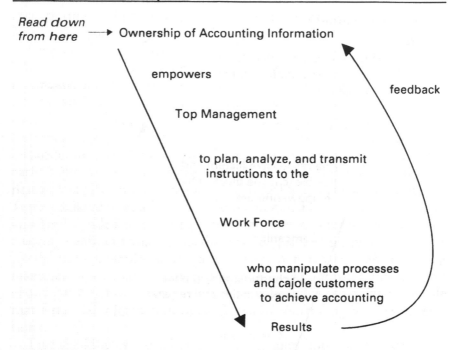

Read down
from here ——▶ Ownership of Accounting Information

empowers

feedback

Top Management

to plan, analyze, and transmit
instructions to the

Work Force

who manipulate processes
and cajole customers
to achieve accounting

Results

customers and who run the processes. Empowerment implies ownership of information—the key to learning. Constant learning by empowered workers is the key to change—the demand for unceasing
change being caused by the power of choice that new information
technologies give the customer.

Managing from accounting information according to the "top-
down control cycle" shown in Figure P–2 has led to two decades of
stagnant productivity and shrinking economic opportunities for
American workers. Accounting systems, focused as they are on financial results, cannot provide information about sources of productivity
and competitive opportunity in today's economy. Accounting systems
do not provide real-time information about customer expectations
and process capabilities, nor does accounting information originate
with the people who carry out the processes that fulfill customer expectations. Instead, management accounting information originates in
systems that top managers maintain in order to pass down instructions
to subordinate managers and other members of the work force who
actually run processes and face customers. For decades American companies have forced employees to fulfill accounting-based targets by

manipulating processes, not to fulfill customer expectations by controlling processes. The result is diminished productivity and lost competitiveness.

If companies are to compete effectively, they must remove accounting information from their operational control systems and relieve their accounting departments of responsibility for providing information to control business operations. American businesses do not have to wait for any new management tools to solve lagging productivity and poor competitiveness. The tools were discovered years ago, by countless companies struggling to be world-class competitors. They encompass actions generally described under the rubrics "JIT" (just-in-time) and "TQM" (total quality management). However, actions consistent with JIT or TQM usually conflict with actions prescribed by traditional management accounting controls. The search for competitive excellence must begin, then, by replacing management accounting controls with information that triggers actions geared to achieving success in today's competitive environment.

Building a new management information base to support global competitive excellence is not an easy, one-step task. Accounting will play an unaccustomed role in the new management information base. Management accounting practice in the past forty years has had companies *control with accounting results* by having people manipulate outputs of processes to achieve accounting targets. Global management information will have companies *check with the accounting result,* while empowering people to control variation of output from processes.[1] In a globally competitive organization, everyone understands that long-term profitability is achieved by improving customer satisfaction, not by trying to sell the largest possible quantities of what the accounting system says are the highest margin products. They understand both the quality imperatives of TQM and the operational imperatives of JIT. Information about customer satisfaction and about variation in processes can move companies continuously closer to achieving the imperatives of competitive excellence. Defining that information and those imperatives is the task that awaits us.

Portland, Oregon
December 1991

PART I

RELEVANCE LOST IN TOP-DOWN CONTROL

To be competitive, businesses must adopt new ways of thinking about business, not new tools and solutions designed to improve on old practices. Preventing businesses from adopting—even from understanding the need for—new ways of thinking are the accounting-based performance measures managers customarily use to control operations. Accounting systems provide important and useful financial scorecard information. However, using their information to control a company's relationships with customers, employees, and suppliers can trigger behavior that impairs long-run competitiveness and profitability.

The first chapter of this book describes the pernicious influence management accounting information has had on business performance, especially in the United States, in the past three decades. Chapters 2 and 3 trace the recent evolution and the adverse consequences of those management accounting practices in American business.

The message offered in these chapters is not that businesses must improve their management accounting practices in order to become competitive in today's global economy. That erroneous prescription has been offered in recent years by countless management experts, consultants, and professional societies. Instead, the new and different message presented here is that businesses must eliminate top-down accounting-based controls. Accounting-based control information motivates the work force to *manipulate* processes for financial ends. Global competition requires companies to use bottom-up information that empowers the work force to *control* processes for customer satisfaction.

CHAPTER 1

INFORMATION, ACTION, AND BUSINESS PERFORMANCE

The basic cause of sickness in American industry and resulting un-
employment is failure of top management to manage. . . . [Reform
requires] transformation of the style of American management . . .
a whole new structure, from foundation upward. . . . Long-term
commitment to new learning and new philosophy is required of
any management that seeks transformation.

—W. Edwards Deming[1]

The transformation of modern management exhorted by W. Edwards Deming must take place at once if American business is to regain
its competitive edge in today's global economy. The question con-
fronting CEOs is not whether they must change, but rather, what kind
of transformation must occur to revitalize American companies. Deming postulates a need to transform the entire structure, style, and philosophy of management—"from foundation upward." Undoubtedly
one of the most wrenching changes CEOs face is to realize that goals
formulated from accounting information no longer permit them to
manage companies effectively.

For the past three decades—a brief period in the history of business—
American business has behaved as if the pursuit of accounting goals were
the underlying force driving business competition. However, that belief
has been a primary reason for American business losing its competitive

edge. Goals reflecting only accounting information constrict managements' thinking, eliminating companies from global competition.

Only if CEOs rely on information that is relevant to the goals of
global competition will their firms survive in the 1990s and beyond.
This book explains why conventional management uses of accounting
information are a major cause of the current predicament in American
business, and it articulates the information and thinking companies
must adopt to become world-class competitors. A key message is that
the current revolution in information technology—based on the computer and the microprocessor—requires and enables CEOs to bring
about the transformation in management practices called for by Deming.

The coming of the computer, the transistor, and the integrated circuit after World War II put in motion forces that gave the customer
enormous power of choice. With customers able to choose the best of
what they want, wherever it is in the world, competitiveness now
means that companies must be responsive to customer wants and be
flexible: able to learn and adapt quickly to changes in those wants.
Top-down command and control information does not motivate the
work force to take actions that make companies responsive and flexible. Adapting flexibly to change requires constant learning and prompt
action by those people in a business who are closest to the customer.

Traditional accounting control systems assume that learning takes place
at the top—far away from customers and processes—and that new knowledge is transmitted down in the form of instructions. The information revolution has turned that assumption on its head. In competitive companies
today, the *entire* work force must be empowered to learn and to act
quickly. That power derives from ownership of "bottom-up" information about customer wants and about the processes people perform to
satisfy those wants. To facilitate learning and change, companies must
respond to real-time information from customers and processes. Fortu-
itously, modern information technology can give workers and managers
ownership of the processes they perform, at all levels, and thereby empower them to constantly improve at satisfying ever-changing customer
wants.

The two concerns of this book are to articulate the shortcomings of
traditional accounting control information and to suggest how new information can motivate behavior that fulfills the imperatives of competitive excellence. The next sections of this chapter highlight the
major themes the book develops as it discusses the shortcomings of the
past and the promise of changes to come. First we describe new
customer-focused approaches to doing business that require new in-

formation. Then we turn to the impediments to change created by existing accounting-based control information. We conclude this chapter by discussing the crucial role of top managers in leading the changes in information and behavior that will restore competitiveness to American business.

NEW APPROACHES TO DOING BUSINESS

"To survive in the global economy, change must become your way of life." Today's CEOs have heard this message and recognize the need for change. Moreover, most businesses are striving to meet this need. They are adopting new management practices at unprecedented rates. Unfortunately, these changes are not improving competitive performance nearly as much as hoped. The reality is that the changes needed are of a different sort—much more than even the most forward-looking CEOs realize.

For nearly fifteen years American businesses have tried a succession of strategies aimed at restoring markets and profits lost to foreign—mostly Japanese—competitors. Well-known acronyms denominate these strategies, most notably JIT (just-in-time), SPC (statistical process control), MRP (material requirements planning), TQM (total quality management), ABC (activity-based costing), TPM (total preventive maintenance), and QFD (quality function deployment). These strategies have helped countless companies improve performance. But the improvements generally seem to go only so far, and then taper off.

This problem appears most often in either of the following two cases: (1) A firm identifies new strategies for organizing work—usually associated with JIT (just-in-time)—which produce breakthroughs that generate substantial one-time gains in productivity, and then stop. Delighted with the results achieved by adopting Kanban-style production systems or by linking people and machines in focused work cells, managers attend seminars and call in consultants in a search for more such breakthroughs. Seldom, however, do they replicate their initial successes, and almost never do the new ideas spread throughout the organization. (2) A company discovers improvement strategies involving team-building and problem-solving processes—usually associated with TQM (total quality management). These strategies boost morale and generate excitement, at least for a while. But the gains in profitability often take a long time to appear. Pressure to get on with achieving bottom-line financial results diminishes enthusiasm for devoting time to the new improvement processes, and people return to business as usual.

What Are JIT and TQM?

JIT. Today, "just-in-time" usually refers to any improvement program that reduces the time needed to get a job done (i.e., lead time) by simplifying work. Once thought to be the exclusive domain of manufacturers in factory settings, JIT now is pursued avidly in service companies and in all parts of organizations, from white-collar functions in the back office to research and design laboratories. In its current guise, JIT originated at Toyota in the 1950s, in factory efforts to produce exactly what the customer wants, when the customer wants it. Many American exponents of JIT stress external features and results of early Japanese JIT, such as Kanban scheduling systems, reduced work-in-process (WIP) inventories, and reduced numbers of vendors. Japanese authorities, however, emphasize American scientific management influence on JIT and they stress the importance of its less visible features, such as the flexibility that follows from lead time reduction.

TQM. "Total quality management" refers to company-wide programs to empower workers and managers to solve problems scientifically with an eye to constantly improving customer satisfaction. Driven by a strong customer-focused mission, all personnel in a TQM environment pursue a well-defined *improvement process*, such as the highly publicized strategies articulated by Motorola and Xerox. TQM should be seen as a people-oriented way of running business, not just another way to achieve better results by pursuing business as usual.

The crucial cause of failure in these two cases is the limited perspective of company leaders. In both cases some change occurs, but nothing changes the basic principles that define a company's fundamental response to business problems. In the first case, company personnel may adopt JIT initiatives to improve productivity, and yet ignore the impact of those initiatives on the company's results-oriented, hierarchical principles of control. Therefore, when top management insists that all resources be utilized "efficiently," this demand clashes with the imperatives of JIT. In the end a few important gains take place, but not the sustained and continuous improvement achieved by a world-class competitor.

In the case of a company practicing TQM, managers introduce team-oriented, self-management techniques in a few processes. However, unless they reject the company's traditional, cost-focused principles when they make decisions, eventually they lose momentum.

Problem-solving teams examining processes do in fact implement changes, but the changes often are designed simply to increase efficiency or reduce cost. This short-sightedness unconsciously guides the organization farther and farther away from achieving world-class performance.

In the United States we see a great many examples of companies incorporating JIT with diminishing returns. Most American companies that have tried to develop strategies to compete globally did so first with JIT-oriented initiatives, beginning in the late 1970s and early 1980s. Relatively recently they have used TQM-style quality improvement strategies. The successful impact of TQM and JIT has often been acknowledged. Laudable efforts to eliminate waste by simplifying work flows, by focusing, and by linking processes, however, have been followed with alarming regularity by new obstacles. Most often human relations constitute the most serious problem for businesses trying to change. Stressed-out and alienated workers and suppliers remain—despite JIT or TQM.

Consider examples of problems created when companies move to JIT. Suppliers invited by their customers to attend JIT-training programs often feel they are receiving a hidden message: "We're shifting to JIT and *you* are responsible for the changes that will let us make the shift." Workers who have contributed time, energy, and brainpower to a workplace improvement campaign aren't given credit for success when the company flourishes. Typically in American firms dividends climb and top managers' salaries and bonuses soar into the stratosphere while "redundant" or "overly costly" workers are laid off or have wages scaled back. In other words, the old polarities of yesterday's business world—us and them—still exist in spite of the reduced WIP, the reduced lead times, and the higher customer satisfaction indexes. Top management must eliminate these polarities.

Whereas firms using JIT often face serious obstacles imposed by their hierarchical, top-down control systems, companies using team-focused TQM problem solving often pursue top-down accounting imperatives that cause them to implement solutions to problems that are antithetical to competitiveness. TQM teams frequently recommend solutions that are designed to achieve efficient use of resources by cutting costs. Problem-solving teams in a TQM company, in other words, seek old cost-focused solutions to problems, addressing imperatives of competition that were popular before anyone heard about Pareto charts and fishbone diagrams. Moreover, solutions designed to cut costs and maximize use of resources often use off-the-shelf management accounting tools for capital budgeting, make-buy analysis, or cost-volume-profit analysis.

For example, I once saw a "TQM guide for team leaders and facilitators" which contained a section on American-style cost-volume-profit break-even analysis juxtaposed to a section on the Seven Statistical Tools (Pareto diagrams, histograms, control charts, etc.) that are basic to Japanese quality programs. This bizarre mismatch is comparable to placing a recipe for Molotov cocktails among recipes for health breads. An equally bizarre mismatch of intentions and tools occurs when quality teams advocate spending time and resources on activity-based costing, an avant garde tool used to compile better product cost information. Activity-based product costs ostensibly focus a company's marketing strategy on profitable high runners rather than costly cats and dogs. This approach seems sound until customers reject the company's "most profitable" products. Eventually the company "efficiently" making "profitable" products must unload them at a discount.

To pursue JIT while keeping hierarchical financial controls in place or to implement TQM-style self-managed processes while equating improvement with cost reduction or increased margins makes no sense. To follow old management principles is incompatible with using well-designed, new strategies to improve performance and quality. Old management principles, left intact, drag down improvement initiatives from one side or the other: top-down hierarchical cost controls drag down JIT initiatives; cost-focused preferences for scale and speed drag down TQM initiatives.

Certainly, initiatives aimed at simplification of work or empowerment of workers will to some extent improve competitiveness. To become truly world-class competitors, however, businesses must simultaneously adopt *both* new ways of organizing work and new ways of organizing people. Unwavering devotion to cost-focused and adversarial management principles thwarts efforts to fulfill simultaneously both the time-focused and the team-oriented imperatives of competition in today's global economy. Hence, we see companies that know how to simplify and streamline work flows (i.e., JIT) or those that know how to lead people into creative, long-lasting relationships (i.e., TQM). But almost never do these companies seem to understand how their continuing attention to obsolete cost-focused imperatives of traditional competition impedes their efforts to achieve global competitive excellence—a state that I define as completely satisfying customers, creating growing opportunities for associates and suppliers (including suppliers of capital), and imposing no undue burdens on third parties in society—while continuously reducing time and resources.

If businesses in the 1990s are to compete, they must not allow misplaced loyalty to obsolete management principles to impair their performance. Companies that adhere to such thinking will follow the cost-focused imperatives that have guided American managers' actions for over forty years—especially the imperative to produce more, faster. Competitive firms, by contrast, will build relationships, empower people to solve problems, and provide satisfaction.

Companies will not follow today's imperatives of competition unless top managers are persuaded to stop using accounting-based information, especially costs, to *control* people, organizations, and work. Companies need accounting systems, surely, to provide information for financial reporting and planning. But the role of accounting systems must not be to supply information to control the work of operations personnel. "Managing by remote control" with accounting-based information perpetuates practices that contradict improvement strategies associated with competitiveness.

Competitive excellence requires constantly improving the ability to satisfy customers and constantly reducing variation in process outcomes. Accounting systems not only provide no information about either customer satisfaction or process variation; as I demonstrate later, cost accounting control targets trigger actions that in fact increase process variation and reduce customer satisfaction. Only companies that replace accounting-based management control information with problem-solving information that focuses on customers and processes will find it natural to adopt practices that fulfill the imperatives of competitive excellence in the global economy.

MANAGEMENT ACCOUNTING DOES NOT SUPPORT NEW APPROACHES TO BUSINESS

Management information affects business performance by shaping a company's goals and by influencing the actions people take to achieve those goals. If being responsive to customer wants and adapting flexibly to changes in those wants are deemed the relevant imperatives of competitiveness today, then management information in today's companies must prompt behavior that satisfies those imperatives.

For forty years *accounting* systems have provided the critical management information that determines goals and actions in American companies. Most companies today use accounting information to motivate actions that are intended to achieve an accounting goal, usually return on investment. But this goal misleads managers into chasing false imperatives. When management accounting information directs businesses, invariably two imperatives of competition emerge: always sustain output at a level to cover all costs, and always persuade customers to buy output at prices high enough to earn the market's required rate of return. A business governed by these two imperatives is misguided. It is comparable to a driver steering a car through the rearview mirror, or to a navigator piloting a ship by looking at its wake.

The point is, quite simply, that excessive reliance on management accounting information inevitably triggers actions antithetical to responsiveness and flexibility—the imperatives of success in the global economy. In pursuit of accounting results, management accounting decrees actions designed to push output and to cajole customers. However, this is not management's proper role today, and this book is intended to help managers reassess how accounting information leads them into such a role. Management information's true function, today, must be to help companies become *responsive*, by building relationships with satisfied customers, and *flexible*, by reducing variation, delays, and excess in processes.

Management information from customers and processes helps companies achieve these imperatives by empowering employees to solve problems and to improve constantly the output of customer-focused processes. Companies need information designed to empower employees to think and act decisively, using their own expertise and experience. Empowerment in this context means simply giving people "bottom-up" problem-solving information and asking them to continuously improve the output of processes. But instead of doing this, accounting controls used by most American businesses in the last forty years encourage people to *manipulate* (or tamper with) processes in order to achieve accounting cost and revenue targets that are dictated by "top-down" command and control information. These businesses view accounting return as their primary goal, not simply as a market-determined constraint they must satisfy by achieving the hallmark of global competitive excellence—exceeding expectations of customers, suppliers (including suppliers of capital), workers, and society at large.

Two premises underlie the use of information that has governed American business practice in recent decades. One is the premise that only managers know enough to translate information into competitive action. For the work force, information consists of instructions and evaluations of performance received from above. The second premise holds that key information to guide actions comes from the centrally-controlled accounting system. Cost and margin information provide both goals and feedback to control people's actions. In the global economy, however, two quite different premises must underlie the information used to guide business practice. The first premise must be that all management control information comes from below, from customers and processes, and it is provided real-time to people who carry out actions. To delay information by compiling and transmitting it through accounting channels is antithetical to the imperative of responsiveness. The second premise will be that *everyone* in a company understands how to translate information into competitive actions. To wait for instructions from above is inimical to flexibility.

People motivated by information that responds to the imperatives of global competition will remove delay, excess, and variation from the output of all processes. Their behavior will be quite unlike that of employees in the average American company of the past forty years who have been kept busy meeting monthly production targets at any price, and who have suffered the effects of a policy that cuts costs by cutting spending—especially spending on wages and salaries.

Companies need management information that will help them capitalize on their two most important resources—people and time. No accounting system is capable of considering either of those assets. On the contrary, when accounting information is used to control business operations, companies lose sight of people and time. The ills of stagnant productivity and shrinking economic opportunities for American workers will be cured only if companies remove accounting information from their operational control systems and relieve their accounting departments of responsibility for providing information to control business operations.

MEMO TO TOP MANAGEMENT: TRANSFORM!

Today's top managers must insure that their companies' management information and management practices fulfill the people-oriented and time-based imperatives of competitive excellence. Otherwise, top management will continue to be, as W. Edwards Deming has said so often in the past, the number one problem in American business. Deming's remark always has been quite appropriate. Unfortunately, few people seem able to correctly define the problem with management. Most see it as the dedication or style of individual managers. I do not believe the management problem is the people who work as managers. The problem is top management's perception of the imperatives that should guide their actions.

An erroneous view of the "management problem" is held by those who say giving free rein to the "market for corporate control" will improve corporate performance. These people clearly see managers, not management thinking, as the problem in American business. They advocate using hostile takeovers or leveraged buyouts to improve laggard corporate performance. Their improvement strategy for American business is quite simple: oust incumbent managers whose dedication to achieving profit seems diminished by a lust for power and perks; replace those incumbents with other managers who will attend ruthlessly and single-mindedly to what stockholders feel is important.

In a recent *Fortune* magazine poll, nearly 70 percent of U.S. corporate chief executives said they think the wave of hostile takeovers in American business during the 1980s hurt the economy.[2] Some might say that this is a self-evident and self-serving opinion, coming as it does from top executives of the companies most likely to be targeted for takeovers. However, I believe their opinion is a correct view of the situation. Changes of leadership can not resolve the management problem that prevents countless American businesses from achieving competitiveness and long-term profitability. Sometimes such changes can wreak chaos and turmoil that drive a company's performance even lower. At best, turnover of top personnel can intensify a company's focus on profit improvement and produce short-term gains in the bottom line. But turnover does nothing to transform the fundamental management thinking adhered to by virtually every business person in our society. Until that thinking changes, there is little reason to hope for long-term improvement in competitiveness and profitability merely by changing personnel at the top.

Management thinking affects business performance just as an engine affects the performance of an aircraft. Internal combustion and jet propulsion are two technologies for converting fuel into power to drive an aircraft. New recipes for internal combustion can improve the performance of a propeller-driven airplane, but jet propulsion technology raises total performance to levels that internal combustion engines can not achieve. So it is with management thinking. Globally competitive businesses require jet (even rocket!) management principles. Unfortunately, internal combustion principles still power almost all American management thinking.

American business people today tend to share similar (and largely obsolete) ideas about how to make a business competitive and profitable. Although individuals differ in the discipline and dedication with which they apply those ideas, all seem to share the same fundamental notions of how people and work should be organized to accomplish the goals of business. Hence, while new, more ruthless managers often generate short-term bottom-line improvements through focusing and winnowing, long-term competitiveness in most cases still eludes their grasp. Managers are not the problem. The problem is management thinking that focuses on the *wrong imperatives* of competition.

To correct management's focus, I believe companies must eliminate accounting-based management information that reinforces attention on irrelevant sources of competitiveness—pushing output and cutting costs. Indeed, erroneous use of accounting information to control business operations since the 1950s has prevented American companies from understanding and adopting the management principles adopted by our leading overseas competitors. It has taken Americans a long time—over twenty years—to realize the profound difference between our management thinking and the thinking of our overseas competitors. The difference between our approach to business—optimizing costs and maximizing profits within constraints—and their approach—continuously removing constraints to profitably satisfy customer wants—is the difference between success and failure in an economy where the customer is in charge of the marketplace and the work force must be in charge of processes. It has taken us so long to understand this difference in large part because our management accounting tools keep our top managers from understanding what it means to run a competitive enterprise in the global economy.

Some people may dispute, of course, the claim I make that information affects business behavior. They might say, "There's nothing wrong with the management accounting information companies use. Problems are caused by the people who misuse that information." I could accept that idea if I saw any evidence that customer satisfaction resulted from improved financial results. In fact, the connection seems to go the other way—satisfying customers leads to improved financial results. I believe that business performance would improve dramatically if top managers eliminated all existing management accounting control systems and, instead, started people talking about "customer satisfaction being everyone's job" and about "new ideas for customer satisfaction being everyone's responsibility."

WRAP-UP

Businesses use information to communicate activities in one part of an organization to decision makers in another part. But information does more than just communicate. The type of information communicated triggers actions that determine a company's performance.

For example, decisions on employee training will be very different if they are based on cost information rather than information about customer satisfaction. If performance evaluation systems put a heavy emphasis on achieving cost targets, of course efficiency-minded managers will attempt to cut costs by spending less on training. If performance evaluations stress customer satisfaction indexes, however, then quality-oriented managers will strive assiduously to increase spending on training.

Whether more or less spending on training will improve performance depends on the imperatives of competition. In a protected market controlled by companies that all do things the same way, such as the American economy for twenty-five or more years after World War II, cutting training costs may improve performance. But in an open and competitive market controlled by customers—the global economy we live in today—improved performance may call for *more* spending on training.

Whenever a sharp, discontinuous change occurs in the underlying terms of competition, companies must reconsider how information triggers actions that shape business performance. When triggered by management information that no longer fits with the market's terms of competition, actions are likely to impair a company's long-term economic performance. Actions to cut training may improve performance when low cost is a key to competitiveness, but may impair performance later, if customer satisfaction (hence, employee flexibility) becomes the key to competitiveness.

American businesses in the 1970s and 1980s experienced a sharp discontinuity in the terms of competition. Comfortably ensconced before the 1970s in an enormously wealthy domestic marketplace of familiar competitors and captive customers, they were buffeted in the 1980s by new and unprecedented global competitive forces. Unfortunately, the management information in most American companies today still triggers actions that are not relevant to this new competitive environment.

Management *accounting* information, in particular, is not relevant to today's new terms of competition. Indeed, it was evident by the mid-1980s that "management accounting information, driven by the procedures and cycle of the organization's financial reporting system, is too late, too aggregated, and too distorted to be relevant for managers' planning and control decisions."[3] Actions triggered by management accounting information have impaired the long-term competitiveness of countless American businesses in recent years. It is time for American companies, and top managers in particular, to base their decisions on truly useful information and to stop depending on accounting information that deflects them from a competitive course.

CHAPTER 2

REMOTE-CONTROL MANAGEMENT IN THE DARK AGE OF RELEVANCE LOST

❖

I look at the bottom line. It tells me what to do.

—Roger B. Smith[1]

American businesses fall short of what is required to compete in today's customer-focused economy primarily because top managers use information from accounting systems to shape and control the actions of company personnel. If American business is ever to restore its lost competitive edge, companies must eschew the use of top-down accounting information to control operations. They must empower workers, and managers, to listen to and respond to the voice of the customers they serve and the voice of the processes in which they work.

Companies that give empowered workers and managers ownership of information about customers and processes are not forsaking concern for profit. Far from it! They simply recognize that long-term profitability is impossible if the bottom line continues to dictate people's actions. Personnel whose actions are driven by the bottom line can not respond flexibly to customers. To motivate behavior that is responsive and flexible, companies require new management information and new management thinking.

It will not be enough simply to reform the management accounting information that companies now use to control operations. Restoring competitiveness will require managers altogether to *stop* controlling business operations with accounting information—even new activity-based varieties of cost management information. Companies first developed the habit of using accounting information to control operating processes—people's work—only during the 1950s. Before that time, companies did not rely on their accounting systems to provide operational control information. The use of accounting information to control day-to-day operations, almost second nature to managers living today, might have seemed strange to generations of managers before the 1950s.

A brief look at the past puts contemporary management accounting practice in perspective.[2] Over the last two centuries, businesses have used financial and nonfinancial information to direct management decisions at two levels:

- to *plan* the extent and financing of the enterprise as a whole, and
- to *control* the work of individuals and subordinate production units.[3]

Until about forty years ago managers generally used accounting information only to *plan* the extent and financing of the firm as a whole. In this context, "extent" refers to both the scale and the scope of a company's activities, including decisions about its input sources and its mix of products, customers, and market channels. This management use of accounting information is seen in forecast statements of income and financial condition, budgets, and "what if" simulations of the bottom-line consequences of alternative choices. To *control* the work of individuals and subordinate production units, businesses, until the 1950s, tended to use nonaccounting information, both financial and nonfinancial. This control information tracked the flow and cost of work by individual workers and organizational subunits in a form that often resembled modern production control and cost accounting information, except that it did not originate in accounting systems.

A striking example of early nonaccounting financial control information comes from the company that virtually invented modern financial management—E. I. DuPont de Nemours Powder Company.[4] DuPont seems only to have planned company affairs, not to have controlled operating managers, with the accounting information from its early return-on-investment (ROI) planning budgets. In the decade before 1920, top managers at DuPont had detailed monthly statistics on the net income and ROI of every operating unit in the company. But they seem never to have imposed net income or ROI targets on managers of their explosives manufacturing plants. Instead, operations managers followed targets dealing with timeliness of delivery to customers, product quality, plant safety, customer training (to use a very dangerous product), and comparative physical (not accounting cost) consumption of labor, material, and power among plants. Secure in their knowledge that subordinate managers would look after those key determinants of competitiveness, top managers took responsibility for the results reported by the company's financial accounting system.

This separation between accounting sources of plan information and nonaccounting sources of control information becomes blurred after the 1950s, when businesses began using accounting information both to control workers and subunits *and* to plan the extent and financing of the enterprise as a whole. The uses of accounting information to *plan* were generally appropriate and no different than what businesses had done for many decades before the 1950s, *with one exception*. Businesses after the 1950s began for the first time to use accounting product cost information to evaluate product profitabilities, product mix, and sourcing decisions.[5] This inappropriate use of cost accounting information impaired the profitability of many companies in the 1970s and 1980s, although new activity-based costing (ABC) techniques now have eliminated most of the problems that make product cost accounting information unreliable for planning and decision making. Aside from improper uses of product cost information, companies followed appropriate and long-established practices in using accounting information for *planning* after the 1950s.

The use of top-down accounting information *to control operations* is the central feature of post-1950s management accounting that has caused it to impair long-term competitiveness and profitability in American businesses during the past thirty years. Combined with inappropriate use of cost accounting information to plan marketing strategies, this use of accounting information to control operating processes constitutes what I refer to as "relevance lost."[6] American business has used accounting information to direct operating processes "by remote control" only since the 1950s—a relatively short time. Nevertheless, the consequences of that practice have been so debilitating that it is not an exaggeration to describe the period from the 1950s

Table 2–1
Primary Sources of Management Information

	Industrial Era: 1800–1950	Dark Age of Relevance Lost: 1950s–1980s	Global Era: 1990s on
To plan extent and financing of company	Accounting	Accounting	Accounting
Marketing and sourcing decisions	Nonaccounting	Accounting	Accounting (modified by ABC)
To control individuals and subunits	Nonaccounting	Accounting	Nonaccounting (customer and process)

to the 1980s as a Dark Age of American business history. As shown in Table 2–1, companies that achieve world-class competitive excellence must stop using management information from their accounting systems to control operations.

Accounting historians have known for a long time that companies did not originally use accounting systems as a source of management control information. Research in the historical records of countless businesses, especially in manufacturing, shows that companies used very sophisticated financial and nonfinancial management control systems between the early 1800s and 1950.[7] However, the *financial* information in these systems seldom was derived from accounting records, even though occasionally it was reconciled with account data. Rather, financial information used to control workers and companies' subunits consisted of cost and margin information derived primarily from "bottom-up" data about work—not primarily from "top-down" accounting-based information.

After the 1950s, double-entry accounting information increasingly became the main source of this financial (and other) information that companies for decades had used to control operating activities at the worker and the business unit levels. Accounting textbook authors after the 1950s expressed the view that this new "management accounting" increased accounting information's relevance to decision making inside complex organizations. However, I believe this growing use of accounting information to control operations indicates a *decline* in the relevance of management control information.[8] Indeed, using *accounting* information to control business processes was a new habit that undoubtedly contributed to declining competitiveness and profitability in many American manufacturing companies in recent years.[9]

Why should this use of accounting information to control operations impair a company's performance? An allegory from a classic of Western philosophy provides an apt metaphorical image.[10] In the *Republic*, Plato articulates a theory of knowledge—that is, how humans go from an unenlightened state in which they take appearances at face value to a state in which they understand reality. We are addressing a similar question; namely, how do people in companies sort out appearance from reality? Specifically, what information is relevant to a company's search for sources of competitiveness and profitability?

In the Allegory of the Cave, Plato considers the condition of men who have lived all their lives underground in a cave:

> Imagine the condition of men living in a sort of cavernous chamber underground, with an entrance open to the light and a long passage all down the cave. Here they have been from childhood, chained by the leg and also by the neck, so that they cannot move and can see only what is in front of them. . . . At some distance higher up is the light of a fire burning behind them; and between the prisoners and the fire is a [barrier] like the screen at a puppet-show, which hides the performers while they show their puppets over the top. Now behind this [barrier] imagine persons carrying along various artificial objects, including figures of men and animals in wood or stone or other materials, which project above the [barrier]. . . . Prisoners so confined would have seen nothing of themselves or of one another, except the shadows thrown by the firelight on the wall of the Cave facing them. . . .[11]

Plato asks us to imagine a prisoner breaking away from his chains and walking out of the cave, passing by the "puppet show" along the way. After overcoming the pain and difficulty of adjusting to light, the freed prisoner would move from the shadow world of appearances, past the barrier where artificial likenesses of real objects cast shadows, to the outside world where he would see real objects for the first time. After living for a very long time in the outside world, the freed prisoner eventually might perceive the highest knowledge, the spiritual reality permeating all objects, represented by sunlight.

We can relate this allegory to post-1950s management accounting practice: the cave and the ground above are a company and its surrounding environment; the shadows cast on the cave wall are accounting numbers. Think of those numbers as money-denominated shadows cast by the resources a business consumes and the products it sells. Resources (e.g., labor , raw material, buildings, machinery, and so forth) and products are the "artificial" objects that cast monetized shadows from behind a barrier. People behind the barrier—perhaps operations managers and management accountants—manipulate products and resources and maintain the fires that cast shadows on the wall. On the floor of the cave, chained in their places, are other people—perhaps finance-oriented top executives and financial analysts—who believe that the accounting shadows passing before their eyes are reality itself, not mere appearances.

Above ground, outside the cave entrance, are real objects represented below by the artificial likenesses—products and resources—that cast financial shadows on the wall. Those real objects above ground are people, especially customers seeking satisfaction of wants and company associates (employees, managers, suppliers, distributors, etc.) engaged in processes that consume resources, in the hope of satisfying customer wants. Thus, a freed prisoner who might break out of the cave and walk above ground would progress from watching accounting shadows on a dark wall, to seeing resources and products used to create those shadows, and, finally, to observing people working in processes that consume resources and cause spending to occur.

Management accounting practice assumes that top managers manipulate accounting shadows in order to plan corporate strategies and to control the operating processes that link employees and other company associates with final customers. Most executives who ran American businesses in the 1970s and 1980s were taught to believe that managers must control reality (i.e., the processes outside the cave) by manipulating accounting variables (i.e., shadows on the wall). Moreover, spending their careers in accounting and finance, instead of working with customers and operating processes only served to reinforce this belief.

In effect, management accounting systems encourage a form of "management by remote control." Managers assume that they control operations with information about the accounting results of operations—like a driver using the rearview mirror to drive a car or a tennis player watching the scoreboard to play tennis. Everyone knows that focusing on the mirror or the scoreboard leads to disaster on the highway or the tennis court. But few people seem to reach the same conclusion about using accounting information to control business operations.

Why did American businesses begin using accounting numbers to control operations (and to evaluate marketing strategies) after the

1950s? I trace this development to two conditions: one is the rapid and pervasive spread of the multidivisional form of business organization (M-form) after the war; the other is the teaching that arose in American business schools after the 1950s. Let's look at each in turn.

As documented in the works of business historian Alfred Chandler and economist Oliver Williamson, the M-form originated in the United States in the 1920s but did not proliferate until after 1950.[12] Large-scale organizations formed divisions in order to economize on the high costs of information needed to manage the complexity of diverse product lines, extensive markets, and diverse technologies. In the 1920s, large companies whose product diversity cut across technological lines (e.g., DuPont) or industry markets (e.g., General Motors) solved the problem of high information processing costs by creating decentralized multidivisional structures. These companies coped with the complexity of diversity by placing the activities of each distinct product line, region, or technology into a separately managed compartment (i.e., division), and all of these were subject to the financial discipline of a strong corporate staff. By lowering the cost of coping with diversity, divisionalization extended the horizontal boundaries of large, complex business organizations.

The M-form, perhaps more than anything else, has legitimated the use of accounting information—especially the use of ROI information—to control operating activities. In multidivisional companies, the "increased structural distance between those entrusted with exploiting actual competitive opportunities [i.e., division management] and those who must judge the quality of their work [i.e., top management] virtually guarantees reliance on objectively quantifiable short-term criteria."[13] Historically those criteria have been defined in financial terms, especially ROI. Top managers in diversified M-form organizations control subordinates inside divisions with the carrot and stick of financial performance.

For the first time in history, top managers in multidivisional organizations unequivocally used accounting information to control the actions of operating personnel. With the coming of the M-form, managers began to regularly delegate responsibility for achieving accounting results, and managing scorecard results, not process results, became standard procedure. After 1960 companies increasingly used accounting results such as costs, net income, or ROI not just to keep score, but also to motivate the actions of operating personnel at all levels.

Not coincidentally, the practice of managing with accounting numbers spread as more and more companies adopted the M-form structure. Large M-form organizations, up to the 1960s, were an important "nursery" for top-level corporate managers—graduate training grounds, as it were, before there were large numbers of graduate business schools. Having learned the virtues of managing through accounting systems, division managers took the lesson with them when they rose to the top or moved to another company. Eventually, say by the early 1970s, accounting results dominated most managers' attention to the point where they no longer knew, or cared, about the production, technological, and marketing determinants of competitiveness.

By 1970, moreover, business education itself reinforced and justi-fied the practice of managing through the accounting numbers. Teach-ing in graduate business schools after the 1950s featured the study of neoclassical economic models of business and psychological models of individual behavior, not the study of real business problems faced by real business people. This emphasis on social science paradigms in business school research and teaching came with the postwar birth and rapid evolution of business PhD programs that piggybacked on exist-ing PhD programs in economics and psychology. By the end of the 1950s, therefore, management accounting professors—mainly ac-countants recently trained in economics—were writing textbooks that showed how to cast accounting information into a form amenable to economic problem solving. Referring to accounting as the "language of business," these professors used the economic model of the firm to show how to make accounting information "managerially relevant," largely by separating fixed from variable costs.

It seems that no one in university business schools stopped to ask if economic models, designed for studying price behavior in market set-tings, were relevant to understanding the workings of a managed en-terprise. People outside business schools may have raised the question. I recall hearing a distinguished British economist in the 1970s refer disparagingly to American business school professors as "second-rate economists chasing third-rate questions." Aside from condescending jibes such as that one, scarcely anything was said to question the social science agenda adopted by business schools after the 1950s. Indeed, the agenda became institutionalized (some might say it became "ossi-fied") in the criteria for business school accreditation adopted by the American Assembly of Collegiate Schools of Business, leading to sim-ilar criteria for faculty promotion and tenure.

Following that agenda, management accounting professors after the 1950s used the neoclassical economic model of the firm to rationalize "management by remote control." The economic model assumes a profit maximizing firm that produces one homogeneous product at the output rate where marginal revenue equals marginal cost. While the highly aggregated view of business activity assumed in that model is appropriate for predicting price behavior in markets, management accountants urged businesses to rationalize micro-level management decisions from the same remote level of aggregation. For example, they equated marginal cost with accounting variable cost and taught businesses to control fixed cost by pushing output to earn short-run contribution margin. This practice viewed customers, if it considered them at all, as objects of persuasion—sponges to absorb output at prices greater than variable cost. Thus, with few foreign competitors to challenge them until the late 1970s, thousands of managers in the 1960s began running companies to generate output, not to satisfy customer wants. In effect, management accounting professors helped these new top managers justify practices that eventually undermined global competitiveness.

These new top managers took a fateful leap after the 1950s that their nineteenth and earlier twentieth-century predecessors had resisted. They used accounting information for a purpose it was not intended to serve—to control people's work in operating processes. Whereas managers before the 1950s seemed content to *periodically check outcomes of properly managed processes with accounting information,* managers after the 1950s encouraged people to *achieve accounting results by manipulating outputs of processes.* Managers increasingly viewed operations through the lens of accounting results. Eventually top managers tended to ignore, even forget, operating processes. That development, more than any other, defines management accounting's lost relevance in recent years.

In effect, the decline into irrelevance of management accounting was a case of putting the cart before the horse. Accounting information about business results—the cart—became the prime object of managers' attention. Managers quickly lost sight of the horse, the underlying forces that produce accounting results. It is no wonder that American businesses in the 1970s and 1980s became absorbed in ultimately debilitating practices such as conglomeration, hostile takeovers, and leveraged buyouts. Although public spending and taxation policies and the onset of high inflation helped catalyze and accelerate conglomeration and takeover practices, the widespread popularity of those practices depended on managers and markets believing that real wealth emanates from manipulating accounting results and financial instruments.

To put this in a slightly different way: by the 1960s, the intrusion of accounting into management control systems was causing top managers to abdicate their strategic responsibilities. Instead of being broad-gauged integrators—conversant in production, marketing, and finance—American senior executives by 1970 were focused excessively on the financial dimension of business. They had adopted, according to Hayes and Abernathy, a "new managerial gospel" that encouraged "a preference for (1) analytic detachment rather than the insight that comes from 'hands on' experience and (2) short-term cost reduction rather than long-term development of technological competitiveness." This new gospel "played a major role in undermining the vigor of American industry."[14]

But "why should so many American managers [by 1980] have shifted so strongly to this new managerial orthodoxy; and why were they not more deeply bothered by the ill effects of those principles on the long-term technological competitiveness of their companies?" To answer the first question Hayes and Abernathy cite the significant change after the 1950s in the typical American manager's road to the top. "No longer did the typical career, threading sinuously up and through a corporation with stops in several functional areas, provide future top executives with intimate hands-on knowledge of the company's technologies, customers, and suppliers." Increasingly top managers came from financial and legal backgrounds, less and less from the technical and marketing sides.

Perhaps this new breed of top manager began to control operations with accounting numbers because they were afraid they might have to discourse about operations they did not understand. If their fear of the unknown caused them to use accounting numbers to control operations, their use of these numbers may have bred another fear—the fear of unfamiliar accounting numbers felt by operations managers whose forte was in the technical, not in the financial, realm. Recently I saw a consequence of this fear. A manufacturing vice president, to please top managers, spent enormous time and resources training operations personnel in "accounting for nonfinancial managers." He could have better spent the time and money training top managers in statistical problem-solving techniques.

To answer the second question—why managers by 1980 were not more bothered by the deleterious consequences of their new financial management practices—Hayes and Abernathy refer to a growing pseudo-professionalism that deprecates the value of industry experience and hands-on expertise as opposed to analytic-quantitative finance training. Helping create and nurture this pseudo-professionalism, of course, was the social science agenda underlying contemporary graduate business education—the training ground for most top and mid-level American managers by the 1970s. This pseudo-professionalism salves the conscience of today's managers by glorifying "an individual having no special expertise in any particular industry or technology who [supposedly] can step into an unfamiliar company and run it successfully through strict application of financial controls [and] portfolio concepts. . . ."

So, a new breed of top managers began to appear in the 1960s—trained in finance, accounting, and law—not conversant with processes or customer wants. Management by accounting—management "by remote control"—became the vogue. Attention of management at all levels focused on costs, profit, ROI, leverage, and other financial results. Not shop floor organization and satisfaction of customer wants. Managers began to manipulate processes to achieve accounting results, instead of monitoring well-run processes by occasionally checking accounting results. Process management—intuitively understood by most managers before the 1950s—was quickly replaced by "managing by the numbers." Worse, top managers increasingly identified and defined "process" in terms of whatever it took to achieve desired accounting results. And that view of things was telegraphed throughout every level of almost every business in the nation.

In their book *Dynamic Manufacturing*, Hayes, Wheelwright, and Clark describe an insidious consequence of this new view of top management's role in business. It eroded, ultimately destroyed, the presence of a central binding core of key managers whose training and experience blended both "the skills and tradition of the craftsman with the thought process of the scientist, the combination of experience and analysis, the mixture of systematic procedure and individual artistry."[15] The erosion of this core left in its wake a dominant strain of top manager who favored "hard" and "scientific" financial-analytic management techniques that eschewed continual improvement through in-house technical leadership in preference to more mechanistic marketing and financial breakthroughs. This new breed of top managers lacked "a long-term, almost organic understanding of how people, both workers and managers, reacted to certain pressures and inducements, how relationships between suppliers and customers could deteriorate or be strengthened over time, how incremental changes in products and manufacturing processes interacted and cumulatively enhanced performance, and how competitors evolved in response to attacks or opportunities. . . ."[16*]

To further amplify how profoundly this "managing by remote control" changed business practices, compare the above description of post-1950 top management with the traits exhibited by exemplars of pre-World War II American management. Three cases in point are Andrew Carnegie in the late nineteenth century, Henry Ford in the 1920s, and Alfred Sloan in the 1920s and 1930s.[17*]

Carnegie was obsessed with production costs and output. He drove his plant superintendents to continuously improve their costs and their output.[18] But he did not focus their attention on driving output by manipulating processes, in order to achieve accounting cost targets. He knew that low costs and high output were no guarantee of profits without satisfied customers. "Carnegie insisted . . . that he be provided with a quality product to sell, for he knew that one adverse comment on his rails circulated by word of mouth among the railroad offices could offset a dozen testimonials in writing that he might distribute throughout the country."[19] There was little chance that plant managers would achieve cost savings by cutting corners that might risk quality. Moreover, Carnegie could inform his plant people about customers' expectations because he knew his customers very, very well and understood what they expected. "There was not a railroad president or purchasing agent in the entire country with whom he was not personally acquainted and few with whom he had not had business in some capacity or other."[20] And he also knew the steel- and iron-making processes so well that he could evaluate his plant managers' cost-cutting efforts and, in turn, keep them apprised of new developments in the world. "The daily communiques [to his partners and superintendents], dealing with every detail of the manufacturing process from the amount of limestone to be used in the blast furnace charge to the relative merits of hammered versus rolled blooms for rails, left no doubt in their minds that Carnegie knew his product probably better than most of the workmen. . . ."[21] In short, a keen concern for his company's financial condition never led Carnegie to manage operations by remote control, by driving subordinate managers to manipulate processes in order to achieve accounting targets.

Echoing Carnegie's concern for the customer and for well-designed, well-run processes are words written by Henry Ford just over a generation later, in the 1920s. I will have much more to say in the next chapter about Ford's famous book *Today and Tomorrow*, in which he articulated his management philosophy (among other things). At this point, it is instructive to compare the quotation at the head of this chapter from recently retired General Motors Chairman Roger Smith—"the bottom line tells me what to do"—with Henry Ford's view on profit: "Business must be run at a profit . . . , else it will die. But when any one attempts to run a business solely for profit and thinks not at all of the service to the community, then also the business must die, for it no longer has a reason for existence."[22] For Ford, service to the community included never-ending concern to meet promises to customers as well as concern (albeit not up to standards taken for granted today in our more environmentally conscious society) to ameliorate undesirable side effects his business operations had on workers (safety) and neighbors in the community (pollution). Moreover, Ford, like Carnegie, knew intimately the dynamics of the manufacturing operations for which his company was so famous. Perhaps for that reason he understood better than most of today's financially trained top managers why "cutting wages does not reduce costs—it increases them. The only way to get a low-cost product is to pay a high price for a high grade of human service and to see to it through management that you get that service."[23] You can be sure that Ford would have equated "see to it through management" with training, process design, and design for manufacturability—not with forcing managers to jump through the hoops of mindless accounting variances and other cost reports.

The same spirit shown by Carnegie and Ford was voiced by Alfred Sloan, chairman of General Motors from the 1920s to the 1950s, when he allegedly said "the chairman['s job] is to control the purse strings, not guide the hands of the artisans."[24] Sloan, like Carnegie, obviously appreciated the value to top managers of having a broad financial view of a company's affairs—controlling purse strings. Like most of his contemporaries before World War II, however, Sloan also seemed reluctant to focus the attention of operating personnel—artisans—on actions designed to achieve accounting results.

Their tendency after 1960 to view business operations through the lens of accounting hid from managers the view of customers and processes that managers once had. Indeed, managing by the numbers culminated during the 1970s in people's viewing a company as a "portfolio" of income-producing assets. Strategists who adopted that view saw top management's job as maximizing the value of a company by balancing the risks and returns of a company's asset portfolio.

While appropriate for managing portfolios of marketable securities, such strategies are totally misapplied when used to manage a business. Managers of conglomerates who followed such strategies turned their attention completely away from internal operations and customer satisfaction and attempted to create value out of thin air by "acquiring stars," "milking cash cows," and "divesting dogs."

By diverting top management's attention from people to finance, managing by remote control caused countless businesses to suffer setbacks, even fail. Andrew Carnegie scarcely would have understood the behavior of America's typical corporate leaders after the mid-1960s. For a vivid example of the ill effects of managing by the numbers in our times, consider the recently published history of a company swallowed up in the conglomeration boom of the 1970s. The company, Burgmaster, was the largest American machine-tool maker west of Chicago when it was bought out by a conglomerate in the mid-1960s. Fifteen years later the financial wizards at Kohlberg, Kravis, Roberts & Company (better known as KKR) helped this conglomerate become the nation's first large leveraged buyout.

Burgmaster's history falls into two phases: twenty years of excellent growth and profitability in the hands of a brilliant, customer-focused engineer who founded the company, followed by twenty years of decline into bankruptcy in the hands of finance-driven, numbers-oriented professional managers. Burgmaster's demise can be attributed in no small way to the lack of interest in people and customers associated with the conglomerate and postconglomerate top managers' obsessive push to manage by the numbers.[25] The company's history after the mid-1960s suggests the very high price a company and society pay when finance-oriented top managers who know little or nothing about engineering or craftsmanship attempt to control both the artisans' hands and the company pursestrings. Founded by a man with the business acumen and instincts of an Andrew Carnegie or a Henry Ford, Burgmaster's demise in the hands of cost-focused financial dealmakers is not an isolated story. It is an allegory for the Dark Age of history that American business passed through in the last three decades.

Another once-great American manufacturing company that crumbled in the 1970s and 1980s as a direct result of top management by remote control was Mesta Machine Company, founded in the late 1800s.[26] Recognized by 1930 as a premier supplier of industrial machinery, particularly to the steel industry, Mesta's skills at innovation, excellent engineering, and customer service later made it one of the top suppliers to the U.S. military during World War II. This tradition of excellence continued for almost two decades after the war, when Mesta made significant contributions to many industries, from steel to aerospace. Then, in 1963, a new generation of top managers came to power. The new group consisted primarily of finance-trained professional managers brought in from outside the company. "Lacking in engineering experience, and therefore unfamiliar with the core of the business, they responded to the competitive challenge by adding new layers of corporate staff, introducing committees for decision-making, and installing new, more stringent accounting and capital budgeting systems. They rarely appeared in the shops or in the engineering centers, and the direct communication that was [pre-1963 management's] hallmark was lost." Focused on financial considerations, the new post-1963 managers "failed to develop expertise in what was probably [the 1960s' and 1970s'] most important process development as far as the steel industry [Mesta's largest customer] was concerned: continuous casting transformed the semifinished stage of steel production and spawned many other developments in related equipment. By the mid-1980s, a company that was not a supplier of continuous-casting equipment (and Mesta was not) was simply not a serious player in steel mill equipment." This failure to keep pace with steel technology as well as "the growing distance and distrust between Mesta's work force and managers, fostered by their remote-control approach to management, proved to be the company's undoing. Crippled by strikes and lost orders, Mesta lost over $60 million between 1979 and 1982 and filed for bankruptcy in early 1983."

WRAP-UP

The chief problem with using accounting information to control operations—managing by remote control—is the tendency for businesses to lose sight of the processes by which people and customers make a company competitive and profitable. What I believe has happened in American businesses since the 1950s is that managers and operating personnel at all levels have lost sight of people, customers, and processes as top management has turned everyone's attention to accounting results. Managers before World War II, such as Carnegie, Ford, and Sloan, seemed to act intuitively as though well-run processes and satisfied customers made their companies competitive and profitable. Moreover, we see the same awareness in actions taken by top managers even in the late 1940s and the 1950s at well-run companies such as Burgmaster and Mesta. While none of these managers eschewed the use of accounting systems to track and budget financial returns, they did not seem to ssuccumb to the belief that focusing everyone's actions in the organization on manipulating processes to achieve accounting cost and net income targets was the way to become competitive and profitable.

Indeed, a sharp discontinuity in business principles and practices seems to occur after the 1950s, associated with the spread of multidivisional enterprise and social science-oriented graduate business education. The discontinuity boils down to one basic difference between the pre- and post-1950s periods. Before the 1950s management information responded to the imperatives of a competitive environment that was defined by real technological and economic forces outside businesses. After the 1950s the order was reversed. Then businesses began to pursue "pseudo" imperatives of competition that were defined by their own accounting-based management information systems. To say that American business after the 1950s became unplugged from reality is not an exaggeration.

By 1970 we see the results of this unplugging. American businesses by that time were defining process—that is, the things you control to achieve results—in terms of accounting results: a cost function, a revenue function, or the accounting determinants of return on investment. No longer were most businesses defining process in terms of work people do or satisfaction customers receive. To reiterate what I said before, that post-1950s change in focus from people, customers, and processes to costs, profits, and accounting relationships—the change brought on by the increasing use of accounting information to control operations—is the main cause of "relevance lost." *Relevance was not lost by using improper accounting information to manage. It was lost by improperly using accounting information to control business operations.*

Proposals to improve the performance of American business by reforming management accounting or by improving business practices of the past thirty years are doomed to fail because they do not take into consideration the sharp discontinuity after the 1950s that brought management accounting and remote-control management practices into being. Improving the cause of what ails us is not going to remedy our malaise! Top managers must have their companies abandon those accounting-based control practices and the remote-control management thinking that they reinforce. Businesses that succeed in the global economy, like those that succeeded in the business world before the

1950s, will pursue imperatives of competition relevant to the external economic environment, not imperatives dictated by accounting-based results.

In other words, America's declining business competitiveness in recent decades was not driven by poor management accounting information so much as it was driven by management accounting practices that caused businesses to ignore new management thinking coming from outside the United States. Indeed, managing by accounting numbers would not necessarily have caused declining competitiveness and diminished profitability for most American companies after World War II, except for one thing: eventually not all our competitors managed by the numbers the same way. If everyone always had managed the same way as American businesses after the 1950s did, we would not talk today about lost relevance and declining American competitiveness. But as we all know, by the 1970s, formidable competitors—Japanese and some Europeans—were paying closer attention than most American businesses did to people, process, and customers. We now know that these competitors were not managing by accounting numbers with top-down financial control systems that treated customers as objects of persuasion and employees and suppliers as cogs in the gears of a deterministic machine. Instead, they viewed management's job as empowering people to control processes and remove constraints that stood in the way of profitably satisfying customer wants.

CHAPTER 3

CONSEQUENCES OF REMOTE-CONTROL MANAGEMENT

If each part of a system, considered separately, is made to operate as efficiently as possible, the system as a whole will not operate as effectively as possible.

—Russell Ackoff[1]

Travel light and make numerous trips—like the water beetle.

—Richard J. Schonberger[2]

Perhaps the gravest consequence of using accounting information to control business operations after the 1950s was to deter American businesses from understanding the new time-intensive, people-oriented, and resource-conserving methods of management developed in Japan—especially at Toyota—during the 1960s and 1970s. After speaking to hundreds of professional and corporate groups around the world in recent years, I am convinced that most business people still do not understand the principles underlying these management methods. Nevertheless, any company hoping to compete in today's global economy must understand why certain management methods—usually associated with Japan but not necessarily Japanese—produce substantially better results than the general management practices that most American businesses have pursued in the past three decades.

As they are known today, those new management methods are embodied primarily in the concepts JIT (just-in-time) and TQM (total quality management). These methods address the need for responsiveness and flexibility that I associate with competitive excellence in an information-based economy. Japanese companies generally are associated with the development of these new management methods. However, the Japanese began to develop these methods when commercial implications of the computer-based information revolution were scarcely a glint in the eyes of those who invented the transistor. Undoubtedly, the immediate catalyst driving early JIT and TQM developments at companies such as Toyota was scarcity in the postwar Japanese economy, not the quest for better ways to serve information-empowered customers and employees.

By the end of the 1970s, however, new management methods, often associated with Toyota, enabled companies anywhere in the world to address competitive requirements of the global economy. Unfortunately, management accounting practices kept American businesses from understanding either those requirements or the methods to address them. Those same practices do not seem to have been used by most Japanese businesses,[3] but they persist in American businesses to this day, preventing companies from seeing the changes they must make to become competitive.

This chapter highlights crucial differences between Japanese and American management principles. The story begins by contrasting Japanese and American manufacturers' approaches to achieving product *variety* at low mass-production cost after World War II. The people-oriented Japanese approach achieved variety, ultimately, through increased flexibility, whereas the more deterministic and mechanical American approach achieved variety with much, much less flexibility, and at much higher cost. But management accounting information prevented American companies from understanding how their chief global competitors by 1980 were able to sell greater varieties of higher quality products at unbelievably low prices. The challenge now facing American companies, and companies located around the world, is to create nonaccounting *problem-solving* systems, both financial and nonfinancial, that trigger actions leading to increased flexibility at low cost.

TWO VARIATIONS ON THE THEME OF MASS PRODUCTION

During the first two postwar decades, from about 1950 to 1965, both American and Japanese manufacturers pursued the same manufacturing Holy Grail: to produce *varieties* of output at mass production costs.

For centuries, preindustrial artisans—tailors, cobblers, wagon makers, and so forth—had manufactured high-quality products in varieties tailored to each customer's wants—but at a high cost that only a wealthy few could afford. By the late nineteenth century, emerging mass-production techniques made low-cost manufactured products generally available, but usually in limited varieties. A few manufacturers, notably General Motors Company,[4] developed techniques for "mass-customizing" goods as early as the 1920s. But these techniques achieve low-cost variety by fine-tuning traditional mass production. Toyota after the 1950s pushed the quest for low-cost variety beyond the principles of mass production, to what I call "flexibility."

The contrast between American and Japanese approaches to variety after World War II is evident in their differing views of Henry Ford's early 1920s River Rouge plant. Both Americans and Japanese in the 1950s referred to that famous plant to define conditions necessary for low-cost "mass production." However, each attributed Ford's low costs to different conditions. For Americans the key to low cost was large-scale capital investment in dedicated machinery that was kept busy producing a high volume of output by workers performing highly programmed tasks. For Japanese—exemplified by Toyota—the key to low cost was to conserve resources by continuously linking processes, identifying and correcting errors as they occur, and relying on workers' brainpower to resolve capital constraints. On those two very different perceptions of mass production hangs virtually all the difference between American and Japanese manufacturing performance since the 1960s.

River Rouge in the Mid-1920s

Ford's River Rouge plant after World War II attracted countless visitors from abroad, mainly from Europe, who saw in it the model of modern industrial production. Japanese truck and auto manufacturers, especially at Toyota, also studied River Rouge in the 1950s, although it is likely the Japanese at first studied River Rouge from a distance by reading translated copies of Henry Ford's 1926 book *Today and Tomorrow.*[5] The book was out of print in the United States after World War II, and scarcely was taken seriously by any Americans who remembered it. Americans reading the book would have been turned away by much of Ford's banal advice for succeeding in life, not to mention many passages that express his rural Midwestern brand of racism and anti-Semitism.

Japanese auto producers would have found the book interesting for Ford's articulation of the logic behind his famous mid-1920s Fordson tractor production system. As Figure 3–1 shows schematically, the system flowed almost continuously from iron ore to finished vehicles, with virtually all processes balanced at the same output rate.

Simple enough in concept, the system Ford created at "Fordson" on the banks of the River Rouge boggles the mind even today! Ships and rail cars delivered steady streams of iron ore, coal, and limestone continuously to blast furnaces from which iron went directly to a casting foundry where engine blocks and other parts were made in a continuous flow. "The foundry is not segregated into departments," Ford stressed. "Instead, every department is coordinated into a continuous system of manufacture by the use of conveyors. . . . The foundry is paved, the floors are kept spotlessly clean, and a system of suction pipes, ventilators, and dust collectors keeps the place cool and free from dust. . . ."[6] Ford writes extensively about eliminating time and inventory from his system. "Time waste differs from material waste in that there can be no salvage. . . . But having a stock of raw material or finished goods in excess of requirements is waste. . . . We do not own or use a warehouse. . . . Our production cycle is about eighty-one hours from the mine to the finished machine in the freight car, or three days and nine hours. . . ."[7]

In *Today and Tomorrow*, Ford attributed the success of his River Rouge system to many factors that would be familiar to any student of "modern" manufacturing in the 1990s, such as self-inspection by every worker, cleanliness and orderliness on the shop floor, frequent deliv-

Figure 3–1
Coupled (Linked) Processes à la River Rouge, Circa 1925

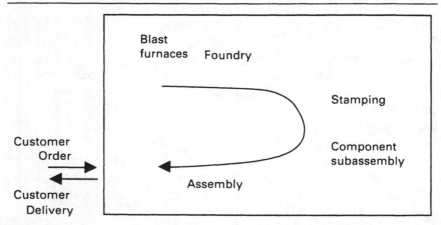

eries from vendors to the production line, preventive maintenance, and an obsession with eliminating waste in all its forms. Ford spoke proudly of turning iron ore, silica, and latex into finished vehicles in less than three and a half days, at the lowest cost in the world. And proud he could be, for the lead times and costs achieved in his River Rouge plant by 1925 had never been equaled before—nor have they been equaled since.

Taiichi Ohno, manufacturing engineer and legendary "father" of the Toyota Production System, always spoke glowingly of Ford's achievement at River Rouge.[8] In 1982, Philip Caldwell, then head of Ford Motor Company, visited Japan. When Caldwell asked Eiji Toyoda, head of Toyota Motors, where Toyota had learned the production methods they employed so successfully in the 1970s, Toyoda replied, "There is no secret to how we learned to do what we do, Mr. Caldwell. We learned it at the Rouge."[9]

Ford's system until the late 1920s was not designed to deal with variety, the problem that American and Japanese manufacturers were trying to resolve in the 1950s.[10] In his original system there was virtually no variety. Until 1927 Ford produced, of course, only one car in one color—the black Model T. In addition he produced one model of a farm tractor, the Fordson, a centerpiece in his River Rouge system. Of course, variety was not a key to competitiveness for mass production manufacturers in the early years of this century. Their competitive advantage derived mainly from the low cost achieved by repetitively producing homogeneous output, and Ford Motor Company led the way in designing systems to do just that. By 1950, however, growing consumer sophistication made variety an important element in any manufacturer's competitive strategy—even at Ford Motor Company. But achieving variety was not enough in a world that was now accustomed to low-priced mass-produced goods. To be competitive, companies now had to produce variety at virtually mass-production costs.[11]

The American Manufacturers' Answer After World War II

To achieve variety with low costs, American manufacturers by the 1950s abandoned the continuous flow of work observed in Ford's River Rouge system. Continuous linking, as exemplified in Ford's 1925–vintage River Rouge system (see Figure 3–1), requires that every process operate virtually at the same balanced rate. However, it is one thing to balance a system to produce one product one way, as Ford did in the early 1920s by building a dedicated system in which all processes operated at one rate. It is quite another thing to keep balance in a continuously linked system of processes that is producing a changing variety of products. Changing to a new variety requires the line to stop and, many times, to be rebalanced at a new rate. Stopping the line to change over and rebalance seemed unnecessarily difficult and costly to the Americans.

To cope with the complexity of variety, Americans decoupled the line, allowing different processes to operate at independent rates, and created inventory buffers and warehouses to absorb production surpluses and deficits between processes. Henry Ford did not require inventory buffers at River Rouge in the early 1920s. Most American manufacturing plants could not operate without such buffers by the end of the 1950s.

In effect, decoupling and buffering does nothing to change the existing organization of work in each process. For example, existing setup times will remain the same, and machines may be dedicated in order to eliminate setting up. Decoupling and buffering simply sacrifices continuous linking of processes in order to cope with the complexity of variety.

To achieve low costs, Americans then ran each decoupled process so as to achieve economies of scale and speed. The theory was simple: the cost of the whole—the finished product—is the sum of the cost of output from each process. Therefore, to achieve the lowest total cost of finished output, produce output in each and every process at the lowest cost per unit. To do this, build capacity in each process as large as feasible and run output through each process in large batches at high speed.

Thus, to get variety, but still enjoy low mass-production costs à la River Rouge, American manufacturers after 1950 decoupled processes, built each decoupled stage to the largest scale feasible, and then ran batches of different things through each process as fast as possible. This often meant centralizing some processes in one place and shipping parts great distances (e.g., locate stamping plants in Michigan and ship frames to assembly plants located closer to the market, say in Texas or California). As shown schematically in Figure 3–2, this decoupled system, unlike River Rouge, did not have workers produce for the next process; now they produced for inventory. Also not like River Rouge, production controllers and schedulers now were required to move things between decoupled processes, and from inventory to final assembly. Moreover, workers did not attempt to identify errors, or

Figure 3–2
Decoupled (Separated) Processes

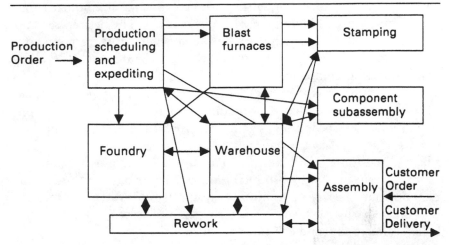

stop to fix them as they occurred. Instead, output was pushed as fast as possible into inventory, where errors would be detected and corrected (as much as possible) later. Not surprisingly, total costs rose and quality in terms of conformance to specifications declined as variety and volume increased.

Decoupling operations into separate processes, as in Figure 3–2, creates a "flight of bumblebees" that increases buffers, space occupied, transportation, and time. At the center of the system is a stockroom—sometimes dubbed "spaghetti junction" for the reason that virtually all work passes through it between processing stages. Work snakes back and forth through the stockroom transfer point at least as many times as there are processes. Decoupling processes diminishes cooperation among departments and allows separate parts of the organization to work at independent rates, not all at the customer demand rate. Over short periods, such as a month or less, rates among various parts of the system can, of course, vary considerably—with the differences going into or coming out of inventory. Theoretically the output from all parts of the system will balance out with customer demand over long periods of time. However, that "balance" is often forced by means such as building inventory, scrapping excess output, reducing prices to clear out excess stock, and, in cases of severe imbalance, eliminating parts of the system by laying people off and selling assets.

It is not inevitable, of course, that decoupling of systems will run toward imbalance and waste. Indeed, decoupling can greatly increase productivity by promoting "specialization and division of labor." The trick is to achieve the benefits of specialization by dividing tasks and to have each specialized unit also work at a rate that harmonizes with the output of the whole system, as in Figure 3–1. The desired result is analogous to the music achieved by the specialized instruments of a well-functioning orchestra. However, the actual outcome achieved by most American companies after the 1950s, shown in Figure 3–2, is analogous to what happens if every instrument in an orchestra tries to play faster and louder than the other instruments. The result is cacophony, not music. Cacophony is achieved when each decoupled unit attempts to achieve scale economies by producing output as fast as possible. A warehouse in the middle of a decoupled system and pressure to "earn" overhead cost by producing output contribute to this discordant outcome. Filling a warehouse to minimize cost variances does not help create harmony; instead, it distracts people from thinking about balance, harmony, and economy.

Balance and harmony are features in the most famous of all illustrations of specialization and division of labor: Adam Smith's pin-making "factory." In that system, workers specialized in each process of pin-making—wire drawing, cutting, grinding, stamping, and so forth. By coordinating the output of their specialized tasks, the group produced much, much more than any one member performing all tasks independently could have done. But the processes presumably were linked in a coherent, smoothly flowing whole. Smith never suggested that the output of individual processes was coordinated through a warehouse. As we see below, manufacturing engineers at Toyota in the 1950s set out to design a system that could achieve the benefits of specialization and division of labor in a continuously flowing system, yet produce variety without waste.

Note that decoupling processes is not the same thing as subdividing and focusing work. Large, multinational, multiplant companies often subdivide an entire multiprocess network, of course, to reduce complexity (and its attendant costs).[12] They focus plants, for example, by coherent groups of product lines and by product age; or they focus full-line plants by geographic region. Focusing by subdividing an entire multiprocess chain of operations along such lines is considered an appropriate way to improve performance, because it reduces costs of complexity. Decoupling operations into processes—as depicted in Figure 3–2—has a different effect. While it can reduce local complexity and local costs in separate parts of a system, it may reduce the performance of the system as a whole. Not only does it create buffers and added work that increase system-wide costs and impair lead times; it also reduces opportunities and incentives for customer-focused teamwork across functions.

It is important to observe that in most American manufacturing plants after the 1950s, where processes had to stop for changeovers to accommodate variety, the capacity of decoupled processes necessarily had to exceed the daily demand rate. No process ever had to exceed the daily demand rate in Ford's 1925–vintage River Rouge system simply because every process was dedicated to producing one thing, one way. In American plants after the 1950s, however, processes frequently stopped to change over between varieties. Hence, less time was available to produce good output than had been the case at River Rouge. To keep to annual output schedules, therefore, processes had to produce at a much faster rate than the daily demand rate during those intervals when they were actually producing, and not down for changeover. With "so little time and so much to do," the rated capacity of machinery (size and speed) had to increase as variety increased. Americans, blessed with abundance after World War II, accepted this connection between capital and variety with equanimity. Moreover, American economic policy makers portrayed capital investment as a driver of productivity, not as an index of wasteful management practices. Hence, U.S. federal corporate income taxation policy placed high priority on incentives to encourage capital spending.

The Japanese Manufacturers' Answer After World War II

Meanwhile, Japanese manufacturers apparently observed that Ford's plant *conserved resources* by having processes linked in a continuous chain and by running slowly enough so people could stop and fix errors when they occurred. In theory, the Fordson plant at River Rouge, by operating every process (from unloading iron ore to assembling finished vehicles) at a rate equivalent to the customer demand rate, about fifty vehicles per hour, allowed humans to keep up and correct errors as they happened. Careful design of product and process, of course, reduced chance for error in the first place. However, with all processes balanced to the daily demand rate, the plant did not require more resources and capacity than the amount needed to make the vehicles customers demanded each day. The only catch, as we noted before, is that every process in Ford's plant was dedicated to producing only one vehicle, one way. How could one preserve the advantages of continuous flow in that system and still get variety?

To answer this question, the Japanese, especially at Toyota, concentrated more than Americans did in the 1950s on continuously linking and balancing processes.[13] Capital scarcity forced them to do so, rather than to decouple to achieve variety. In Japan, of course, manufacturers after World War II were struggling with scarcity, not abundance. Scarcity precluded the Japanese adopting scale and speed in decoupled processes as their pathway to variety at mass production costs. They could not seek variety by buffering between decoupled processes, nor could they seek low costs by running high-volume batches in large-scale, high speed equipment. They had to work on a smaller scale than Americans could afford, with fewer buffers, but still achieve similar mass production costs. Their answer: work very, very carefully. At Toyota, this led Ohno and his colleagues to consider fast changeover as the key to keeping processes linked, but capable of producing in variety.

Ohno and Toyota did not take existing ways of organizing work as given. They thought: what if it took *no* time to change over any process from producing one variety of something to another? In that case, one could vary the work passing through multiple processes and still require scarcely more capacity than if the processes were linked in a line dedicated to making just one product one way. They realized, of course, that zero changeover time in processes would not be achieved in the near term—perhaps never. But they recognized it was possible to achieve variety with enormous savings in resources if they adopted a goal of continuously and forever reducing time to set up and change over.

Moreover, it took little or no capital to reduce changeover times, whereas decoupling (especially with a high degree of imbalance) required inventory buffers, larger machinery, and a host of additional capital and "overhead" resources. Reducing changeovers took human ingenuity—the effort and brainpower of people on the line who carried out setups and other changeover steps in processes. This line of thought led Toyota (and others) to conclude, eventually, that it often is more profitable to empower workers to be flexible "learning machines" than it is to invest in new capital equipment. Meanwhile, American companies invested heavily in capital equipment, satisfied they could always cover the higher cost with more output. As suggested in Figure 3–3, these investments in capital and other "overhead" resources eventually pushed manufacturing costs much higher in America than in Japan.

So, the Japanese proceeded to manufacture for variety at low cost with systems that were designed to cope with scarcity. Their systems,

Figure 3–3
Managing Changeover

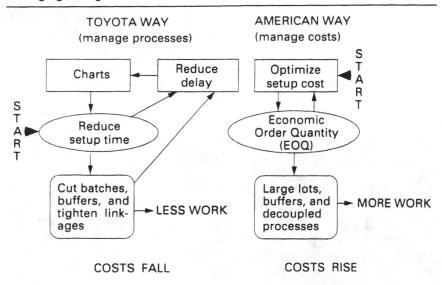

not designed to allow waste in the belief that you can always control costs with more output, produced output at just the rate needed to satisfy demand—as Ford had done in 1925—and to stop and take corrective action whenever defects occurred. Instead of a discontinuous, decoupled system that featured large, fast machines producing output in long runs at high speed for inventory, they strove to create a continuously linked system featuring much smaller machines operating at much slower rates—just enough for consumers' current needs. Like the water beetle, Japanese plants were designed to carry small loads and make frequent trips. And every trip had to count. Therefore, they always attempted to do things right the first time, a message Dr. W. Edwards Deming reinforced in his famous presentation to Japanese manufacturing executives during the summer of 1951.[14]

After World War II, then, we see American and Japanese manufacturers following divergent paths to the goal of variety at mass-production costs. Cost-focused American manufacturers were geared up by the 1960s to allow waste. But it didn't matter, because Americans saw every relevant (i.e., domestic) competitor doing the same thing and, besides, they believed they could always recoup higher cost by producing more output. Scale economies and volume of output were regarded as key imperatives of competition. Process-minded Japanese manufacturers, however, were geared up by the late 1960s to work no faster than demand required, to change over quickly, to run balanced, linked processes with little interruption, and to do work right the first time. As we now know, by 1980 they produced more variety in smaller quantities, at higher quality, and at lower cost per unit than the Americans.[15] The Japanese did it by designing and managing flexible processes to satisfy customers, not by pushing output through rigid processes, regardless of customer wants, merely to satisfy top-down accounting cost targets.

MANAGEMENT ACCOUNTING PUT AMERICAN BUSINESSES IN THE DARK

Management accounting practices adopted in American business after World War II motivated companies to make decisions that systematically put them at a disadvantage compared to focused and flexible competitors that began to appear, mainly from overseas, during the late 1960s. These practices concerned primarily the handling of indirect costs, or overhead. One practice, discussed later in Chapter 8, concerns the allocation of overhead cost to products. Accounting procedures for allocating overhead costs prevented companies whose marketing strategies led to more and more variety from seeing the causes and costs of the complexity arising in their increasingly imbalanced systems of decoupled processes. In short, overhead allocation procedures caused distortions in product margin information that deceived American companies into thinking it was much less costly than it actually was to proliferate varieties of products. Thus many companies failed to see the threat posed by their more focused competitors, and were lulled into pursuing self-destructive marketing strategies in the 1970s and 1980s.

Far more damaging to long-term competitiveness, however, was the practice companies followed of viewing overhead as a cost they could control by driving people to push output through fixed processes. This practice epitomizes the remote-control management that arose after the 1950s when American companies for the first time took to controlling operations with accounting numbers. The most prevalent example of this practice, standard cost performance evaluation systems, prevents companies from seeing the long-term benefits of striving continuously to achieve flexibility. Accounting-based performance evaluation procedures motivate actions that unwittingly increase complexity and overhead costs in systems of decoupled, unbalanced processes.

Management accounting practices of the past few decades, reinforced by principles taught in American university schools of business, have kept most American managers from understanding the long-term economic benefits of reducing changeover times and continuously linking and balancing processes. These accounting practices disguise the cost of decoupling, buffering, and flowing work in discontinuous batches. Worse, management accounting controls cause people to focus their attention on *rates of output,* not on the *flexibility of resource inputs,* especially "human resources." The reason is clear. American manufacturers who have pursued decoupling strategies since the 1950s have recognized, of course, that higher "overhead" costs were implicit in the larger transport distances, more buffers between processes, more storage, scheduling, inspecting, and rework. But they apparently believed they could always "make it up on volume" by producing more output. Volume of output, by definition, determined unit cost in each and every process. Spreading "overhead" costs over more output meant lower cost per unit of output in each process. Presumably that also meant lower total costs per unit of finished product—assuming the whole to be equal to the sum of the parts.

Of course, producing more output to achieve lower costs also meant one had to sell more finished product, presumably at a price at least equal to out-of-pocket variable costs. The answer there was to aggressively *persuade* the customer to take off your hands what you produce, with care never to discount price below variable cost. Helping to make this strategy work, of course, was the fact that every major (domestic) competitor was doing things the same way—at least in the 1960s and 1970s.

By focusing people's minds on rates of output, management accounting contributed greatly to the creation of waste in American business after the 1950s. It reinforced a general theme throughout American history—the idea that economic development entails expansion onto a frontier of virtually limitless resources. Scale and speed, seen in large-scale capital investment justified by high volume output, was not just an economic imperative. It was also a cultural and social norm.

Contributing particularly to waste was the management accountants' concept, popular after the 1950s, of controlling "fixed" overhead costs by concentrating on variable cost, contribution margin, and the "break even" rate of output needed to "cover" fixed cost. In other words, instead of looking for better ways to manage overhead cost itself, management accounting controls caused people in American business to think the real issue was how to drive output rates fast enough to *cover* overhead costs caused by scale and complexity. This imperative to control costs by sustaining output was enshrined in cost-volume-profit (CVP) analysis, a central theme in MBA courses for the past thirty years. CVP analysis, put simply, relates a company's profits to the revenue margin each unit of output contributes above its variable cost. With most overhead costs defined as a fixed constraint, profit is presumed to result directly from that contribution margin and from the number of units sold: more units and more margin per unit mean more profit.

A by-product of CVP thinking, referred to by management accountants as contribution margin pricing, has insidiously generated enormous sums of excess capital in American industry for decades. Management scholar John Shank has recounted three excellent examples of contribution margin pricing folly:[16]

1. In the years immediately following deregulation, few airline companies really knew how to operate in a free market. Braniff was one that competed itself to death with contribution margin concepts. "The notion which led Braniff into Chapter 11 is that you can prosper selling $100 tickets based on the zero-variable-cost concept." Everyone knows that concept—if a plane is about to take off and one seat is empty it costs nothing to put on one more passenger. Conclusion: Any money collected from that passenger above the price of a bag of peanuts and the extra fuel consumed by his or her weight is pure profit to the bottom line. Right? Absolutely wrong! When contribution margin pricing is built into regularly advertised tariff schedules, long lines form and airports become overcrowded, disrupting service and creating numerous frustrations for full-fare paying passengers. Eventually no one but the bargain seeker enjoys flying, and the airline ends up in the long run covering *only* short-term variable costs.

2. Contribution margin pricing also took a heavy toll on American steel firms such as Jones & Laughlin, Wheeling Pittsburgh, and Youngstown Sheet & Tube. Their downfall was the seductive belief that higher contribution margins resulted the more highly the steel is processed: slabs are more profitable than ingots, rolls are more profitable than slabs, cold rolls are more profitable that hot bands, and galvanized sheets are the most profitable of all. "Product mixes in the

steel industry moved in the direction of those higher margin items, but the result was not higher profit. The fallacy is simple . . . further processing of a band of steel requires extra investment and extra fixed costs but very little extra variable costs. . . . So then the more processed the steel, the higher the contribution margin for those products—but also the greater the long-term losses when prices do not cover those fixed costs."

3. Perhaps the paper industry provides the most egregious example of wasteful capital spending prompted by the contribution margin pricing mindset. According to Shank, "per capita paper consumption in the United States is about [twice] what it is in Europe [outside Scandinavia]. Wow! The paper companies hear that and they see a tremendous marketing opportunity in Europe. . . . But is it a tremendous marketing opportunity? [Selling] prices are on average about twice as high in Europe. The higher prices certainly have something to do with the lower consumption rates. [Moreover,] the growth of paper consumption in this country over [the last 25 or so years] matches the period of the growing use of the contribution margin mentality in thinking about pricing strategy in the industry. The aggregate return of the paper industry now ranks 23rd out of 31 in the latest Forbes five-year ROE history. [In] the early 1960s it was in the top third in profitability. . . . It's dropped from the top third to the bottom third, and the aggressive pricers rank near the bottom of the industry. [Companies such as] Champion International, International Paper, Weyerhaeuser, and Georgia Pacific [all] think in contribution margin terms, and the bottom line is those companies are eating their seed corn."

Cultivation of waste is a general result of *all* management accounting tools, not just the contribution margin pricing tool. Perhaps the most vivid example of this claim is the management of *costs* reported by the accounting system—one of the principal tasks of operating managers in most American manufacturing companies during the last forty years.[17] In traditional management accounting systems, the controller's office "rolls down" cost targets from top-level planning budgets to lower-level operating reports. Cost targets, reminiscent of shadows on the wall of Plato's cave, are seen as an important tool to "control" the work of plant managers and department supervisors. Like the setting on a thermostat that keeps a furnace working at the rate needed to maintain a desired room temperature, cost targets are viewed as a desired outcome to compare against actual performance. Variances between actual and desired results provide "feedback" that is supposed to prompt operating managers and other employees to adjust their actions.

The typical actions this cost accounting information motivates are ones designed to sustain output in order to achieve cost targets. For example, department supervisors act to keep machines and people busy producing output, regardless of market demand, in order to minimize standard cost variances. By using such targets and variances to encourage high utilization of worker and machine time, financially oriented companies often cause unnecessary inventories of finished and in-process merchandise to accumulate. They see product lead times increase, and their dependability at keeping schedules decrease. To achieve their separate cost targets, each department impairs the company's overall ability to compete. *People left to their own devices produce better results.* But people can not move a company toward competitive excellence if they are rewarded for meeting top-down accounting-based targets, not for continuously seeking better ways to satisfy customers, internal and external.

The ultimate irony is that actions prompted by traditional management accounting systems to keep local costs under control actually increase total costs in decoupled systems. As we noted before, the practice of controlling output costs in decoupled processes by having each decoupled unit produce more output, faster, actually increases overall work and total costs. This increase in costs, often referred to in the financial press during the early 1980s as "overhead creep," reflected additional work, or transactions, caused by increased volume and diversity of output in unbalanced and decoupled systems.[18]

These consequences of decoupling are exacerbated by cost measurements that induce people to gain local advantages at the expense of systemwide results. Companies do that when they use traditional standard cost variance incentives to control "efficiency" in decoupled systems. Indeed, standard cost variance reporting systems deserve special attention because of the contribution they themselves make to cost and complexity.[19] Believing that total cost in the whole system is equal to the sum of the costs in each separate process, management accountants created standard cost variance systems to monitor costs in each and every process of a company's production system. For direct costs they devised labor and machine tracking schemes that reported direct costs per hour or per unit of output. For overhead costs they devised reporting schemes to track the percentage of overhead "covered" or "earned" by units produced.[20]

The goal of these reporting schemes is to have all direct labor hours or machine hours go toward production of standard output and thereby "absorb" or "cover" all direct and overhead costs, a condition referred to as "efficient." Intelligent department managers beat this system by scheduling workers and machines to produce output in long runs. That eliminates time spent on changeovers and setups—categories of indirect or "nonchargeable" time. Don't have workers and machines idled for changeovers; keep them busy producing output, because output enables a department to "earn" the direct hours incurred each reporting period. Every unit produced—including the equivalent of full units in partially finished work—entitles the department to a standard allotment of machine or man hours. If a department produces enough equivalent finished output to "earn" all the direct hours reported in the period it is declared "100 percent efficient." It doesn't matter if the output is saleable. In fact, hours spent on "allowable" rework are often considered to be "efficiently covered." With so flawed a system, people sometimes put in hours creating defects, just so the department can report enough direct labor hours to be classified as "efficient."

Therefore, achieving standard direct cost "efficiency" targets leads to larger batches, longer production runs, more scrap, more rework, and less communication across processes. Ironically, managers' efforts to achieve high standard cost efficiency ratings have tended over time to increase a company's total costs and to impair competitiveness, especially by increasing lead times. In any plant striving to achieve manufacturing excellence, standard cost performance systems are anathema—especially if incentive compensation is geared to controlling standard-to-actual variances. Those systems encourage waste (excess production), delay (longer lead times), and imbalance (end-of-period production spurts to reach "efficiency" targets). Moreover, they do not provide motivation for continual change and improvement in the methods and parameters of production.

Indeed, motivating people to act in response to standard cost variances will, in most cases, throw processes farther and farther out of control. It is safe to say that most top managers and management accountants in America do not understand this consequence of overcontrol. The phenomenon was articulated years ago by W. Edwards

Deming, among others, and today is well known to statisticians acquainted with statistical variation in processes. A good description of the phenomenon comes from quality expert William Scherkenbach who points out that workers' efforts to compensate for any and every variation in a process (such as the compensations made to eliminate standard cost budget variances) in fact changes the process.[21]

The point is that output characteristics, such as cost, should be expected to vary within statistically normal limits. Those limits are indigenous to a process and can be reduced over time by improving the process. But if someone "tweaks" the process to compensate every time there is a variation, the process is changed and the limits of normal variation grow wider and wider. I don't believe any management accounting textbook or any management accountant has ever pointed out that adjustments people make to reduce standard cost variances destabilize processes and add to the costs of doing business.

Perhaps an even more insidious consequence of standard cost performance evaluation systems is their tendency to downplay—even ignore—what customers want. Indeed, customers scarcely fit into the world of standard cost performance. The customer is merely someone the company persuades to buy the output managers are driven to produce, at prices it is hoped exceed variable costs.

Companies that understand manufacturing excellence know these things. Harley-Davidson knows this. General Electric knows this. Both companies used traditional standard cost performance measurement systems years before they ever heard of JIT. When they began to implement JIT systems in their plants in the 1980s, both companies discovered that traditional performance measures clashed with the imperatives of satisfying customers "just in time."[22]

The clash occurs as soon as plant personnel begin to spend their time eliminating waste and increasing flexibility, not just producing output. In a JIT system, employees expend extra effort to do things right the first time, pitching in wherever need arises, and to train—all of which traditional labor reporting systems usually classify as "nonchargeable" time—that is, time not "earned" producing output. Hence, doing what it takes to send customers the *right* output *on schedule* can reduce the department's "efficiency" rating. That's the "clash."

As we discuss in Chapter 7 of this book, the answer, or at least a good part of it, at companies like Harley-Davidson and GE, is to evaluate shop floor performance in terms of things that matter to customers—such as keeping promised delivery schedules and reducing calls to repair defects. However, they also monitor cost—*total actual* costs controlled by the entire plant, not standard unit costs of pieces and subcomponents tracked in separate departments by the accounting system.

Ironically, when plants in GE's Medical Systems Group first moved toward JIT in the mid-1980s they discovered the corporate accounting system could not produce information about the total actual costs. Now those plants bypass the accounting system and track total payroll (direct and indirect, not just direct payroll) and total material costs at the plant level. The company evaluates plant managers on their success at driving down total cost—an unambiguous index of something that adds value both to the customer and to the company, like reducing defect rates and meeting delivery schedules.

In American companies during the 1960s and 1970s, added complexity and cost caused by efforts to achieve departmental cost performance targets did not impair any one company's competitiveness and profitability because most businesses in the marketplace followed basically the same procedures. Most manufacturers by the 1960s used standard cost targets to "control" decoupled systems through which work lurched toward completion in discontinuous batches. The complexity of these systems caused added time (the time from iron ore to finished vehicle went from less than three and a half days at Ford's River Rouge plant in 1923 to five or six weeks in most automotive plants by the 1960s) and cost (cost of people and resources consumed in storing, moving, inspecting, expediting, scheduling, monitoring, accounting, and waiting; not to mention the cost of investing in larger and faster equipment). But no one minded this added time and cost as long as all competitors did things the same way.

That condition changed after 1970. By then many American manufacturers faced the competitors, largely from Japan, who had discovered how to achieve variety by achieving flexibility, without decoupling the processes in a production system. The change began with automobiles. Companies such as Toyota recreated what Henry Ford had done at River Rouge in the 1920s, but this time they made it possible to achieve variety. The need to link processes and to achieve variety with flexibility was scarcely understood in the Western world, of course, until the early 1980s. Unfortunately the traditional cost performance systems which blinded managers still prevent many companies from understanding this change, and taking the steps necessary to make the change themselves.

WRAP-UP

Using accounting information after the 1950s to control business operations and to evaluate marketing and sourcing decisions caused American business to overlook two developments: (1) the cost of complexity implicit in organizing people and work in unbalanced, decoupled systems, and (2) the savings in cost and improvement in flexibility and reliability resulting from Japanese efforts to remove constraints, such as changeover time, in order to link work and people in balanced, continuous flows. Failure to understand the costs of complexity and the benefits of flexibility caused American companies to lose market share and profitability to more focused and flexible competitors in the 1970s and 1980s.

Many people express the belief that the worst is over, that the hard times of the 1970s and '80s were due largely to war-torn competitors returning to their rightful place in the world's economy. American business, they say, could not expect the halcyon days of the 1950s and '60s to last forever. They believe that for the most part ground lost will not be regained. They are nonetheless confident that further setbacks such as those they suffered in the last two decades will not recur. Presumably Americans have learned some hard lessons about wasteful management practices, as evidenced by their efforts to become "lean and mean," to "downsize" and to "scale back" the excess spending of the past. These steps, many think, will enable U.S. companies to march forward profitably and competitively.

I wish I shared this optimism. Unfortunately I doubt that top management in American businesses understands fully the principles and imperatives of competitive excellence in the global economy. Unless these imperatives guide them, companies will continue sanctioning management actions designed to fulfill the wrong competitive goals. If this occurs, the devastation visited on American business in the 1970s and 1980s may look tame compared with what is coming in the next decade.

American business leaders must recognize that a change in fundamental ways of managing processes—not incremental improvements on traditional business practice—lies behind the dramatic success of the world-class companies, especially those in Japan, that rose from nowhere to conquer world markets in autos, consumer electronics, machine tools, and other industries in the last twenty years. A shift in methods of this magnitude creates a discontinuity that leaves people with an unsettled feeling until they come to terms with—make unconscious—the new method. A company that pursues business as usual to compete in today's global economy faces the same fate as an athlete who tries to stay competitive by honing and improving the old way of doing things, like a high jumper in the early 1970s who might have tried to compete by improving the Western roll when other people began using the Fosbury flop. That jumper surely would have failed.[23]

Unless managers adopt new methods and new thinking they will be thwarted. Merely improving their skill at doing things the old way will not salvage their companies and make them competitive.

RELEVANCE REGAINED BY BOTTOM-UP EMPOWERMENT

New information technologies impose new demands on businesses desiring to compete in today's economic environment. The next six chapters describe those imperatives and outline the new thinking and new management practices businesses must adopt to compete in the global economy.

Chapter 4 describes the imperatives of competition today and compares them with the principles that guided business competition both before 1950 and during the period from the 1950s to the 1980s. The remaining five chapters in Part II discuss the management information and the actions required to run a competitive business today. Chapters 5 and 6 discuss how businesses can meet today's demands for responsiveness and flexibility. Chapter 5 discusses customer relationship building as the key to becoming responsive, while Chapters 6 discusses the need to empower the work force to continually simplify work processes, to achieve flexibility. Chapter 7 describes the changes in management information that motivate the work force to build responsive relationships and flexible processes. Chapter 8 discusses the strengths and weaknesses of management information derived from a popular accounting innovation known as activity-based cost management. Finally, Chapter 9 rounds out this section of the book by outlining tentative steps companies can follow to fulfill the imperatives of competition in the global economy.

Time: A Note on Terminology

In Part II of this book I use the term "lead time" to mean the elapsed time, from start to finish, that it takes to complete a job—to design a product, deliver on a promise, prepare an invoice, whatever. The term "cycle time" is often used instead of "lead time," as in the application guidelines of the Malcolm Baldrige National Quality Award. I prefer to follow traditional industrial engineering terminology and use "cycle time" to mean the time between recurring events, such as between units on an assembly line. (For more on the different definitions of "lead time" and "cycle time" see Robert W. Hall in the Summer 1989 issue of *Target*, pp. 2 and 29–33.) As I use the terms here, "lead time" is an inclusive measure of time to perform a process (or a series of processes) while "cycle time" refers to the time to generate output from a process (or a series of processes).

CHAPTER 4

IMPERATIVES
OF COMPETITION
—PAST AND PRESENT

Information technology . . . raises a vision of a sort of corporate
utopia—the "learning organization," which uses technology ceaselessly to refresh its knowledge of its customers' wants and to devise
new ways of satisfying them.

—John Browning[1]

A business performs adequately in the long run only if its goals and
the actions of its personnel address relevant imperatives of competition. A key to insuring competitiveness is management information
that links the goals and actions of company personnel to the appropriate imperatives. Top management's job is to know what these are and
to insure that the work force has proper information and uses proper
methods to achieve competitive operations.

The imperatives of competition normally are defined by underlying
technologies that create business opportunity. Peter Drucker argues
that business opportunity in the past two hundred years has derived
from two underlying technological revolutions.[2] One is the industrial
revolution, lasting until the late 1940s, when businesses profited by
tapping energy sources created by the sun—wood, coal, oil, and nuclear sources of energy. The second is the information revolution,
started by the invention of the mainframe computer in 1946, which

allows businesses to profit by capitalizing on computer technologies. Associated with each revolution are distinctive demands for long-term business competitiveness. Successful long-term performance requires a business to link its management information and practices to those imperatives.

The model in Figure 4–1 suggests how the information that guides people's goals and actions connects business performance with the imperatives defined by underlying technological opportunities. Using that model as a framework, this chapter discusses the imperatives of competition and the management information used to control operations in American business over the last two hundred years. The next section compares the management information used to control business operations before the 1950s (Age of Energy) with that used from the 1950s to the 1980s (Dark Age of Relevance Lost). This discussion is a prelude to the central topic of the next six chapters—the imperatives, actions, and management information required for long-term competitiveness in the 1990s and beyond (Age of Information).

Figure 4–1
Structure of Business Performance

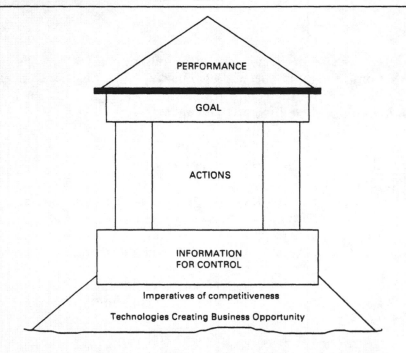

PERFORMANCE

GOAL

ACTIONS

INFORMATION
FOR CONTROL

Imperatives of competitiveness

Technologies Creating Business Opportunity

IMPERATIVES OF COMPETITION BEFORE THE 1990S

Until the 1950s, well-run American companies addressed the imperatives of industrial competition, particularly the demands for scale and speed. After the 1950s, however, the coming of new computer-based information technologies radically altered the nature of business competition. Unfortunately, American businesses from the 1950s to the 1980s — the Dark Age of Relevance Lost — failed to address the new imperatives of information-based competition. Instead, they began to address imperatives defined by accounting and finance, not by the economic opportunities offered by new information technologies. Indeed, the remote-control management practices of the past forty years simply parodied the old imperatives that had been relevant to competition in the industrial era down to the 1950s. In effect, American business after the 1950s floundered aimlessly, virtually oblivious to the fundamental technological forces that were shaping global business competition.

The Age of Energy: Circa 1800 to 1950

Before the 1950s, according to Peter Drucker, companies competed by tapping economic opportunities offered by energy-using technologies. Businesses organized production in mechanical systems where "the whole is equal to the sum of its parts and therefore capable of being understood by analysis."[3] In such mechanical systems, metaphors for which are the steam engine or a turbine electric generator, "greater power means greater output: bigger is better."[4] Thus, the key imperatives of competitive business performance in energy-based mechanical systems are scale and speed: performance is improved by scaling up. Figure 4–2 portrays the relationships between the imperatives of competition, the actions of management, and the goals that prevailed in American business before the 1950s, whether in the early nineteenth century water-powered textile mills of New England or the mid-twentieth century industrial giants such as General Motors.

Several features of pre-1950s business practice discussed in earlier chapters are implied in Figure 4–2. For instance, American business leaders before the 1950s did not seem to allow their quest for scale, speed, and division of labor to create wasteful imbalances in systems of decoupled processes. Andrew Carnegie and Henry Ford, for example, seemed to understand the virtues of balanced, continuous flows far better than do their post-1950s counterparts in American business.

Figure 4–2
Structure of Business Performance: 1800 to the 1950s

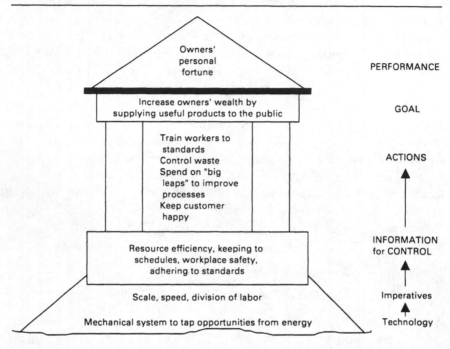

Their organizations—Carnegie's Edgar Thompson works in Pittsburgh and Ford's River Rouge system outside Detroit—exemplified the relationships portrayed in Figure 4–2. Both plants epitomized the pursuit of scale and division of labor. Neither achieved division of labor by decoupling tasks and activities into a hodge-podge of processes, each bent wholly on producing output at their peak capacities.

Top managers before the 1950s, such as Carnegie and Ford, also expected their operating managers to devote attention to training workers properly according to well-defined standards, to minimizing waste of time and resources, and to pleasing customers. Their employees, while having no mandate to improve processes continually by identifying and solving problems, were exhorted to perform processes to the highest standards. Employees were not to manipulate processes to enhance the bottom line.

Top management in nineteenth and early twentieth century companies also took primary responsibility for improving processes, by searching for and implementing new technologies embedded in new capital equipment or new methods to organize work. Their motivation for these "big leap" investments, in most cases, was to improve processes, not simply to cut costs. Carnegie and Ford, in particular, never let cost calculations stand in the way of capital investments that they believed would significantly improve products or processes and thereby enhance their companies' long-run competitiveness.

These pre-1950s business leaders, driven in business not by altruism but by the plain wish to make money, as their vast personal fortunes testify, clearly understood that their business success depended upon the value their products and services provided to society. Not financial manipulation, but quality performance dictated their business leadership. It is not surprising, then, that these customer-focused entrepreneurs should have a social conscience. In *Today and Tomorrow* Ford waxed eloquent about the social implications of mass production and automobile transportation. And Carnegie, after selling his business to J. P. Morgan in 1901, spent the rest of his life giving virtually all his money back to society, to build libraries and to improve educational opportunities for people around the world. Their examples were not unique. Many early business leaders such as Carnegie, the DuPonts, and Ford detested the financial community and went to great lengths to avoid dealing with financial markets. They focused their attention on markets for products and services, not on markets for securities. Evidently few business leaders before the 1950s held to the view that their wealth should emanate from astute financial manipulation.

These observations suggest that the torch passed down by prewar American business leaders such as Ford, Sloan, Carnegie, and the DuPonts has been carried on by the Japanese, such as Ohno at Toyota, and not by the wizards of remote-control financial management in post-1950s American companies. Ohno himself in the 1970s spoke of that difference when he said, "I have long doubted that the mass-production system practiced in America and around the world today, even in Japan, was Ford's true intention. . . . I think that if [Henry Ford] were still alive, he would be headed in the same direction as Toyota. . . . I think [Ford's] true intention was to extend a work flow from the final assembly line to all other processes . . . Ford's successors, however, did not make production flow as Ford intended. . . . A major reason is that Ford's successors misinterpreted the work flow system. The final process is indeed a work flow, but in other production lines, [they] force the work to flow. . . . America's system of mass production . . . generates unnecessary losses in pursuit of quantity and speed."[5]

Probably the single most important difference between the approach to production that Ohno developed at Toyota and the approach followed by his peers in America was Ohno's willingness to remove certain constraints that his American counterparts assumed were fixed and immutable. Chief among those constraints, discussed above in Chapter 3, was changeover time in production processes, although removing other constraints such as product and process design and layout of work (discussed later in Chapter 6) should not be overlooked. Ohno's brilliance was to ask questions no one had asked before, such as "what if it took no time at all to change over processes?" Business historian David Hounshell notes that Ford himself often had the same insight, to remove constraints rather than take them for granted,[6] but Ford did not carry the thought process as far as Ohno would some thirty years later. In contrast, Ford's successors in the United States, after the 1950s, made a religion out of mathematically optimizing within constraints, not removing them (see Figure 3–3).

The Dark Age of Relevance Lost: From the 1950s to the 1980s

After the 1950s, American businesses stopped pursuing externally defined imperatives of competition. They began to pursue "pseudo" imperatives defined by their new accounting-based management information systems. This practice marked a sharp break from the past. Before the 1950s, companies designed management information to trigger actions that would fulfill the energy-based imperatives of the industrial economy. After the 1950s, accounting-based management information was designed to prompt behavior that fulfilled the goals of management accounting's own making. Lacking any connection with the external imperatives of information-based global competition, these accounting-based imperatives took on a life of their own. In a very real sense, accounting became the "language of business."

Figure 4–3 portrays relationships between business performance and management information after the 1950s, during the Dark Age of Relevance Lost. The relationships in Figure 4–3 differ in several key aspects from the pre-1950s relationships portrayed in Figure 4–2. First, the figure depicts performance, measured by securities markets, as the result of everyone focusing their actions on an accounting artifact—return on investment—not as the end result of providing socially useful products or services at a profit. Secondly, the underlying principles of business competition are not defined in the marketplace. They

Figure 4–3
Structure of Business Performance: 1950s to 1980s

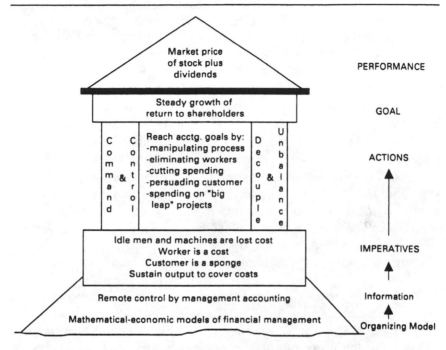

are defined by financial models and accounting relationships. Thus, the foundation on which business performance rests is not information that links actions and behavior to real imperatives of competition in the marketplace. In Figure 4–3, it is not technological opportunities but mathematical-economic models of financial management that define the imperatives of business competition. Management uses remote accounting controls to trigger actions and behavior that are intended to fulfill those "pseudo" financial imperatives.

As a consequence of this remote-control management, businesses lost a clear sense of purpose. Their vision became myopic, narrowly defined by accounting information. Ernest Huge describes the implications of this consequence:

> To maximize return on investment is an inadequate statement of purpose. It fails to accomplish the paramount responsibility of leadership—to provide meaning and inspiration to those who are expected to follow. The mass of people within our corporations are not primarily motivated by maximizing private gain. Many firms are structured as if they were. . . .

Financial objectives also are an inadequate statement of purpose because they fail to recognize the social justification for the corporation's
existence. Business enterprises do have a noble purpose, and they should
recognize and proclaim it. The purpose of business is the creation of
wealth—not for a few, but for all. The creation of genuine wealth in the
form of goods and services [and jobs] must be the corporations' primary
purpose. Financial results will follow as the corporation succeeds in this
primary aim.[7]*

Business as it has been practiced by most American companies in the
past forty years lacks this large purpose. Figure 4–3 portrays the fundamental purpose of business in terms of a deterministic set of financial-
mathematical relationships—what economists refer to as a production
function. Those relationships resemble a machine in which employees,
suppliers, and customers are merely cogs in the gears. To attain competitive costs, the machine is built to the largest scale permitted by resources available, and all parts of the machine are run at the highest
speed possible. Output is sold, hopefully at a profit, by persuading a
customer to take merchandise off the company's hands without com-
plaining.

Many management authorities before now have described and in-
veighed against these deficiencies in American business practices of the
last four decades. What I have reiterated is how sharply those practices
depart from the more rational and defensible practices of American
business in the Age of Energy, before the 1950s. When people say businesses today do not pay enough attention to customers, to quality, to
worker training, to broader goals than shareholder returns, and so
forth, they are venting criticisms that apply to American business only
since the 1950s. Before then, businesses did not routinely ignore people and time. This relatively recent development in American business
had its origins in the growing use of accounting information to control
business operations after the 1950s.

Until top managers stop controlling people's behavior with accounting
information, remedying the problems American businesses faced in the
1970s and 1980s is inconceivable. With proper management information, however, they will do many things the same way their predecessors did them before the 1950s. They will also do many things differently, because the organizing basis for business competition is not
the same today as it was when energy-using technologies provided the
basis for competition. Today companies must capitalize on information-
based technical and marketing opportunities in the global economy.

*©1988. Used with permission of Dow Jones-Irwin, Inc.

THE AGE OF INFORMATION: IMPERATIVES OF COMPETITION IN THE 1990S AND BEYOND

According to Peter Drucker, information became the new "organizing principle of production" after 1946.[8] With the coming of the computer and technological developments associated with it, information replaced energy as the basis of competitive opportunity in the business world. The tremendous availability of information has increased the power of the customer by revealing new, abundant opportunities for choice. The enormous array of information accessible to businesses permits learning about individual customers and analyzing processes. Once thought too costly to gather, real-time information is now easily available as a by-product of making a sale or performing work.[9] Whereas information was always an important tool to help businesses plan and control their use of resources, now information is an important resource in its own right that contributes to competitiveness and profitability.

To capture the potential implicit in information, businesses must do more than alter or improve present-day management practices. New management principles are needed to tap the possibilities created by virtually limitless information. Information brings to the table an entirely new set of competitive opportunities that require companies to radically overhaul the way they organize work and people. Imperatives that must guide businesses in this information-based economy are quite different than those energy-based imperatives that guided successful businesses before the 1950s. They differ, too, from the "pseudo" financial imperatives most American businesses have followed since the 1950s. As shown in Figure 4–4, the overriding imperatives of competition in the global economy are *responsiveness* and *flexibility*. The information (and communication) technologies spawned by the computer give power to the people—to customers, workers, investors, and to members of the general public affected by a business. In general, people adapted to the company (and to the state) in previous eras. Now companies (and nation states) find more often that they must adapt to people in the information-based global economy.

Businesses today must understand what it means to have the customer in charge of the marketplace and the work force in charge of processes. Having the customer in charge of the marketplace requires companies to be responsive, an imperative with which most American businesses are unfamiliar. In the last four decades, the customer played a minor role in American management decisions. Capacity constraints,

Figure 4–4
Structure of Business Performance: Global Economy

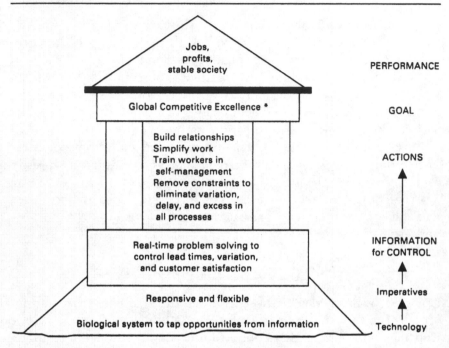

* Continuously reduce time and resources needed to completely
 satisfy customers, associates, suppliers (including shareholders), and society

output rates, and cost targets—not customer wants—dictated how much a company should produce. The customer was no one in particular; just anyone the company could persuade to buy products at an adequate price. No more. New information technologies now give customers unprecedented power. Customers know about myriad options and possibilities. They can choose. Companies must do more than just persuade—they must respond to customers' wishes. Responsiveness necessitates building relationships, trust, and loyalty among customers by keeping promises. After forty years of viewing customers as flexible buffers—mindless sheep who responded to price stimuli and absorbed the output that a company rigidly produced to cover its costs—now businesses are forced by global competition to view customers as a lodestar guiding the company's very flexible operating system.

The corollary of customer power is that business processes and systems must become *flexible*. This means giving the work force ownership of processes. By tapping the power of new information technologies, especially the microprocessor, real-time process information can be placed directly in workers' hands. By empowering workers to access information and initiate action, and by building relationships with suppliers and customers, companies can compress time within and between processes. World-class companies reduce lead times primarily by removing constraints and by altering the way work is organized. They do not reduce lead times simply by accelerating the speed with which people and machines perform tasks.

The quotation at the head of this chapter expresses the new imperatives imposed by modern information technology on global business. Companies must "ceaselessly refresh their knowledge of what customers want" and "ceaselessly devise new ways to satisfy these wants." Thus, competitive excellence requires that companies pay attention to two imperatives that are totally antithetical to the financial imperatives of competition companies have pursued since the 1950s.

Achieving Responsiveness: "Managing with the Customer in Charge"

Increased "customer power" has changed the terms of competition in most markets since the 1970s. Until the 1970s, most companies defined competitiveness in terms set by other companies, not in terms set by customers. Focusing on a captive market, companies studied local competitors' products and processes to understand what they had to do to compete profitably. Reflecting this behavior are practices such as reverse engineering (taking apart the competitor's product to see what makes it tick) and traditional benchmarking (calibrating one's own performance against competitors' standards). The primary purpose of these practices in the past was to surpass competitors. In the global economy, however, these practices must aim above all at satisfying customers.

To succeed globally, beating the competition has increasingly meant since the 1970s discovering and providing what customers want, not just matching or surpassing what competitors can do. As barriers to interregional and international trade diminished and access to information grew dramatically during the 1970s, customers became increasingly able to locate and acquire the best of what they want, at an acceptable price, wherever it is *in the world*. Consequently, customers have displaced producers from the driver's seat of many markets. In wresting control of the marketplace from producers, customers in effect ushered in the global economy. Competitive excellence in a global economy is nothing more nor less than having the power to profitably satisfy and exceed the expectations of customers who can secure the best of what they want wherever it is in the world.

Previously limited to choosing among local and national suppliers, customers today select among a global array of suppliers who not only offer them more, but also respond faster to *changes* in their wants. The shift in the locus of power from competitors to customers compels companies to satisfy an immeasurable array of customer wants faster than ever before. Most companies before the 1970s had to satisfy customers only up to a point. They only had to meet standards set by "the usual suspects"—familiar local or national competitors. Today's new "customer power" forces companies to respond quickly to the best that customers can locate anywhere.

For example, North American or European bicycle makers must respond now to customers in Kansas City or Munich who can fax orders to Kokubu, Japan where the National Bicycle Industrial Co. builds Panasonic bicycles for Matsushita—and can ship the finished product almost anywhere via air express. National Bicycle is a company that has discovered and is pursuing the vision of global competitive excellence.[10] The company places top priority on satisfying the customer. Its system "puts the consumer at the beginning rather than at the end of the process . . . [giving consumers] what they crave most: unique products." This small (twenty-person) company can hand-assemble over 11 million possible varieties of custom-made bicycles in lots of one! To be so responsive to individual customers' wants the company has redesigned radically the way everyone works. They use modern computer-aided design (CAD) equipment and employ welding robots, but their manufacturing process is *not* highly automated. "The factory looks a little like a traditional workshop, with crafts people hand-wiring gears and silk-screening the customer's name on the frame with the same care that would be given to the finest kimono or lacquerware." The people at National Bicycle have transformed mass production into flexible *personalized* manufacturing. To compete globally, they manage the business as though the customer is in charge.

Achieving Flexibility

Businesses all over the world are being told that to succeed in the global economy they must "listen hard and respond fast."[11] Is this message new? Hasn't success in business always hinged on satisfying customers? It has up to a point. The major difference today is that global competitors must focus totally on listening and adapting. Companies do not succeed merely by adding more service, smiles, and guarantees on top of business as usual. Instead, competitive excellence depends on "organizing entire companies—from research to manufacturing, from information systems to pay incentives—around giving customers what they want."[12] Running a business with the customer in charge requires total dedication to becoming flexible.

How does managing a business to be flexible differ from the management practices that have guided businesses for the past forty years? Basically, flexible organizations focus on total time to get work done (lead time), whereas cost-focused organizations in the last four decades have concentrated on the rate (speed) at which work is done. Steps to reduce lead time involve removing constraints that cause delay, excess, and variation in processes. Steps to increase speed involve optimizing within unchanging constraints. Lead times are influenced by many constraints, such as the design of products and processes, plant layouts, vendor relations, and employee relations. Since the 1950s, American businesses have tended to see these constraints as more or less immutable, usually caused by external forces beyond a company's short-run control. Taking these constraints for granted, they have focused day-to-day attention on optimizing rates of work in every part of the company.

Companies in many industries, such as the bicycle maker referred to above, have already adopted changes that address information-era imperatives of responsiveness and flexibility. Competing with such companies forces other businesses to do the same or fall by the wayside. Eventually no industry will be left untouched. The change is already visible in consumer electronics, computers, telecommunications, industrial machine tools, and automobiles.

Indeed, the automobile industry offers particularly stunning examples of the profound change that occurs when companies pursue flexibility in order to be totally responsive to customer expectations. The change was evident by the mid-1970s in cars made by Japanese companies such as Toyota, Nissan, and Honda. In the 1980s it began to take hold in North American automobile companies such as Ford. Now European automakers are striving to join the list.

This change brings pleasant surprises to automobile consumers, if not to automakers who fail to adapt. Consumers of small and midsized cars in the 1970s and early 1980s enjoyed unheard of improvements in quality without paying higher prices to get it. The first quality improvements were limited to "fit and finish," but they quickly grew to include improved mileage without loss of engine performance, increased wear and durability, improved serviceability, and greater reliability. Companies that first offered these improvements did so on a narrow range of models and option packages. But that did not remain the case for long. By the mid-1980s these quality improvements, especially from Japanese automakers, were appearing on a wider array of model choices, including midsized vehicles. Clearly, global competitors were learning to master quality as well as flexibility, in terms of variety and time to introduce new designs. Still, consumers were not paying a great deal more, in real price-adjusted terms, for the additional satisfaction. By the mid-1980s, companies that had mastered these lessons enjoyed growing market share and profitability.

The recent introduction by Japanese companies of new luxury automobiles indicates that leading Japanese automakers are as determined as ever to extend the frontier of customer satisfaction. A July 1990 report claims that Acura (Honda), Lexus (Toyota), and Infiniti (Nissan) have "redefined the meaning of luxury."[13] After achieving new standards of customer satisfaction in economy and midsize cars in the 1970s and 1980s, these automakers are now bringing "exceptional product quality, reliability, and value with superior sales and service" to luxury car markets. The result is a new breed of "totally trouble-free, care-free cars" that redefine the concept of luxury automobile in terms of what customers want, not what competitors have customarily provided. People who buy these cars "get the greatest luxury of all—no hassles." Moreover, they enjoy surprisingly low sticker prices. Who's worried? North American makers of luxury cars such as Cadillac and Lincoln are, of course. But they've already learned a lot from earlier battles in the economy-class and midsized wars of the last decade. Relative newcomers to the fray now include famous European luxury automakers such as Mercedes, Ferrari, BMW, and Porsche.

WRAP-UP

To achieve competitive excellence today, companies must stop employees and managers from attempting to manipulate outputs of processes in order to reach accounting targets—the insidious practice that emanates from "managing by remote control." That practice reinforces behavior that is antithetical to the terms of competition in the global economy. Top managers must have a clear understanding of the difference between that remote-control behavior and the behavior that leads to flexibility and customer satisfaction.

Managers can not articulate practices that will lead to flexibility and satisfaction merely by extrapolating from practices of the past. They must work back from a vision of a future state they hope to achieve. That vision must enable them to portray *the present as the past condition of the future*—not an incremental transition from the past.[14] Defining a vision of what that past condition must be is, in a sense, the goal of this book. Table 4–1 briefly summarizes the characteristics, or earmarks, of business behavior today that reflect the "past condition" of competitive performance in the global economy tomorrow. The figure contrasts those earmarks with the remote-control management practices of the past forty years. Quite different behavior is called for when customer satisfaction and worker empowerment drive operations than when accounting "shadows on the wall" drive operations.

The behaviors listed in Table 4–1 reflect very different assumptions about the roles of people and time in a business. Remote-control be-

Table 4–1
Earmarks of Business Behavior

Remote Control	Global Excellence
Behavior	**Behavior**
Accept constraints as given	Remove constraints continuously
Follow finance-driven rules	Create environment for learning
Manipulate output to control costs	Provide output as needed, on time
Persuade and sell	Build customer loyalty
Build for scale and size	Build for flexibility
Increase speed within parts of system	Decrease lead time of entire system
Specialize and decouple processes	Link speciaized parts into teams
Utilize resources fully	Keep idle resources ready
Results in today's global economy	**Results in today's global economy**
Costs rise	Costs fall
Satisfaction falls	Satisfaction rises
Profit declines	Profits increase

havior assumes that the primary business of management is finance. Operations are guided by mathematical relationships that are fairly fixed in the short run. People influence costs, revenues, and profit primarily by varying the rate at which the system operates, not by trying to change constraints such as plant layout, product design, work rules, purchasing policies, or marketing plans. Underlying remote-control behavior, of course, is the belief that it is easier to cajole a customer than it is to alter the dynamics of the operating system. In terms of the earlier analogy to Plato's cave (see p. 20), remote-control managers try to improve performance by manipulating the resources and the products that cast accounting shadows on the wall, not by empowering the work force to satisfy customers. They manipulate resources and products by varying the rate at which the company uses capacity, by manipulating the rate at which people and machines work, and by using incentives to stimulate sales. Manipulating accounting shadows inside the cave, remote-control managers project no compelling vision of business's social purpose or of the competitive advantage that comes from building human relationships.

Although remote-control manipulation of processes may lower unit costs and improve short-run profits, it is seldom conducive to achieving competitive excellence. Global excellence assumes that the only appropriate operating rate is one that satisfies customers. Taking that rate as given, managers in global enterprises come "above ground" and lead with vision. They influence people to improve processes continuously by removing constraints, and to adjust the operating system as new customer wants unfold. They recognize that continuously reducing constraints in order to flexibly satisfy more customer wants is the key to achieving competitiveness and profitability.

Global competitors believe the business of management is people, not finance. They see profit as something achieved through human relationships, not by slavishly bowing to mathematical relationships. This is quite different than remote-control behavior that views customers and operating personnel only as robots who purchase products and consume resources strictly according to financial stimuli. Globally competitive companies don't eschew profit or financial well-being, but they do not believe businesses achieve financial goals by using accounting variables to control people's work. They see employees as a source of learning, not as a cost.

CHAPTER 5

BECOMING RESPONSIVE BY BUILDING LONG-TERM CUSTOMER RELATIONSHIPS

The relationship between a seller and a buyer seldom ends when the sale is made. . . . The sale merely consummates the courtship. Then the marriage begins.

—Theodore Levitt[1]

The purpose of a business is to create a customer.

—Peter Drucker[2]

To be competitive in the global economy, companies must be responsive to customer wants. The best way to become responsive is to build long-term, mutually dependent relationships with customers. In recent decades, however, most American businesses have faced the customer from a radically different perspective. As cost-focused enterprises, where operations are controlled by remote accounting numbers, American businesses have viewed customers simply as sponges to soak up the company's output. Managers assume they will be able invariably to persuade the customer to purchase the output the company must produce to achieve its cost targets.

In the customer-focused enterprise, by contrast, management knows that the customer provides the company's very reason for being. The company's every action, every moment is directed toward profitably creating, satisfying, and keeping a customer. A truly customer-focused global competitor understands that its profits come from *customers,* not products.

Harvard marketing expert Theodore Levitt has documented the adverse impact of a myopic focus on product with two well-known examples: the American railroad industry and the Hollywood movie industry before the 1970s. According to Levitt, railroads incorrectly assumed themselves to be in the railroad business, not in the passenger and freight transportation business. He says, "the reason they defined their industry wrong was because they were railroad-oriented instead of transportation-oriented; they were product-oriented instead of customer-oriented." Similarly, the early Hollywood film companies were nearly all wiped out by television because they defined their business incorrectly. Hollywood, says Levitt, "thought it was in the movie business when it was actually in the entertainment business. 'Movies' implied a specific, limited product. This produced a fatuous contentment which from the beginning led producers to view TV as a threat. Hollywood scorned and rejected TV when it should have welcomed it as an opportunity—an opportunity to expand the entertainment business."[3]

Overcoming a misdirected focus on product rather than on customers does not in itself insure, of course, long-run business success. Countless companies pay lip service to the "marketing concept"—the belief that a company must identify and satisfy customer wants to succeed. But too many companies view satisfying the customer as "getting closer to the customer" in order to remedy *dis*satisfaction caused by putting products and competitors ahead of the customer.[4] They fail to consider how they must do things differently now that the customer, empowered by information technology, is in charge of the marketplace.

A brief summary of three stages through which marketing has passed in the last forty years puts in perspective the enormity of the change that is in store for global competitors. The first stage emphasizes selling, not marketing. Here companies begin with production and then follow up by trying to persuade customers to buy what has been produced. In the second stage, something more like marketing appears—the company first identifies segments of the population who are more likely to want what the company produces and then goes after them. In effect this is still persuasion, just more efficient persuasion. In the third stage we begin to see customer focus. It often begins with studying segmented groups of people, for efficiency, to learn what they want *before* deciding what to produce. Eventually it moves toward communicating with each and every customer on an ongoing basis. That is the relationship-building stage when, to become responsive to "empowered" customers, companies begin building long-term, mutually satisfying relationships with customers.

Perhaps companies would find it easier to understand what global competition entails if they first explored the implications of building serious customer relationships. This chapter explores three such implications:

1. Commit to building loyalty. Believe that profits result from loyal customers, not one-shot sales of products.
2. Direct every process in the company toward the goal of finding, satisfying, and keeping loyal customers.
3. Make sure that all members of the company know how their work fulfills customer wants, and make sure everyone shows it.

The second and third implications build upon the first—the primacy of building customer relationships rather than making sales. The second implication follows from the fact that customer relationships are not built by waving a wand—they require astute management of every process a company performs. The third implication is simply a reminder that processes are people doing work. People in a customer-focused enterprise do not work according to strategies planned on high; rather, the company's strategy is to have each person in the company working only to satisfy a customer's wants. Ultimately a customer-focused company literally becomes one with the customer—by *pulling* inspiration from and creatively answering the customer, not by *pushing* the company's expertise and insight onto the customer.

BUILDING LOYAL RELATIONSHIPS

Critics who fault businesses for having a "short-term" viewpoint usually refer to the obsession of business people, especially those in the United States, with achieving short-term financial results. Invariably the criticism focuses on Wall Street's worship of quarterly income performance. But even if Wall Street and quarterly reporting disappeared, a *much* deeper and more pervasive source of "short-termitis" is the attitude that profit emanates from "making a sale."

A sale can be viewed as a transaction that occurs at a price where the supply and demand curves intersect.[5] Some business people call this the (only) "moment of truth." But in reality, the connection between buyer and seller neither begins nor ends at the time the sale is made; in fact, the connection can intensify after the sale, as it has before the sale, whether either party chooses it or not. A relationship orientation recognizes that the connections between buyer and seller involve *time*, and that these connections can intensify over time. Thus, the customer-focused enterprise considers a sale just *one moment* in the course of a relationship, not as a "moment of truth" that defines the buyer-seller interface. This *involvement over time* is what distinguishes the transaction orientation from the relationship orientation.

Signs of a relationship orientation are visible in well-known slogans such as "the sale begins after the sale" (Harley-Davidson) or "we do more than make parts—we manufacture solutions" (Eaton). Companies such as Harley-Davidson and Eaton articulate a desire to become each customer's trusted supplier, not merely vendors of products. A similar desire to put building relationships ahead of selling products is seen in the shift toward "systems integration" or "enterprise services" in the computer business of the 1990s.[6] There are good reasons for this shift: dramatically decreased margins on hardware sales, combined with users' demands for more simplicity and standardization in interfaces and architecture, mean that computer vendors increasingly should seek competitive advantage (and profits) via software, services, and support as well as the development of full-function solutions (not piece-part components) customized to end users' industry characteristics. Because of what is being sold and bought, the customer is ultimately seeking a trusted supplier, that is, a vendor whose internal capabilities can deliver the customized package of product and service support, rather than a series of products or services.

A good example of the payoff from putting customer before product and doggedly striving to satisfy customer wants is NCR wiping out IBM in the world market for automated teller machines (ATMs).[7] NCR, famous for computers and office equipment, turned to ATMs in 1980 as a product to revive the fortunes of an inefficient forty-year-old cash register plant in Dundee, Scotland. The Dundee plant's 1980 ATM output placed it a lowly ninth in the world, behind IBM, Diebold, Docutel, and NCR's main plant in the United States. But James Adamson, the Dundee plant's new general manager, believed he could do better by visiting customers constantly to find out what new features they wanted and to learn what their own customers liked. He also brought a different customer to Dundee *every working day* to be interviewed by marketers, engineers, and executives. Hearing his customers repeatedly emphasize the importance of quality and reliability, Adamson asked his engineers to design an ATM twice as reliable as any on the market. They responded with a rugged, simpler-to-build machine three times as reliable as any in the world.

Meanwhile, IBM viewed the ATM as a "mature product" and responded in 1985 with a more "sophisticated" and complex model that could read magnetic check codes and cash customers' checks to the penny. Unfortunately for IBM, banks' customers didn't care about a machine that cashed checks. Moreover, banks wanted greater reliability and lower cost. Working closely with customers to give them what they wanted, NCR by 1985 was the world leader in ATM sales (all coming from the Dundee plant) and by 1987 had the largest installed base of ATM machines in the world.

An organization such as the Dundee plant of NCR has learned to think of itself "not as producing goods or services but as *buying customers,* as doing the things that will make people want to do business with it."[8] They ultimately hope to build a base of customers who buy from them as much because *they* sell it as because of what they sell. This is quite different than the transaction-oriented belief in building product switching costs—barriers that cause customers to commit because it is too costly to change to other products they like better. And it is more than simply "getting close to the customer," a policy companies promote in too many cases to placate angry or frustrated customers who have been persuaded to "soak up" products that the company produced to suit itself, not the customer.

Putting customer relationships ahead of making sales undoubtedly raises a company's profitability in the long run, although little empirical research exists yet to prove that claim unequivocally.[9] However, the case for increased profitability can be argued in two ways. One is to compare the profitability of selling indiscriminately to large numbers of indifferent customers with the profitability of selling only to carefully nurtured and loyal customers. The other way is to compare over time the profitability of building loyalty with the profitability of selling products.

First consider the differential profitability of selling to a loyal few. Compare Alpha and Beta, two hypothetical companies illustrated in Table 5–1 below. Both companies enjoy the same *competitive position* in terms of market share and total sales. However, Beta Co.'s *customer position* allows it to spend more sales dollars (and time) *per customer* without necessarily spending *in total* as much as or more than Alpha Co. The greater resources per customer that Beta can devote to rela-

Table 5–1
**Two Avenues to Profitability: Market Share Versus
Customer Relationships**

Amounts Sold to	Amounts Sold by			
	Alpha Co.	Beta Co.	Others	Total Market
Customer A	$ 1,000	$10,000	$ 4,000	$ 15,000
Customer B	1,000	10,000	4,000	15,000
Customer C	750	5,000	1,250	7,000
Customer D	750	—	5,000	5,750
Customer E	500	—	3,000	3,500
Customer F	500	—	2,500	3,000
Customer G	300	—	1,500	1,800
etc.	25,200	5,000	218,750	248,950
Totals	$30,000	$30,000	$240,000	$300,000
Presumed profitability	*Lower*	*Higher*		

tionship-building activities is the key to creating loyal customers who become both an important source of new ideas and a major source of new customers. Such loyalty is a sustainable source of competitive advantage and superior long-run profitability.

Next consider the time-path of profit in two companies such as Alpha and Beta. Figure 5–1 compares the different profitability over time from nurturing relationships, as in Beta, versus selling products, as in Alpha. Alpha, assumed to be a transaction-oriented company, views its profit stream in terms of the life cycle of products it sells. Products follow a path of increasing, level, and then decreasing profitability as they travel from birth through maturity to death. A successful new product, pulled by heavy spending on advertising and promotion, first generates excitement and high prices, then reaches market saturation as competitive alternatives come on stream. Much later the oft-copied mature product, now a commodity, generates steadily less revenue and profit, but new products may well have come on line to bolster the company's shrinking cash flow. The company's lifeblood is a continuing flow of new products to replace those coming to the end of their life cycle. Beta, assumed to be a relationship-oriented company, views its profit time-path entirely differently. For Beta there are no commodity products, only differing degrees of customer loyalty.

Figure 5–1
Transaction versus Relationship Orientation

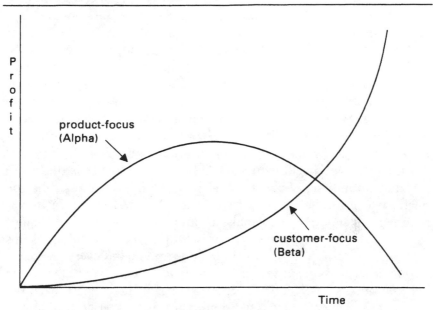

Beta views products as opportunities to satisfy each customer's never-ending needs and wants. Their efforts are directed primarily toward finding and staying in contact with customers whose wants they can profitably satisfy and whose word-of-mouth endorsements lead to increased revenue. Their goal is to satisfy, eventually, 100 percent of every customer's requirements for what it is they sell.

Indeed, one of the key measures of performance in a customer-focused company such as Beta is the share of each customer's requirements purchased from them as opposed to their competitors. I once observed this in a Japanese manufacturer that continually monitors the percentage of each of its customer's purchases that its products comprise. Their goal is to be number one or two in every product line they sell to every customer. Gathering these data keeps them constantly in touch with all customers and encourages them to continually explore customers' reactions to their own and their competitors' products. Similar information is gathered by Milliken Company, one of America's leading textile manufacturers and recent winner of the Malcolm Baldrige Award for excellence in quality.

To see the impact that relationship-building activities have on profitability, customer-focused enterprises may find it useful to compile customer-specific information on costs.[10] Few companies have ever done this. Indeed, one rarely sees compilations of product-specific cost information (except for cost of sales); almost never does one see such information by customer. To compile this information implies, of course, that one has a reliable means of tracing specific types of costs, such as relationship-building costs, to customers. One possible means is the activity-based costing technique discussed in Chapter 8. This cost information, by showing the impact of relationship-building activities among customers, can help companies spot "bad customers." Such information shows differences in margins among customers and documents patterns such as those depicted in Figure 5–1.

The advantages of cultivating and depending on loyal customers are not had without risk, of course. The cost of losing a customer may be much greater for Beta Co. than it is for Alpha. Relying on fewer customers (or suppliers) may make a company hostage to the threat of broken relationships. However, the risk of terminated relationships can be mitigated if everyone in an organization makes *every* customer encounter an opportunity to create *mutual* dependence between the company and its customers. This means not only listening to what the customer says, but also actively listening for unspoken or even unrecognized needs and actively informing the customer about opportunities the company can offer of which the customer may be unaware. Sony, for instance, did not simply listen to what customers wanted in turntables or portable tape players. While developing the CD player or the Walkman, they would apprise customers of the new concept's superior capabilities—before customers had ever heard of CDs or the Walkman.

Mutual dependence underlies the concept of switching costs as it will come to be known in the global economy. A customer-focused global company creates switching costs by generating opportunities lost by switching *suppliers*, not by creating nettlesome barriers that make it inconvenient to switch *products*. Such opportunities increase over time as customer and provider learn more about *each other's* wants and opportunities and become more mutually dependent. Mutual dependence arises from both listening and informing. A manufacturer of precision-machined parts, for example, after prodding one of its customers for years, finally gained access to the customer's plants to study how the customer used their parts. On seeing how one part was used, the supplier asked, "Why do you require polished-surface finished tolerances in noninterfacing areas?" The customer could only say, "We don't know; that's always been our spec for that type of part." It turned out they really didn't need that finish, so the spec was changed and both the customer and the provider saved money. Thereafter, the customer invited the supplier to its plants regularly.

By taking advantage of opportunities in every customer encounter, the customer-focused enterprise creates mutually advantageous relationships that transform customers into loyal advocates. Customer encounters are seen as opportunities to learn and inform, not just as opportunities to present and sell. The customer-focused global enterprise is continually poised to create and adapt to change. Keeping apprised of changes in customer wants, and keeping customers informed, provides a "relationship advantage"—an important source of its competitive edge in the marketplace.

DIRECT PROCESSES TOWARD BUILDING CUSTOMER RELATIONSHIPS

Obviously a company does not develop close involvement with customers simply by waving a magic wand. Customer relationship building requires self-conscious design and deployment of people and resources. The entire company, in Ted Levitt's words, "must be viewed as a customer-satisfying organism . . . as providing customer-creating value satisfactions. *It must push this idea (and everything it means and requires) into every nook and cranny of the organization.*"[11] Ideally, every process performed in a customer-focused enterprise is directed toward finding, satisfying, and keeping a customer—no more, and no less. Obviously this is not easy to do.

I have heard companies that take this step seriously say it is not wise to begin by having everyone focus on the final consumer—the buyer who ultimately pays all the bills. Instead, they recommend having workers begin by focusing attention on *their own customer*—the user in the next process. Eventually everyone must, of course, justify individual efforts to satisfy internal customers by the satisfaction those efforts deliver to the final customer. Aside from recommending that everyone in a company begin by "building a chain" of internal customers,[12] it is difficult to say precisely how a company should go about focusing all its processes on the customer, because so few documented examples of customer-focused global enterprises exist at this time.

At a minimum it seems safe to say it would *not* follow the "remote control" practice of assigning activities to specialized functional departments (silos) that communicate with each other sporadically "over the wall," and communicate with the customer only through the selling, invoicing, and collections departments. Presumably it will resemble what existed in small companies years ago where everyone knew all the customers, and customers knew everyone in the company. Companies of all sizes must achieve that effect to compete in the customer-driven global economy. Consider examples of two companies—Toyota Motor Company, the Japanese automobile colossus, and Direct Tire Sales, a small automobile service firm in Watertown, Massachusetts—that seem to have moved farther than most in the direction of focusing activities on creating, satisfying, and keeping customers.

Toyota Motor Company: Finding and Satisfying Customers

I have alluded several times to Toyota as a model, perhaps the most advanced in the world today, of what I mean by competitive excellence in the global economy. Their famous JIT production system, implemented in the production side of Toyota's business between the late 1940s and the early 1970s, was transferred aggressively to the marketing and selling side of the business in Japan during the 1980s. Toyota probably spends much more money to retain existing customers' business than it spends to attract customers in the first place. Moreover, Toyota also seems to realize that the best way of attracting new customers is by referrals from existing customers who endorse their products and service. Here are highlights of how Toyota's distribution and selling system in Japan are directed toward satisfying customers:[13]

1. Toyota distributes cars through nationwide dealerships, usually owned by Toyota, that do not exist as much to create brand identity as they do to link the customer closely with the company's manufacturing system. For example, members of a dealership work closely with Toyota product-development teams; and all dealer employees, usually hired out of university, are centrally trained at Toyota.

2. The sales staff in a Toyota dealership is a multiskilled team who are trained in products, order taking, financing, insurance, solving myriad owner problems, and information gathering. Traditionally the team members sell door-to-door, systematically visiting every household in the dealership's area. During these visits the team members gather extensive data about the householders' automobile wants and needs. When a family expresses an interest, the team drops by with a demonstration model. Orders are placed with the sales teams who transmit them directly to the factory—most cars are custom ordered.

The team also handles the buyer's needs for insurance, financing, and trade-in of the old car. Ten to twelve days after an order is taken, the team delivers the finished car to the owner's house. Similar service is provided subsequently for scheduled maintenance and, should the need arise (which is very rare), for repair work. Dealers generally repair defects for free as long as the car is in service, regardless of the terms in any warranty.

3. Toyota's sales teams do not spend time haggling with the potential buyer about price. No one is trying to push onto the buyer a car he or she does not want. The team's goal is to make the buyer feel that a full price is a fair price. Moreover, the team wants to maximize Toyota's long-term income stream from the customer, not squeeze the best one-shot deal from someone they will never see again. No effort is spared to satisfy the customer's wants. The customer is considered a member of an extended "family" who will call on and be visited by the Toyota team many times over the years.

Toyota is more customer-driven than perhaps any other company in the world today. Their selling system bespeaks an effort to direct every process toward satisfying and retaining customers. However, an integral part of Toyota's ability to keep its promises and retain loyal customers is the remarkable production system that stands behind the selling teams. Indeed, the selling and producing parts of the business support each other in a close symbiotic relationship. To promise and deliver cars exactly as the customer wants when the customer wants requires a carefully balanced and flexible production system. But the constant stream of accurate and timely customer information flowing from the selling teams' efforts helps create the smooth flow of production in the factory. In this sense the apparent high costs of dealers' activities is offset not only by customer willingness to pay more, but also by costs saved in the factory. But in time Toyota will undoubtedly take advantage of information technology to reduce the cost of door-to-door selling and information gathering. Then cars can sell for even less, with no loss of customer satisfaction.

Direct Tire Sales: Satisfying and Keeping Customers[14]

Direct Tire Sales in Watertown, Massachusetts is a one-shop, one-owner $4 million a year automobile service establishment that sells and installs tires and also does brake and alignment work. In an industry chronically plagued by oversupply and rife competition, Direct

Tire incurs substantially higher costs and charges higher average product prices than anyone else. Traditional product-focused competitors might conclude that Direct Tire's higher costs and prices should lead the company into a death spiral of shrinking revenues and rising deficits. Instead, this twenty-six-year-old company consistently earns a net margin on sales that is twice the industry average. How? They link every process and every dollar they spend to creating, satisfying, and keeping customers.

Direct Tire continually identifies exactly what service its customers expect and then *keeps its promise to deliver that service,* without fail. Here are some examples of what they promise and how they systematically focus activities and spending to keep those promises:

1. Schedule appointments and complete work on schedule. To fit work into customers' schedules Direct Tire has a fleet of seven loaner cars and one full-time chauffeur who ferries customers to and from work. There is no charge either for a loaner or for a chauffeured ride. On rare occasions when a customer shows up for scheduled work and the promised ride or a loaner isn't available, Direct Tire calls a private taxi and pays the full fare just to be sure the customer gets what was promised.

2. Guarantee all service work against defects forever. To insure that work is done right the first time, Direct Tire hires only the best people and provides them the best equipment and working conditions. They use headhunters, not newspaper want ads, to hire mechanics and alignment specialists who are paid 15 to 25 percent over the industry scale. It all costs more, but the people they hire are experienced, dependable, and committed. Helping to make their jobs more attractive is Direct Tire's policy to spare no money equipping workers with state-of-the-art diagnostic machines. Direct Tire's turnover is virtually zero; some tire changers have been employed for seven years.

3. Provide customers, 40 percent of whom are women, with a pleasant and reassuring environment. Waiting rooms are immaculate, stocked with a wide range of current reading material and freshly-brewed coffee, and lined with windows that overlook a clean, well-organized shop area where cars are being serviced competently and quickly. All staff dress in clean, crisp company-supplied uniforms.

4. Have tires and parts the customer wants when the customer wants them. In addition to a full line of standard tires, Direct Tire carries a larger than normal inventory of unusual tires, such as special rear tires for the Porsche 928S. To avoid making customers wait while they track these items they have a $48,000 customized software program that also prints work orders and receipts.

5. Make customers *know* you care. Not only does Direct Tire place the customary comment card in the front seat of serviced cars, the CEO personally calls every customer who registers a complaint. Moreover, all salespeople are empowered to reduce the charges on a bill if the customer is dissatisfied or has been inconvenienced.

6. Surprise customers with services they haven't even thought of yet. Direct Tire rents a trailer to store apartment-dwellers' snow tires in summer and regular tires in winter.

Keeping these promises costs a lot of money. That's the point. They know exactly what they promise and they spend what it takes to keep those commitments. They don't grouse about high costs nor do they see spending as a way to differentiate—*they spend because it's the most profitable way to run the business.* It's profitable because the money they spend is on processes that transform everyone who enters the store into a repeat customer. Loyal, satisfied customers are glad to pay for the services they receive. Indeed, "there are few bargains at Direct Tire, but customers don't seem to mind. On the contrary, [Direct Tire] has found that—if you keep your promises—customers are more than willing to pay for value, service, and convenience, and [they are] constantly looking for new ways to let them do just that."[15]

Direct Tire knows the reason it earns margins far above industry averages is its policy of turning onetime buyers into repeat customers. They have information to prove it. Of the eighty-five transactions they handle on an average day, about three-quarters are with repeat customers. Repeat customers tend to spend on average about twice as much per visit as first time customers who are responding to newspaper promotions (about $173 versus $90). But a first-time customer who has been referred by another customer spends an average $224 on the first visit! It seems these are people who have put off service hoping to find an outlet they can trust and when they find Direct Tire they spend. Direct Tire "invests in customer service, and that wins over customers, who bring in their friends, who spend even more money and are won over and tell their friends, and on and on. Small wonder that Direct Tire's revenues continue to increase steadily, as they have every year since its founding in 1974, despite generally flat sales for the industry as a whole." [16]

Both Toyota and Direct Tire bring to mind a point made years ago by champions of quality—that money and effort invested up front to "do things right the first time" usually is saved many times over downstream in avoidance of rework, repair, and other clean up. In that sense quality is "free." A similarity to this in customer relationship building is the much higher payoff from money and effort invested in retaining present customers rather than in attracting new ones. While it is vital always to attract new customers, the lion's share of activity and money should be spent to draw existing customers back again and again. Many studies show that it costs much more—five to ten times as much—to attract a new customer as it does to keep an existing one. [17] Even worse is to so displease an existing customer that he or she not only leaves, but also drives other potential customers away.

Obviously it makes good sense for Direct Tire and Toyota to spend as much as they do to retain old customers. That carefully designed spending is the driving force, I believe, behind the higher profitability attributed to "Beta Co." in Figure 5–1. Customers who come back are willing to pay more for what they get from companies such as Toyota and Direct Tire, because they know those companies can be depended on to keep promises. Moreover, they refer other customers who are willing to pay more for promises kept. Building customer relationships is more profitable than merely selling product to an anonymous procession of skeptical new customers.

"EACH MEMBER REPRESENTS THE COMPANY"

Every process in a globally competitive company must be directed toward building profitable long-term customer relationships—toward buying customers, not selling products. Everything in the business must be run in contemplation of the customer, especially in contemplation of what the customer sees. The customer does not see a company in terms of its parts. The customer sees only what he or she is promised by the system as a whole and what any given part contributes to that promise. Given the customer's vision, it follows that in the customer-focused global enterprise every person must understand, and continually demonstrate, that his or her work fulfills customer wants. Each employee must think in terms of making a contribution that ultimately develops customer loyalty.

That understanding instilled into every person in the company resembles the DNA "code" that infuses the architecture of the whole into every cell of a biological organism.[18] The living organism isn't the sum of its parts—each cell reflects the whole and in a sense is capable of replicating the whole. So it must also be in global businesses. Each person must have a clear vision of how his or her work fulfills customer wants. Such vision keeps a company from being "merely a series of pigeonholed parts, with no consolidating sense of purpose or direction."[19]

Every member who understands how his or her work fulfills customer needs has a personal sense of mission. This sense of mission inspires employees to excel in their efforts to build enduring customer relationships. This vision drives and directs the attention of empowered employees. Instilling such vision is the job of leadership. The ideal globally competitive company ultimately has no "managers" who issue commands and manifest control in the traditional manner. Rather, in the ideal company leaders and employees share efforts to fulfill customer wants in the light both of the leader's vision and workers' ideas. A key step to achieving the "flatness" displayed by this type of organization is to articulate a mission that instills in every person in the company an obsession with focusing all their work and spending on fulfilling customer wants. Direct Tire, for example, has dispensed with the need for supervisors by gearing recruiting and training activities of all shop floor personnel toward customer service. This move makes some traditional supervisory activities unnecessary, thereby cutting costs.

WRAP-UP

To develop long-term, mutually dependent relationships with customers, organizations must commit themselves to building customer loyalty, directing every process in the company toward that goal, and instilling in each employee an obsession with that goal.

To manage operations in a company focused on customer relationships, new information is essential. Having the customer in charge puts a premium on information that concerns just what it is customers want. To learn this, talking to and observing customers on a one-to-one basis is an excellent practice. For example, Toyota goes door to door gathering information in Japanese households. That canvas takes people, and people, say traditional remote-control managers, cost money. Where will the people and the money come from? They will come at no cost, from workers who are continuously eliminating their own jobs by removing constraints and eliminating work. Eliminating constraints, simplifying work, and creating resources redundancies— topics covered in the next chapter—are all steps on the pathway to flexibility.

CHAPTER 6

BECOMING FLEXIBLE BY EMPOWERING WORKERS TO REMOVE CONSTRAINTS

[With flexible manufacturing], the prime task of management . . . is to create and nurture the project teams whose intellectual capabilities produce competitive advantage. What gets managed is intellectual capital, not equipment.

— Ramchandran Jaikumar[1]

Building relationships to achieve long-lasting customer loyalty takes a company well on the road to global competitive excellence. Learning how to turn on a dime to meet shifting customers' wants is also crucial. The need to be flexible, not just responsive, is an implicit imperative of competition in the Information Age. Customers' tastes and needs change over time, and their opportunities to buy what they want from others increase over time. Companies must be prepared to adapt to these changes or go out of business.

Perhaps the most unfortunate consequence of American companies adopting remote-control management practices after the 1950s was the tendency those practices had to divert managers' attention from the added work required to decouple, buffer, and batch—work added in large part to achieve variety. Remote-control management practices caused businesses to ignore the competitive advantage of flexibility—

the power gained in the marketplace by being able to change over quickly and do something new or different. American businesses after the 1950s paid little or no attention to the merits of a production system that could meet and exceed customers' expectations by empowering workers, suppliers, and managers to be flexible.

FLEXIBILITY DEMANDS NEW THINKING

The global imperative to be flexible introduces a goal that most American businesses today would regard as nearly impossible to attain, and in any case very costly to deliver. The concept of flexibility is defined as producing on the spot, or in a period of time that satisfies the customer, exactly what the customer requests—from scratch, not from stock and not by assembling to order. Moreover, the product or service must be sold at a price similar to that of a mass-producer who sells it "off the shelf." As Figure 6–1 suggests, modern flexibility combines the best of the preindustrial artisan's ability to produce customized quality with the best of the early twentieth-century mass-producer's ability to sell at a low price in short lead times.

Japanese auto manufacturers such as Toyota are fast approaching the day when customers sit in a dealer's "virtual reality" simulator and experience the look of different color choices, the feel of different in-

Figure 6–1
Product Features, 1750 to 2000

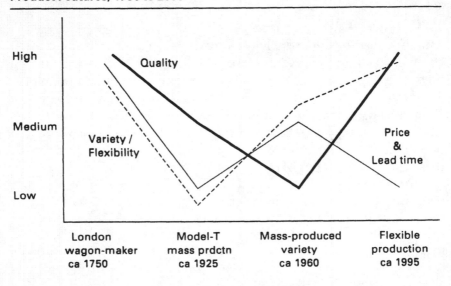

terior compartment configurations, the sound of various audio systems, and the road handling of various suspension and power train combinations. With choices based on more comprehensive information than that provided by any road test, the customer's order will go directly to the factory where his or her "fingerprint" car will be made from scratch and delivered in about five days—at a highly competitive price.

Most executives in American businesses today, especially in large companies, are not familiar with this concept of flexibility. Indeed, Robert W. Hall and Jinichiro Nakane conclude from their extensive field research in both Japanese and American companies that flexibility in people and organization is not equated with corporate survival in the United States, whereas it is in Japan.[2] Here is the view American business leaders have of flexibility from both the customer's and the producer's perspective:

- From the customer's perspective, they generally define flexibility as having variety—options or capacity—available on demand. In this sense, being flexible for customers is being able to deliver many variations and quantities of products, either from stock or by assembling to order. Such "flexibility" has an obvious appeal to customers, but it entails holding costly inventory or capacity buffers. Companies that pride themselves as "full-line" suppliers tend to charge more to cover the cost of providing variety on demand, even though they strive assiduously to minimize such costs.
- From the producer's perspective, companies define flexibility in terms of speed and expediting. Speed usually means automated or faster machinery and equipment, while expediting means extra people. Once again, flexibility is seen as costly.

Perhaps the best known American example of a customized product or service at mass-production prices is Burger King's promise to deliver a fresh-cooked hamburger "your way." Other examples exist in fast food, in clothing, in house paints, and more. Many of these examples entail what is commonly described as mass customization—mass production of a basic plain vanilla version of the product or service with ingenious customized tailoring of "trim" options added at the final assembly or delivery stage. The variety provided by mass customization often provides sufficient "spice" to attract and hold large numbers of customers. From the producer's standpoint, such mass customization seldom entails a major shift in the way work gets done. It requires only paying attention to clever schemes for customizing at the end of the line. American producers see mass-customized products as somewhat costlier than homogeneous mass-produced goods. But they assume that the perceived differentiation in the marketplace will justify charging higher prices to recoup such costs.

The flexibility required for global competitiveness—rapid creation from scratch of the fingerprinted product in a "lot size of one" at mass-production costs—will require a radical change in the way companies do work. The prevailing American approach to flexibility presupposes no fundamental change in the way companies organize work; it attempts to achieve variety by modifying long-familiar techniques of mass production. The one dramatic change most Americans associate with flexibility is computer-driven flexible automation. However, new approaches to the way they organize work enable companies to achieve very high degrees of flexibility without turning to computer-based automation.

Indeed, world-class Japanese flexibility has its roots in the precomputer approach to production that we discussed in Chapter 3. Taiichi Ohno once described that approach as "limited" production, which he contrasted with "lean" production. In Ohno's words, "The idea [of 'limited' management] is to produce only what can be sold and no more. The idea is to *limit,* not necessarily to *reduce* the quantity. The important thing is to . . . produce what can be sold at the lowest possible cost."[3]

American managers show little appreciation of what Ohno meant by "limited" management. He meant the creation of conditions that make it *economically feasible* to do only as much as customers want you to do, when they want it done, and then to stop. Who would waste time doing any more? I know a lot of American managers who would. They not only will produce more than is needed at the moment, they will do it persistently, will spend resources moving and storing the excess, and then refer to the excess as an "asset." When told that reducing setup times dramatically reduces the cost of producing smaller-sized batches of output, they often say "why should I want to produce in smaller-sized batches, and have to set up more often, to produce what I make now?" They don't see that setup-time reduction strategies, by creating the conditions that make "limited" production economically feasible, enable one to do something different from what has been done. Such strategies improve one's ability to do whatever the customer wants, when the customer wants it, at little or no extra cost. *That* is flexibility. That is *competitiveness.*

How does one achieve this ability? Limited production entails a very different approach to doing work than either lean production or the remote-control approach taken in most American businesses. By "lean" production Ohno meant a slimmed-down version of existing remote-control ways of doing things. However, companies do not achieve limited production by going on campaigns to downsize, flatten, and trim. Just as people trying to lose weight usually don't succeed in the long run by crash dieting, but must adopt a new lifestyle, so is it true in business—flexibility is achieved in the long run only by changing lifestyle and ways of thinking.

REMOVING CONSTRAINTS IS THE PATHWAY TO FLEXIBILITY

Flexibility through limited production is achieved by continually removing constraints. Constraints are practices and assumptions that cause delay, excess, and variation in processes. They make work necessary and, therefore, increase the time it takes to accomplish jobs. In other words, constraints increase lead time, the enemy of flexibility. Removing constraints improves flexibility by eliminating the need for work that is caused by delay, excess, and variation. The simplification achieved by removing constraints, not taking them for granted, eliminates work and costs that otherwise seem necessary. Removing constraints eliminates work (and resources) that remote-control companies add when they optimize within constraints in the decoupled and unbalanced systems we discussed in Chapter 3.

The following list describes several examples of constraints that make work necessary, the types of added work they spawn, and the steps people can take to remove the constraints and eliminate the needed work:[4]

1. *Setup and changeover.* Long lead times necessitated by changeover, setting up, and other delays tend to generate a demand for added scheduling, forecasting, and buffer inventory. Any steps to remove delay from work will improve lead times. An extensive literature now exists that describes steps to reduce elements of changeover time such as setting up. As Figure 3–3 suggests, reducing setup time almost automatically triggers a chain reaction of steps that eliminate work, space, and time. Moving this constraint wherever it is

found—in the factory or in the front office—simplifies work and reduces resource requirements.

2. *Work layout (including process design).* Poor layouts of systems, plants, and processes generate a demand for transporting, work-in-process inventory, inspection, rework, unscheduled maintenance, and additional setup time. As a general rule, the first step in improving layout is to map work flows and study opportunities to locate upstream suppliers close to downstream users. The changes that would take place in a hypothetical move from Figure 3–2 to Figure 3–1 suggest the impact of putting this rule to work, although our discussions of setup time reduction in Chapter 3 and elsewhere indicate that making such a move requires attention to more than just layout.

3. *Product design.* Poor product design generates a demand for parts ordering, work-in-process inventory, rework, and after-sale costs of service, repair, and lost customers. Steps to improve product design must encompass both user-friendliness and manufacturability. Moreover, user-friendliness also should take into consideration the person who may someday have to repair the product for the ultimate consumer.

4. *Performance evaluation systems.* Standard cost variance targets encourage workers to throw processes out of statistical control and generate demand for inventory, inspection, and scheduling. Information for evaluating processes should encourage people to improve, not impair, the capability of a process to satisfy customer wants. At a minimum, all standard cost variance reports should be replaced by statistical process control charts.

5. *Vendor relations.* Regarding vendors as adversaries whose charges reduce your bottom line leads to policies and practices that generate added storage, rework, machine downtime, and unhappy customers. Deming's instruction to "end the practice of awarding business on the basis of price tag alone," strikes to the heart of this issue. Becoming competitive is impossible unless vendors are treated as partners whom you trust and depend on for ideas, and savings.

6. *Employee relations.* "People power," says Robert Hall, "is the ultimate source of competitiveness." Viewing employees as a cost rather than a valued resource is the costliest of all practices engaged in by remote-control managers.

This list—not meant to be exhaustive—indicates many possibilities to eliminate work (and reduce lead times) by removing the underlying sources of delay, excess, and variation that make work necessary. As we discuss further in Chapter 9, efforts to remove constraints should be a major item—perhaps *the* key item—on the process improvement agenda in any quality-minded company. In fact, eliminating constraints is tantamount to removing systemic, or common, causes of variation from processes, as that concept is referred to in the statistical process control literature. Removing constraints improves customer satisfaction by eliminating causes of variation, delay and excess in people's work. In other words, it improves the satisfaction customers receive by improving processes. Removing constraints is the antithesis, therefore, of manipulating processes to achieve accounting targets.

WORKERS EMPOWERED TO LEARN
WILL REMOVE CONSTRAINTS

In a flexible ("limited") organization, everyone from the top down is obsessed with removing constraints that make work necessary and, therefore, increase lead time. Removing constraints may in fact be the single most important difference between the remote-control management style that has characterized American business for the past forty years and the time-focused, people-oriented management style that increasingly characterizes global enterprises.

A work force empowered to learn and innovate must be the backbone of a strategy to create flexibility by removing constraints. The idea of such an empowered work force is alien to the world of remote-control financial management. Top managers regard a business as a system of fixed accounting-defined relationships in which people play passive roles. In that world, companies often follow many steps on the road to flexibility, such as linking processes continuously, as in work cells or in so-called focused factories. Such linking can, of course, remove much of the work companies add when they decouple processes, buffer, and batch work to cope with the complexity of variety. But linking processes—even the linking achieved by computer-integration (i.e., CIM)— does not *itself* increase flexibility.[5] In addition to linking processes, flexibility also requires putting control over processes *in the hands of people doing the work* .

As experts in TQM realize, people and brainpower—not machines, imposed systems, and capital resources—make a system tightly linked and flexible. That is the main point that management accounting practices and principles have kept American businesses from seeing for the past three decades. In top-down accounting systems as we have known them since the 1950s, employees manipulate processes for fear of not achieving accounting results. American management accounting systems do not put real-time process information (especially information on variation in processes) in the hands of people who do the work, with the intent that they will strive steadfastly to *improve* processes, not manipulate them to achieve accounting results.

Indeed, remote-control management practice puts what I call constraints under the heading of "fixed costs." In that setting, companies manage fixed costs by driving workers, and managers, to earn contribution margin by producing and selling output. There is virtually no attempt to encourage people to root out causes of work that causes such costs. In contrast, a flexible organization that practices what Ohno referred to as "limited production" does not view any cost as "fixed." There, all costs are seen in terms of work that can be managed, somehow. The main thrust of everyone's attention in the flexible organization is eliminating work by locating and removing sources of delay, excess and variation that make work necessary. The purpose, of course, is to achieve a state ("limited production") where you can *efficiently produce output only when it is needed* by a customer, not be forced to produce output in order to seem to be efficient.

Empowering the work force by giving people ownership of the processes in which they work is the key, then, to the learning and innovation that create flexibility. I believe the essence of organizational learning is the discovery of new and innovative ways to remove constraints that stand in the way of flexibly answering customer wants. Such innovation and learning will come only from people who are in touch with the voice of the customer and the voice of the process. It can not come from people who act only on instructions from top managers who are immersed in a fog of information about financial results.

FLEXIBILITY CREATES REDUNDANCIES THAT OPEN DOORS TO OPPORTUNITY

By eliminating the need for certain work and thereby reducing lead time, constraint-removing improvement processes not only increase flexibility and quality, they make existing resources redundant. Companies that focus on eliminating constraints create opportunities to reduce lead time, to use less space, less (and smaller) equipment, and fewer people. And these benefits accrue not from large-cost investment programs, but from tapping the relatively low-cost brainpower of people who do the work that is being constrained.

Management guru Tom Peters has described a good before-and-after example of the redundancies a company can create by removing constraints and linking process:[6]

Before. In 1988, Titeflex, an industrial hose maker, entered new customer orders into an MRP (materials requirements planning) system that initiated paperwork for purchasing, production, storeroom schedules, engineering, and costing. There followed a series of meetings to cover purchasing, quality review, make-buy issues, and so forth. Order entry took around three to five weeks. On the factory floor paperwork was generated for numerous departments—the basic hose area, five different fittings departments, cleaning, three assembly departments, a fifty-person quality assurance department, and then shipping. A production control planning unit handled transfers of product into and out of the stockroom six times. Manufacturing added another six weeks to the three to five already spent in order processing.

After. In 1991, new orders come into a cell, dubbed "Genesis Team," consisting of six people in one circle. The six people represent all relevant functions who review orders, do design work, and handle problems as a group. One of the six stays in contact with the customer. No more meetings to process orders. Total time to process orders ranges now from ten minutes to no more than a few days. The factory has also been reorganized into cells of five to fifteen people each. The Genesis Team makes direct contact with necessary factory cells and arranges work on the spot. Each factory cell handles its own quality work. Work passes into the stockroom once—when it is finished and ready for final assembly. Total manufacturing time now is about two days to one week.

The result of these changes at Titeflex is, of course, less lead time, fewer people and less space needed to get the job done, less inventory, happier customers, and probably worried competitors. However, people often overlook the new opportunities to increase revenue, at less cost, that these redundancies create. As I suggested at the end of the last chapter, the opportunities that flow from customer relationship building are not had by waving a magic wand. They come from people spending time and money to contact, observe, and analyze customers. Now you can begin to see where these people and resources can be found—for free! They come from the people, time, and resources made redundant by removing constraints wherever delay, excess, or variation exist.

Unfortunately, the average American company usually sees most improvement processes as a way to cut costs, not a way to increase competitiveness by improving organizational learning, lead times, and flexibility. So, we see countless stories in the press of companies where "improvement processes" lead to layoffs and downsizing. These companies, invariably eager to improve their accounting measures of return to investors, forget that the more they cut, the less they have. Not a good way to march into the global economy.

Removing constraints instead of optimizing within "fixed" constraints is a potential source of enormous productivity improvement in the factory, the office, and the corporate staff. Constraint-removing improvement processes can be among the highest payback ventures a company ever pursues! A one-time cost of removing a constraint (usually nominal) can be offset by a permanent reduction in the cost of work eliminated and by a permanent gain in customer satisfaction from shorter lead times, better quality, and quite often, lower price. But the gains in customer satisfaction do not come automatically. Relationship building takes hard work. Anticipating how to employ redundant resources in new opportunities should be a key part of any campaign to improve flexibility by removing constraints.

THE MYTH OF "NONVALUE ACTIVITY"

Work made redundant by removing constraints often is referred to as "nonvalue activity." Everyone has seen lists of "nonvalue" classes of work, such as moving, storing, inspecting, expediting, rework, and so forth. I believe the term "nonvalue" is unfortunate. Encouraging people to eliminate "nonvalue activity," rather than removing constraints that make work necessary, can impede and delay efforts to become flexible. Let's briefly examine this issue.

Work made redundant by removing a constraint can be viewed, of course, as source of added cost that presumably gives customers no added satisfaction. However, this work is necessary to getting the job done until the constraints that cause it are changed. If setup times are not reduced, the work caused by large batches—moving, storing, inspecting, and so forth—is necessary. Therefore, it really is not correct to say that companies will achieve global excellence by exhorting people to eliminate nonvalue activity. Too often, in fact, such exhortations lead to people *econ-*

omizing on the "nonvalue" work that constraints make necessary—shipping larger batches, for instance, to economize on transportation resources—rather than removing the constraints that make the work necessary in the first place. To be competitive, companies must eliminate constraints that make work *necessary.* Once constraints are removed and the work becomes unnecessary, then it can be called "nonvalue" and the resources eliminated or, preferably, redeployed to better use.

Indeed, the next time consultants tell you how important it is to eliminate nonvalue activity—often referred to as NVA—take them into your workplace and perform this simple experiment.[7] Ask everyone there to stop working for a moment and ask all those who are performing nonvalue work to raise their hands. Agree to buy an hour of the consultant's time for every hand that goes up. You can be sure you won't have to buy many, if any, consulting hours on that basis, because most of the work will be necessary, given the constraints management is taking for granted. It would be better to ask the consultants if they see any work-causing constraints and, if they do, to please tell you how the constraints might be eliminated.

REMOVING CONSTRAINTS MAKES TRADE-OFF THINKING EXTINCT

An important effect of removing constraints that is not well understood by American business people is the opportunity it creates to *simultaneously* reduce costs and improve other dimensions of customer satisfaction such as flexibility and quality. By eliminating constraints, rather than optimizing within them, managers effectively eliminate *trade-offs* among sources of customer satisfaction such as quality, flexibility, service, and price. Trade-off thinking, very common among American managers, explains why so few companies put the customer first and pursue relationship-building strategies. It would seem that most American businesses resist focusing seriously on customer-relationship building because they feel that satisfying more and more customer wants creates more and more cost. The traditional remote-control company assumes there is a trade-off between improved customer satisfaction and cost. This belief in the inevitability of a cost-satisfaction trade-off I call the "yes, but" syndrome. "*Yes* we would like to give customers more, *but* to do so drives up costs and, unless our competitors do the same thing, makes us uncompetitive."

A trade-off means that more of one thing requires giving up some of another thing. The trade-off mindset portrayed by the balance-scale in

Figure 6–2
The Cost-Focused Trade-Off

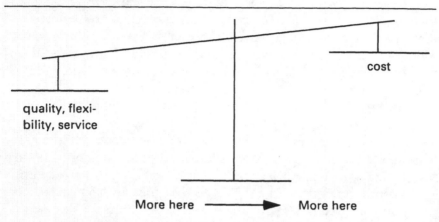

cost

quality, flexi-
bility, service

More here ⟶ More here

Figure 6–2 has permeated American business practice in the past fifty years. To keep such a scale in balance means adding equal amounts of weight to both sides of the scale at any time.

For example, adding more customer satisfaction to the scale on the left requires adding more cost to the scale on the right. In other words, you can always give customers more of what they want, but only at a cost. Similarly, if customers expect more of any one thing on the left-hand scale—say more quality—they must either expect to sacrifice some other things on the same side, such as variety, service, or reliability—or else expect more cost on the right-hand scale.

Trade-offs arise from taking for granted the constraints that generally were associated with "business as usual" in the United States after the 1950s. Belief in those trade-offs is the main reason, I think, that American managers ignore the earmarks of management behavior I associate with global competitive excellence (see Table 4–1). Managers accustomed to business as usual generally reject these earmarks of global excellence as being too costly, too difficult to implement. And indeed they are correct—as long as constraints associated with doing business as usual are left untouched. In doing so, traditional managers focus efforts on cutting cost by doing more efficiently that which they have always done, or they focus attention more narrowly on fewer product lines and fewer processes. They don't get the point. To behave as a global competitor, they must remove constraints, not optimize within them. That's the secret to achieving the flexibility that makes a company a global competitor.

It is time to challenge the trade-off mindset and to begin removing constraints that prevent companies from achieving higher and higher levels of customer satisfaction without incurring higher costs. The trade-off mindset can't survive in the 1990s. Early quality crusaders such as W. Edwards Deming, Joseph Juran, and Philip Crosby challenged the trade-off mindset, saying it always costs less to do a thing right the first time than to do it wrong and fix it later. I would go even further and say that a company always improves its long-run performance by doing what suits the customer rather than doing what suits the company and then trying to make the customer like it. From now on, the strategic choice is not *either* beating competitors on cost *or* differentiating from competitors enough to offset higher cost with additional revenue. Competitive excellence in the global economy means companies must differentiate *and* beat competitors on cost. No trade-off.

However, one *real* trade-off in achieving flexibility is the increased attention to detail and discipline that is required to work with smaller batches, tighter lead times, and generally closer tolerances throughout. That attention and discipline are the point of much of the training that accompanies the never-ending march to flexibility and customer responsiveness in the global economy. Absent that training and the discipline it engenders, a company may find that its march to global competitiveness leads to increased stress—and higher costs.[8]

FLEXIBILITY AND COMPUTER-INTEGRATED AUTOMATION

You have heard the admonition to simplify before automating. Sometimes the theme of this advice is to avoid automating "messes"—that is, simply automating work as we do it at the moment. It becomes clear what people mean by this admonition once we understand the implications of removing constraints. A great deal of work becomes unnecessary once constraints are reduced. Automating such work is foolish and wasteful. For example, automated storage and retrieval where the storage reflects buffers between badly designed process linkages. Or, automatic guided vehicles carrying things between processes that should be linked directly. Automating often leads to doing with greater speed, efficiency, and reliability many things that should not be done in the first place—the work associated with optimizing around a constraint. Remove the constraint, eliminate the work, *then* automate.

Stories about the failure of General Motors's massive effort to adopt

robotics and computer-aided automation in the early and mid 1980s
are legion. They appear to be a classic example of what happens when
a company ignores the imperatives of global competitiveness and tries
to improve performance by pursuing financial imperatives of remote-
control management defined by scale, speed, and cost. It seems that
the company failed to take seriously the need to empower workers and
transform the workplace, despite the opportunity to learn from
Toyota first-hand in a jointly run California assembly plant. Instead,
billions and billions of dollars were thrown at automating existing processes. Ford Motor Company, by contrast, seems at the same time to
have improved processes much more, with far less spending, in the
launch of its famous Taurus line. To be sure, the final chapters of both
companies' attempts to compete with Asian and European manufacturers have yet to be written. But their experiences to date lend
strong support to the claim that bringing automation to old remote-
control management practices simply accelerates the creation of work
and waste, not additional customer satisfaction.

Nevertheless, computer-integrated automation undoubtedly is the
final leg of the journey to global flexibility. No noncomputer
human system can match the lead times achieved in an integrated
system that combines the speed of computer networks with the reliability of computer-aided machinery. The key is to approach automation with a clear sense of why it is necessary. Computer-aided automation is necessary when the time comes to push flexibility to its
farthest limits—after everything has been done that can be done without computers to achieve flexibility. Unfortunately, Americans too
often view automation as a way to do existing work faster, not more
flexibly.

A clear, almost brutal, statement of the failure of American business
to address the potential offered by flexible automation was provided
over five years ago in a *Harvard Business Review* article by Ramchandran Jaikumar.[9] Citing research in which he compared the practices of
ninety-five flexible manufacturing systems in the United States and
Japan, Jaikumar concluded that "with few exceptions, the flexible
manufacturing systems installed in the United States show an astonish-
ing lack of flexibility. In many cases, they perform worse than the conventional technology they replace." But he went on to note that "the
technology itself is not to blame; it is management that makes the difference." In particular, he noted that the American plants produced
"an order-of-magnitude less variety of parts"—on average, ten different parts in the American plants versus ninety-three different parts in

the Japanese plants. In essence, the American plants "used [flexible automation] the wrong way—for high-volume production of a few parts rather than for high-variety production of many parts at low cost per unit." It seems that remote-control thinking is alive and well even in American companies that employ the most advanced technology of our age. In Jaikumar's words:

> The battle is on, and the United States is losing badly. It may even lose the war if it doesn't soon figure out how better to use the new technology of automation for competitive advantage. This does not mean investing in more equipment; in today's . . . environment, it is how the equipment is used that is important. Success comes from achieving continuous process improvement through organizational learning and experimentation.[10]

WRAP-UP

Top managers of American companies who would adopt the new thinking face a particularly difficult transition. They must throw off three to four decades of viewing a company as assets and products rather than as people and opportunities. Forty years of emphasizing accounting-style control over things has seen American businesses do little or nothing to develop the capabilities of people. Workers have been viewed as a source of energy and cost, not as a source of ideas. It is time for American top managers to stop viewing a business as a mechanical contrivance, somewhat like a Swiss watch, where the determination of optimal output comes from outside, from above. In the usual view of those mechanical systems, the purpose of workers is to keep the system running as close as possible to peak rates of throughput. Workers simply follow orders, monitored by top-down control systems and motivated by output-oriented incentive procedures. Similarly, customers are not viewed as a source of ideas for the company. The global economy compels companies to recognize that their most important asset is the power of people—workers, managers, suppliers, and customers—to remove constraints that impede flexibility.

CHAPTER 7

MANAGEMENT INFORMATION FOR COMPETITIVE EXCELLENCE

———◆———

[Knowledge management] entails investing in the problemsolving skills of the workforce and then focusing their attention on those problems that they are in the best position to solve. . . . To operationalize this view in an organization, workers' problemsolving skills must be developed and the needed information provided so that they can determine what the problems are and how they ought to be solved. . . . This, of course, requires a very different kind of information system, one that is real-time—and problem-identifying/problem-solving—oriented.

— Steven C. Wheelwright[1]

Companies require new management information (perhaps we should say *self*-management information) about customer expectations and flexibility of processes in order to reinforce actions that fulfill the imperatives of global competition. The actions companies must take to become global competitors do not entail new and highly sophisticated technology. People in American companies have known for decades how to build customer relationships by returning customers' calls, following up on complaints, calling unexpectedly to ask if a customer was satisfied with a product or service, and so forth. And they have known for decades how to increase flexibility by simplifying work and eliminating causes of waste. However, few American businesses in recent years seem willing to execute the relatively simple, straightforward steps that global competitive excellence demands. We already know the reason: management accounting information invariably suggests it is too costly to pursue actions that are in synch with imperatives of information-driven global competition.

Discussions of management information and business behavior often start by invoking the old adage: What you measure is what you get. Measures used to evaluate performance presumably drive what people do and shape the results they achieve. I don't think anyone seriously disagrees with that idea. But new performance measures themselves will not prompt companies to adopt new attitudes about the purpose of being in business, and about the role of people in helping a business fulfill its purpose. To become a people-oriented, time-conscious competitor in the global economy, a company first must be filled with the spirit of employee-driven customer service. That spirit comes from forceful leadership, not from tinkering with performance measures or management accounting information.

However, vestiges of remote-control information systems can subvert the goals of well-intentioned performance improvement programs. Therefore, businesses must eradicate all performance measures and any other management information that does not trigger behavior congruent with the imperatives of global competitiveness. Earmarks of behavior that fulfills these imperatives were listed in Table 4–1. This behavior will always diminish delay, excess, or variation wherever they exist. It won't rationalize longer lead times or added waste by producing more output. It will reflect a sincere belief that everyone in the company is responsible for the customer, and for how the customer views their performance. The excellent global company will not resort to top-down controls that separate the organization in two camps—us and them. Everyone will be part of everything, and everything will matter to everyone.

What information might a company want if all it could wish for were handed to it on a silver platter? How does that ideal information compare with some of the old tools of management accounting, and certain modifications now being proposed to improve those tools? These questions, and more, are the subject of this chapter.

INFORMATION TO PROMOTE IMPERATIVES
OF COMPETITIVE EXCELLENCE

A key deficiency in traditional management accounting information is its failure to promote relationship-building with customers. Accounting systems provide almost no information about customers, other than revenue data. And revenue data simply tell what customers paid for items received. They say nothing about whether customers wanted or liked what they received. Revenue data never indicate if the customer would have preferred something else, had it been available. Nor do they say anything about the company's importance to the customer. It's no surprise that users of traditional management accounting information usually return a blank stare when asked what they know about customers.

Information about customer satisfaction will be ubiquitous in the global enterprise. But it provides only a periodic check on results—like the doctor taking a patient's pulse or temperature. New or reconstituted information about customer satisfaction itself does not elicit the responsiveness companies must achieve to be competitive. The results of customer surveys, focus group sessions, and the like can be gratifying, of course. But everyone knows that actions designed to achieve high customer scores may not always be in the interest of long-term customer relationship building. Employees can cajole and coax customers to achieve high scores on a satisfaction survey. Such actions usually do not build relationships for the long haul. Only customers who believe that employees' actions reflect a genuine effort to be responsive are likely to become the company's loyal long-run advocates.

The catalyst driving people to build lasting customer relationships will not be customer satisfaction surveys and the like. It will be top management's expressions of strong commitment to the importance of serving the customer. Everyone in the company must project a sense of the central place customers occupy in the organization's mission. We mentioned in Chapter 5 the importance of having a shared concern for customer service throughout an organization. Like the code of a biological organism that DNA implants into each cell, a shared sense of an organization's mission helps focus every action in the business on satisfying customer expectations; it also enables every person in the company to represent the entire organization to any customer.

A mission statement is not what one normally thinks of when asked to describe management information. But I believe a well-crafted mission statement does more than anything to trigger actions that are relevant to the global imperative of responsiveness. For one thing, it can prompt people to think *first* about the customer, before doing anything else. What a change that attitude will bring to most companies! The mission also provides a gauge against which each employee can judge his or her efforts to satisfy customers. If employees navigate with a strong inner compass, every action in an organization will more likely be directed "ceaselessly to refresh its knowledge of its customers' wants and to devise new ways of satisfying them."

Federal Express Corporation's U.S. operation has a short but powerful mission statement: "Absolutely, Positively Overnight!" Everyone in the company knows what that statement means. Almost nothing more has to be said to insure that everyone directs every process, every moment toward total customer satisfaction. Here is a mission statement that puts the emphasis on serving "the best interest of all those who see us as a means to an end," including customers:

> We, here at Johnsonville Foods, have a moral responsibility to become the best food company ever established. We will accomplish this as each one of us becomes better than anyone else at serving the best interest of all those who see us as a means to an end. We will accomplish our mission by setting near-term objectives and long-term goals that will require superlative performance by each of us. We will change any objectives or goals that no longer meet these requirements to ones that do. We understand that this is a never-ending process. This is the Johnsonville Way, and we are committed to it.[2]

A company that imbues its people with a strong commitment to serving customers, as outlined in these statements, can periodically track many measures of customer satisfaction to confirm results. The CEO of Johnsonville Foods, Ralph Stayer, suggests measures that reflect on "every way we touch the customer. Is the product delivered on time? Is it easy to use? Do they like our billing and credit and discount system? How well does the truck driver perform when he takes the product to their warehouse? Does their buyer look forward to our salesman coming, or does he say, 'Oh no, not that again!'"[3]

Another measure of a company's responsiveness to customers that we mentioned previously is the share of each customer's purchases from the company. As someone once said, the only market share that ever matters in the long run is the share you have of each of your customer's purchases in your market. A company that supplies nearly 100 percent of the relevant needs of every customer it serves probably has focused its attention more assiduously on relationship building than a company that satisfies only a few percent of many, many customers' needs. It should be no surprise if the former company sells more in the long run, at higher profit.

One additional measure of successful relationship building is the share of revenue from repeat sales to old customers as opposed to new sales to first-time customers. To succeed in the long run a business needs both, of course. But most American businesses tend to focus almost exclusively on creating new customers, not retaining old ones. Indeed, information systems often focus on problems that existing customers *create for the company*. The typical accounting system can track a customer's overdue payment, for example, but it never will indicate if the delinquency is linked to customer dissatisfaction caused by a still-unresolved shipping error or product defect.

It is important for a customer-responsive organization to track many indicators of potential or actual customer dissatisfaction. Some of these indicators should track external developments such as competitors' plans, new product or process announcements, and studies of changing consumer tastes and habits. Often consumers themselves are the best source of this information. Here is a good reason to invest in focus group research. But many internal indicators of dissatisfaction also should be tracked. The literature is filled with examples of this type of information: first-pass failure rates; defect rates at final assembly; error rates in filling orders, invoicing, and recording payments; warranty and service calls; timeliness in handling inquiries; and so forth.

In addition to measuring success at building customer loyalty, companies also need performance measures that promote the imperative of flexibility. Here the literature offers a great deal of guidance, primarily as a by-product of American business's growing interest in and experience with JIT in the 1980s. Listed below in the left-hand column are three measures that track people's overall success at removing delay, excess, and variation—the enemies of flexibility. The right-hand column suggests the central issue addressed by each ratio.[4]

| Total time / necessary time | How much does the time spent to do something (e.g., prepare an invoice, assemble a product, or answer a customer inquiry) exceed the time one ought to spend if there were no delay? |
| Use rate / demand rate | How evenly are processes balanced to the final demand rate? |

| Number of pieces per workstation | How much does work in process exceed what is needed to exactly supply what the customer wants, when he or she wants it? |

A company that steadily pushes these ratios toward a value of one certainly must be manifesting the earmarks of behavior leading toward flexibility. These measures can be taken at almost any level in an organization, and they do not have to be taken frequently, perhaps only as often as once or twice a year.

On a less global level, individuals and teams everywhere in an organization should be tracking what processes accomplish, the time and resources it took to get a job done, and where problems are lurking for further study and resolution. These tracks—made by people everywhere using marker pens, flip charts and so forth—are the primary badge of each person's ownership in processes and results.[5]

In a well-led company, all the above information—from external indicators of customer satisfaction, to internalized signals from a mission statement, to handmade marks on a flip chart—can trigger actions that support customer responsiveness and flexibility. American companies gradually are beginning to take such measures seriously. But too often the information represented by these new measures—the information that should herald actions aimed at achieving competitive excellence—is cultivated alongside the old accounting-based information that heralds remote-control management. An example of whipped cream piled on to a serving of moldy pie? Let's examine in more depth the insidious impact of traditional management accounting's lingering presence in American companies.

TRANSFORMING OPERATIONS CONTROL INFORMATION FROM SHADOWS INTO SUNLIGHT

As I said above, the accounting information used to control operations in most American businesses in the last forty years resembles shadows cast on the wall of the cave in Plato's famous allegory. Those shadows are the reflected dollar magnitudes of products sold and resources consumed. The information in those accounting shadows tells nothing about the capabilities of processes to satisfy customer wants, nor does it say anything about customers' attitudes and desires. Hence, this accounting-based management control information does not speak to the imperatives of responsiveness and flexibility. In most cases, this information sets targets that motivate people to manipulate processes, producing results that are antithetical to those imperatives of competition. We already have shown examples of this where traditional management accounting controls, especially standard cost control systems, encourage people to generate output to cover costs, not to satisfy customer expectations. To those points made earlier, let's add some additional examples of dislocation caused when companies use accounting information to trigger people's actions by remote control.

The first example shows how cost accounting information often confounds efforts to control costs simply because it shows only where money was spent, and how much, not why it was spent.[6]* A hypothetical company's production department in Cleveland records costs in two separate lines for resin and maintenance incurred in running extrusion machinery. These cost accounts do not indicate, however, that *both* the resin and the maintenance consumed in Cleveland reflect a company-wide policy, carried out by the purchasing department in Baltimore, to "buy in large quantities from vendors that quote the lowest price." A dumpster full of defective extrusions and extra maintenance to unclog gummed-up extrusion machines simply show up in the accounts as extra costs of production in Cleveland, not as the price paid for a Baltimore purchasing agent's efforts to win a bonus by acquiring raw material at the lowest cost. Attempts to control the costs recorded in such accounts will not affect purchasing policies executed in Baltimore. Instead, favorable price variances on raw material purchases will encourage more of the same policies, while unfavorable production cost variances will focus attention on "inefficiencies" in Cleveland, perhaps prompting a decision to reduce costs by outsourcing extrusion to a Third World country.

How much better it would be if operators of the extrusion machines in Cleveland maintained SPC (statistical process control) charts and formed problem-solving teams that search for constraints as soon as symptoms of delay, excess, and variation appear. Because these operators are intimately involved with the process, it should not take them long, using fishbone diagrams, histograms, and other problem-solving tools, to pinpoint their resin supply as a major cause of machine stoppages (delay) and defective parts (excess). Moreover, their search for a constraint will likely lead to the purchasing office in Baltimore. At that point the machine operators and the purchasing agents (not higher ups) will consult with each other on the phone or fax to define and to discuss ways to remove the constraint. Undoubtedly they will connect Cleveland's problem with top management's purchasing and incentive policies (buy from the lowest bidder and show favorable purchase price variances every month). At that point, the team will approach top management. But now, unlike times past, operations people will go to top management with hard facts—irrefutable information about processes that points a clear finger at the need to change management policies. Presumably top management should recommend that they scrap the "lowest bid wins" policy, apply SPC to incoming materials, and purchase only from vendors who pay explicit attention to variation, not just price. Long-term result: costs fall, quality improves, customers and employees are happier. Nobody has to begin the arduous and costly processes of establishing a supply source for extruded parts in the Third World and laying off machine operators in Cleveland.

In Chapter 3 we observed how the imperative to "earn direct labor hours" and report favorable standard cost overhead variances puts pressure on managers to produce output for its own sake, rather than to concentrate on the work needed to satisfy customers. Similar pressure to produce output for its own sake also results from companies using net income or ROI targets to control divisional and departmental profit or investment centers. This pressure to produce output for its own sake emanates to a large degree from accountants' "matching" rules for attaching production overhead costs to manufactured goods.[7]* Only overhead costs attached to products sold are deducted against revenue in the income statement. The rest stays in the balance sheet, reported as inventory. Therefore, the more units of output produced in a period and the more of those units that remain unsold (but marketable) at the end of a period, the less overhead cost is deducted from revenue in the period. Smart managers who need to temporarily boost income know what to do: go into overtime, rent temporary warehouse space, and get busy producing output.

Obviously this practice has a backlash. In the next period, unless sales continue to equal or exceed production, income is reduced by the prior period's costs carried forward in inventory sold in the next period. Managers usually assume, however, that they can build inventory to boost income in one period and then spread the effect of the backlash over several future periods, meanwhile hoping no one notices the added inventory carried over from the first period.

But it is not just steps that operations managers take to produce output for its own sake that impair company-wide competitiveness and long-term profitability. Other steps can be taken to manipulate financial performance that impairs a company's long-term economic health: deferring discretionary expenditures for research and development, postponing maintenance programs, encouraging employee turnover as a way of holding down direct labor costs, cutting back employee benefit programs, cutting employee training programs, postponing capital investments in expensive new technologies (i.e., scrape by as long as possible on old, fully depreciated assets), and more.

Astute business analysts have long recognized the pitfalls inherent in relying on accounting reports for indications of a company's long-term financial health. Along those lines, an eminent British financial analyst, David Allen, has said:

> If this year's return on capital is the overriding objective, it will always appear preferable to chase low-margin business to put through underutilized facilities, rather than face the high front-end outlays (investment on both capital and revenue account) required to adapt those facilities to the real needs of the market-place. Failure is shored up, and opportunities are neglected, leading to an undisclosed weakening of the business in terms of its ability to face the future. In short, as indicators of long-term financial health, accounting reports not only have little positive value, but can be seriously misleading. Other things being equal, for example, a shrinking business will show better returns on capital than an expanding one. With such a measuring system, the likelihood of resources being misdirected is just too great to be ignored.[8]

Managers are not unaware of these weaknesses in accounting information. An image of executives mindlessly responding to accounting shadows in a cave does not accurately portray, of course, the remote-control approach to management followed by most businesses in Western industrial countries since the 1960s. Managers and financial analysts in the past forty years have adopted very sophisticated tools to "get behind the numbers." Four examples of these developments since the 1950s, in chronological order, are as follows: DuPont's ROI formula, originated at DuPont by Donaldson Brown in 1912, was widely publicized after 1950 as a tool for analyzing the impact any element in the balance sheet or income statement has on ROI;[9] variance techniques for assessing the impact on net income of changes in price, volume, and mix of products and resource inputs became widely taught in

American business schools after the 1950s;[10] after the 1970s, shareholder value analysis stressed the importance of using cash flow and debt leverage information to roll back clouds of obfuscation created by the accounting information used in corporate financial reports;[11] finally, in the 1980s, activity-based costing (discussed in Chapter 8) became a widely heralded technique for eliminating distortions from traditional cost accounting information.

However, each of these tools, from ROI analysis to activity-based costing, simply "looks behind the barrier" from which the shadows are being projected. The tools do not go outside the cave, above ground as it were, to examine real processes, the people working in them, and the customers being served by them. The tools analyze products and resources—analogous to what Plato in his allegory calls "artificial objects"—that create accounting "shadows." While the use of these tools reflects managers doing much more than reacting passively to mere accounting signals, their use still reflects managers focusing on artificial objects in the cave, not real objects above the ground.

How can we modify or discontinue use of these management accounting tools, and develop information that directs managers' attention toward improving processes that build relationships and create flexibility, not toward tampering with processes to achieve accounting targets? What role will *accounting* information play in companies that develop appropriate management information? What role is there for *financial* nonaccounting information in controlling operations?

IS THERE A PLACE FOR ACCOUNTING AND FINANCIAL INFORMATION OUTSIDE THE CAVE?

Will companies that "come out of the cave" and empower workers to control processes in the light of customer expectations still have a use for accounting and financial "shadows?" For a long time to come, yes. Perhaps indefinitely. The main problem I trace to management accounting information is using the information as a target to motivate inappropriate goals and actions. Even if everyone in the company acts as though customers are in charge of the marketplace and workers are in control of processes, *accounting* information still has a role to play in planning and in tracking results. And *financial* (nonaccounting) information has a role to play in managing operations.

To reiterate what I said before about the different roles for management accounting and financial information in planning and control, here is a brief recap of the management information that developed in three stages of American industry's development over the past century and a half:

Stage 1. Very low complexity. The earliest managed business organizations in America, such as early nineteenth-century textile mills, limited their attention to coordinating and controlling labor-intensive tasks in a few closely linked manufacturing processes that tended to produce fairly homogeneous product lines. Management information systems focused on the collection of financial and nonfinancial data about the efficiency of input/output conversion activities in processes, including nonaccounting data about the cost of process outputs. Ford's plant at River Rouge in the early 1920s represented the ultimate extension of this stage.

Stage 2. Medium to high complexity. By the late nineteenth century we see both large-scale organizations whose activities integrate mass production with mass marketing and large metal and machine-making manufacturers whose activities span a complex variety of intermediate and finished products. Prominent examples of these developments just before World War I include the DuPont Corporation and Yale & Towne Manufacturing Company. Management information systems for *planning* the economic performance of entire industry-spanning companies and their subunits focused on measures of margin, net income, and return on investment.

Stage 3. Between the 1920s and the 1980s we see large business organizations cope with growing complexity in two ways. To cope with organizational complexity, large organizations focus internal activities along product lines or geographic regions by creating multidivisional structures. To cope with product complexity, companies decouple functions and processes. Developments at General Motors between the late 1920s and the 1980s epitomize both divisionalization and process decoupling. After the 1950s, management information systems focus on the growing use of *accounting* targets to *control* operating processes.

There are several ways for companies to modify or discontinue management accounting information that motivates people to manipulate or tamper with processes, and still track financial results. Some we have already discussed and others are mentioned below for the first time. Let's examine some of these ways to modify or discontinue existing management information: first, information used to control operations; secondly, information to plan and track overall financial results.

Controlling Operations

In businesses of all types, whether they deal in manufacturing or services, the most urgent need is to eliminate all management information that encourages people—at any level—to manipulate processes in order to achieve accounting results. Undoubtedly the most prevalent examples of such information are the myriad performance and budget reports that controllers' offices "throw over the wall" at regular, frequent intervals to managers at all levels. These reports invite (often require) managers and employees to reconcile the outcomes of their work with financial outcomes compiled from the accounting records. They force operations people to view their work primarily through accounting categories. Their use to measure performance also forces people insidiously to manipulate work, to fulfill financial imperatives that are antithetical to competitive excellence in the global economy.

I am not the first person to propose that companies scrap accounting-based operations control reports. Operations management experts for years have urged manufacturers to run their operations without the traditional cost accounting control information. Perhaps the most strident advocate of dispensing with accounting cost control information is Thomas Vollmann, co-director of Boston University's Manufacturing Roundtable. Vollmann equates recent activity-based efforts to reform manufacturing accounting systems with ancient warriors' attempts to untie the massive knot on the yoke of King Gordius's chariot.[12] An oracle had prophesied that whoever loosed the Gordian Knot would rule the world. After countless challengers failed in their attempts to untie the knot, Alexander the Great came up to it with his sword and cut it in two. "Companies," says Vollmann, "have similarly discovered that the simple, bold move of cutting the knot between accounting and [operational] performance measurement is much more effective than trying to untie it."[13]

In a similar vein, Richard Schonberger says that a company using continual improvement and total involvement to control the causes of cost "does not need to rely on cost information for management control." Schonberger believes most companies are reluctant to accept this idea because they have "relied on costs so long that [they] cannot yet imagine using costs [even activity-based costs] just for making product-line and pricing decisions and not for cost control."[14] Finally, Robert Hall believes that "financially oriented management must be weaned from thinking that detailed financial goals stimulate operating improvement. [Over time] it becomes obvious that actions improving quality or reducing lead times will reduce operating costs."[15]

Although authorities such as Vollmann, Schonberger, and Hall advocate using nonfinancial performance indicators of time, space, distance, and quality rather than cost information to manage operating activities, they are not opposed to collecting cost information for planning and evaluating events in the workplace. Obviously companies may keep financial score. But the financial score is like the score in a tennis match. As tennis players know, it is necessary while playing to keep one's eye on the ball, not on the scoreboard. But nonfinancial measures of operating performance, unlike traditional cost measures, often *are* the ball, not just the score. Controlling processes in order to improve many nonfinancial measures undoubtedly will improve a company's competitive position. But manipulating processes in order to achieve accounting cost targets is not likely to improve competitiveness at all.

An example of a company that uses accounting cost information to *check* scorecard results while simultaneously tracking real-time outcomes of processes to *control* process results was shown to me by Kenneth J. McGuire, a consultant who has taken American executives on study tours of Japanese companies since the early 1980s.[16] The company is a well-known Japanese manufacturing firm—call it Company J. People everywhere in Company J compile operations control information by product line in a series of twelve graphs that appear on walls all over the company. The data on all but one of the graphs come from operations people on the line. Those graphs depict variables such as average setup time per job by department, process times per minute of elapsed time, number of defect claims from customers (i.e., next users), downtime percentages, number of line stops per day (one worker oversees on average about fifty unattended devices in Company J's plant), and amount of inventory.

One graph reports cost information from the accounting department. Its title is "total costs down," and it shows percentage change from month to month in total costs by product line. Everyone in the company hopes to see total costs go down. The title on this one cost graph expresses both a goal and, for the year's results that I observed, an actual fact. However, according to McGuire, Company J's personnel devote their primary attention to process variables that affect total product cost (the variables on the other eleven graphs), not to the total cost statistic itself.

In effect, accountants in Company J report total product-line cost information to operating personnel so that they can look over their shoulders to be sure costs are where they are supposed to be as everyone in the company races forward to perform processes according to what it takes to make the company competitive. "Total cost down" is a scoreboard, not a primary object of control. Company J's accountants keep the usual double-entry books for external reporting purposes. Top managers, of course, do not ignore financial results. Indeed, Company J has an enviable record of long-run profitability. But they have achieved that record by focusing operations control on determinants of competitiveness, not on the financial results that come from being competitive.

Richard Schonberger has documented numerous examples of American companies where operations departments prominently display "charts on the wall" on which line personnel record real-time nonfinancial process data.[17] These charts reflect true ownership of causes and results by people on the line who observe process outcomes and customer reactions as they occur, not as they appear many weeks or months later in garbled translation through top-down accounting reports. These charts, as kept by Company J and by the many American companies Schonberger documents, are the front line of operations control in a globally competitive enterprise.

An observation one can not ignore, however, is that process improvement efforts to drive out causes of variation, delay, and excess — the efforts whose results are tracked in the "charts on the wall" referred to above — do not automatically generate cost savings in the accounting records. Indeed, successful process improvement programs first create resource redundancies, then reduced costs. Perhaps the main exception to this generalization is the savings from reduced inventory caused by a successful program to reduce lead times and batch sizes in a manufacturing establishment. Reduced inventory shows up immediately in the accountants' records. But most other benefits of process improvement show up as less space needed, fewer people needed, less time needed, and so forth. Those redundancies show up on the books as financial improvement only after someone takes steps either to sell or lay off the excess resources or, better yet, to employ those underutilized resources in some previously untapped opportunity.

The redundancies created by successful process improvement programs test top managements' ability to lead and discover opportunities for growth. I once heard an executive say "we have no problem generating ideas for cutting $60 million of costs in this company; the real difficulty is coming up with ideas for generating $60 million more revenue." This difficulty should be felt less in companies that build strong customer relationships, in companies that focus R&D on developing well-defined core competencies, and in companies whose leaders are committed to the idea of empowering people to control customer-focused processes, not using people to achieve financial results.

A step any company can take to focus managers more intently on creating opportunities for redeploying redundant resources is to create what I call a "process improvement account." I have seen variations of this idea referred to as a "JIT bank" or "TQM bank." This idea is to systematically identify anticipated resource redundancies at the start of a process improvement program and locate the dollars associated with those resources on the books. As improvements occur, the dollars associated with freed-up resources should be transferred to the process improvement account. A regular report on the status of this account should be a constant reminder to management of untapped resource potential going to waste. A key indicator of top management success should be the speed with which resources in the improvement account are redeployed to revenue-generating opportunities. An index of management failure would be a decision to lay off people listed in the improvement account, or to write off redundant assets.

Returning to our discussion of enterprises that maintain visible indicators of process improvement in charts on the wall, it is important to ask if such organizations will have any place at all for *financial* control information? Perhaps they will, just as companies in the nineteenth and early-twentieth centuries did. But the type of financial information must be carefully defined. Probably these companies will have no *accounting-based* cost or other financial performance information in the operations domain. And I define "accounting-based information" to include any driver-based activity cost information, discussed in Chapter 8, that merely reconfigures existing accounting costs.

The key point is to free operations from any information that encourages people to manipulate processes to achieve results other than continuous improvement at meeting the imperatives of global competitiveness. Accounting information, of course, does not have to motivate behavior antithetical to competitive excellence. However, that has been its role in management accounting control systems for the past forty years, and there is little to suggest that role will suddenly change if controllers' departments continue to generate periodic operating performance reports. Besides, even if people stopped using accounting information to manipulate operations, I see no positive contribution accounting control reports make to operations that would justify their continued production. *They provide no control information that is not otherwise better supplied by real-time charting of information from processes and customers.* This is not to deny that accounting still has a role to play in planning and checking results. But just because plans and summary reports are denominated in financial accounting terms, it does not mean it is best also to denominate operational control targets in the same terms.

However, financial *nonaccounting* information sometimes may be useful to operations managers. This is particularly true of complex continuous flow operations that make extensive use of modern microsensor and microprocessor technology to track real-time process data. The primary example of such operations is a computer-integrated manufacturing, or CIM, plant. Ramchandran Jaikumar has articulated the conceptual framework for process control costing in a CIM environment.[18] The key element of his framework is the power of the computer to act as an "omniscient observer" of a production system, capturing information about every possible event that affects process outcomes. By adding appropriate economic values to a virtually infinite array of process information, the computer can supply information with which to evaluate economic consequences of ignoring or acting upon events as they unfold. Jaikumar refers to this as process control costing information.

Using an analysis of wire breakage in a wire-drawing factory as an example, he says process control costing can provide a model with which to assess the impact of different causes on breakage. In Jaikumar's words, "The model needed for process control costing is precisely the model we need to control a process. A process control costing system adds to this model the economic value and economic cost of reducing or eliminating the different causes of failure."[19]

While Jaikumar's process control costing information is financial, it is not derived, necessarily, from the accounting system. In a sense, it comes "bottom up" from processes, not "top down" from central accounting records. There is all the difference in the world between traditional standard cost accounting information used to control processes and Jaikumar's process control costing information. With the latter, decisions affecting processes are based upon sound process information that has been adjusted with financial coefficients. That information does not lead to tampering with processes to achieve desired accounting results. Instead, it reveals financial consequences of sound process control. On the other hand, standard cost accounting information provides financial information unrelated to processes. It encourages people to manipulate processes—in effect, throw them out of control—in order to alter the financial accounting results.

A glimpse into the future of process control costing is provided by Texas Eastman Company, a chemical manufacturing subsidiary of Eastman Kodak located in Houston, Texas. In a recently published teaching case, Robert S. Kaplan describes a fascinating experiment in which production people at Texas Eastman use process control information, generated for quality management purposes, to produce a daily income statement in a complex CIM-type chemical plant.[20] This plant-wide income information has provided a stimulus to operating personnel to accelerate their already very successful quality improvement process. Striving to improve on each day's net income has caused people to improve the plant's quality indicators at a faster rate than ever.

It is significant, however, that the plant-wide income information does not come from Texas Eastman's central accounting records. It comes "bottom up" from process control information. Hence, *there is no temptation for operating personnel to tamper with processes to improve unrelated accounting results.* The impetus now at work is to reduce variation in processes faster than ever in order to improve the resultant financial outcomes reported by the plant!

Someone might ask: Do these plant-wide income numbers "tie-out" with the central accounting ledger's "bottom line?" Not at the moment. But whether that matters probably depends on what you view as the primary management information—the accounting ledger or the "process ledger." Traditionally the controller's office has thrown accounting results "over the wall" to the plant and has expected plant managers to reconcile operations data to accounting financial results. This is what monthly standard cost variance reporting is all about. Now, at Texas Eastman, the possibility exists for plant managers to compile process control financial results that they throw "over the wall" to the controller's department and expect the controller to reconcile those process results to the general ledger results. The transition from accounting-generated control information to process-generated financial information that one sees unfolding in this experiment at Texas Eastman symbolizes perfectly the turning away from "shadows in the cave" that managers must make in the global economy.

It may seem ironic that the plant manager at Texas Eastman urges his operations personnel to improve *daily* plant net income, calculated from dollarized process control data. After all, isn't Wall Street's alleged pressure to achieve *quarterly* earnings targets one of the reasons American companies suffer, by trading off future well-being for short-run gains? Quarterly earning targets seem infinitely long-term as compared to daily targets. In fact, one very important lesson of the Texas Eastman story is that competitiveness may not be impaired so much by people paying attention to short-run process-based financial information as by people manipulating processes to achieve short-run accounting targets. If financial results are calculated from quality process improvement data, driving hard to improve processes should quickly improve financial results, especially if the "process improvement account" mentioned above is in place. It seems that is what has been happening at Texas Eastman. But when people drive hard to improve accounting results by tampering with processes, short-run financial gains almost inevitably show up later as long-term economic sacrifices. That is the story of remote-control management in most American businesses since the 1950s.

Planning and Tracking

None of the comments made above about limitations of accounting information in the area of operations control should be construed to mean that accounting has no place in a globally competitive organization. On the contrary. Accounting has as important a role as ever helping companies evaluate the extent and financing of their operations. Companies have long used, and for the indefinite future will continue to use, accounting tools for planning and tracking financial results. In a well-run company, top management always must have a continually evolving sense of the likely financial consequences of plans and decisions. It was for that purpose that DuPont developed its famous ROI chart system nearly eighty years ago; and for that purpose people developed sophisticated modes of variance analysis and shareholder value analysis in the last thirty years. These planning and forecasting tools are as useful today as they were originally.

Companies also must know the *cash* implications of plans, decisions, and ongoing operations. Nobody likes surprises, at least not the type that lead a company toward bankruptcy. To avoid preventable mistakes companies must have sound cash budgeting and cash flow tracking systems. Traditional accounting tools have served this purpose for many, many decades and will continue to for years to come.

The point of everything said above is that *information from systems designed to enforce fiscal responsibility*—what Alfred Sloan referred to as top management's responsibility to control the pursestrings—*should not also be used to control operations*. The ironic result, as the last forty years of American business history suggests, is to court fiscal disaster. As a general rule, then, top managers should resist rolling plan and budget information down to control operating processes. They should not invest resources in creating elaborate information systems to "tie-out" operating performance indicators with financial account-

Figure 7–1
Old Management Information System

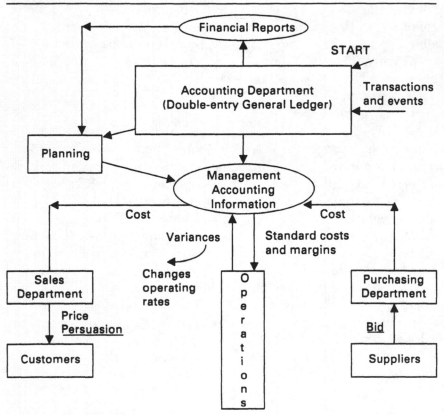

Figure 7–2
New Management Information System

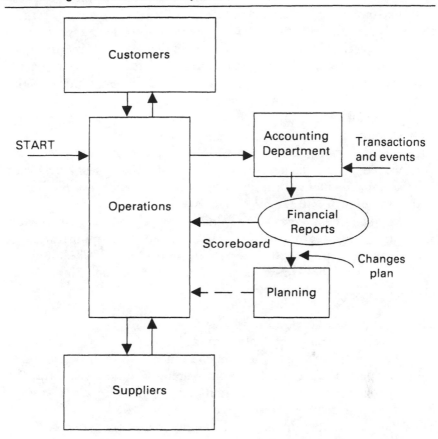

ing performance indicators. Instead, they should invest in special studies as needed to explain unforeseen financial performance variances. And if special studies indicate that by running existing processes as well as possible a company can not generate desired financial results, they should resolve to adjust their plans, not beat up on the operating people and not step up efforts to cajole reluctant customers.

Figures 7–1 and 7–2 compare the relationship of accounting-based information to operational control information that has prevailed in most American businesses in the past forty years with the relationship that I believe will prevail in competitive businesses of the 1990s and beyond. In the old era, portrayed in Figure 7–1, operations control information came largely from accounting information that the accounting department made "managerially relevant" in standard cost variance reports, budgets, and so forth. There was no feedback from customers, nor any information but price bids from suppliers. Operations personnel manipulated processes to fulfill cost or income targets that had been "thrown over the wall" by the controller's department.

In the new global company, portrayed in Figure 7–2, operations departments will link with customers and suppliers and strive to get all processes in control. Information will flow from operations to the controller's department, to help accountants prepare financial reporting and planning documents. But control information never flows from accounting to operations. Costs and income are not ignored, of course. Like runners in a race, operations people look over their shoulders once in a while to check on total costs and bottom-line performance. Companies maintain accounting systems to *check results* of operations, but not to *control* operations.

The two figures above bring to mind four special topics that concern accounting information used for planning, and the administration of accounting departments that prepare this information. The four topics, discussed briefly here, are target costing, capital budgeting, cost of quality, and accounting simplification.

Target Costing.   An important idea from Japan, target costing recently has received a great deal of attention, not all of which is based on a clear understanding of the concept. It is not another type of standard cost performance measurement system. It simply identifies the price customers seem willing to pay for a thing (final product or component part) and subtracts the necessary return a company must receive from selling that thing. The difference, called the target cost, is a measure of the upper bound of the company's own costs in the long run.

Target costing is the antithesis of traditional American cost-plus thinking. If you define strategic as anything that affects competitiveness vis-á-vis customers, target cost reinforces the idea that cost is not strategic. In effect, it says the customer doesn't care about your cost, only about the customer's own costs. So, you had better get the customer's costs—the price the customer pays you—into your management information system as a sort of benchmark to define the upper bounds of your own costs. As for identifying and measuring your own costs, to compare with a target cost, target costing prompts a legitimate use for activity-based costing tools. Although few people yet have explored the application of activity-based costing concepts to target costing, the idea is beginning to catch on.[21]

Capital Budgeting. A great deal has been written already about the limitations of traditional finance approaches to capital budgeting in the global economy. This traditional approach usually assumes the future will be an extrapolation of the present.[22] Financial investment analysis considers how new investments reduce current costs, but it usually assumes that current benefits will continue to flow whether or not new investment is made. A new investment is justified, then, largely by the present value of cost savings, primarily the displacement of direct labor. This assumption may be valid where investment entails replacing old with new equipment embodying the same technology. But it overlooks the radically different benefits inherent in today's state-of-the-art technologies. This oversight biases against investments that offer improved quality, dependability, service, or flexibility.

Indeed, costing systems that stress direct-labor performance measures reinforce the tendency for American companies, in particular, to invest primarily in short-term cost-reducing or labor-saving projects. Information from those systems, used in traditional capital budgeting techniques, tends to bias against any investment that promises to develop the company's people or to build customer satisfaction in the future without reducing current costs or direct-labor hours. To overcome this bias when evaluating investments in new technologies, companies must extend the time horizon and broaden the scope with which they view costs and returns.

However, companies probably should abandon traditional financial analysis altogether when evaluating R&D expenditures.[23] R&D is a special class of spending that often is equated, mistakenly, with investment spending. Investments presume knowledge, albeit imperfect, about future costs and returns. R&D represents an effort to gain a stake in future opportunities before anything is known about future costs and returns. Uncertainty about future outcomes has the opposite effect on current values of investments and R&D. Companies facing a future of new and often unexplored technological opportunities will impair their long-term financial well-being if they judge R&D with the same financial tools they use to evaluate investments.

R&D spending resembles the stake in the future one acquires by purchasing options in financial markets. Downstream benefits affect the value of an option quite differently than they affect the value of an investment. When evaluating an investment, downstream benefits are more heavily *discounted* the more uncertain and the more distant in time they are. However, the value of an option is greater the more uncertain the outcome and the longer the time horizon in which to capture the outcome. Uncertainty and timing of future outcomes can never increase an option's downside risk; that risk is limited to the amount spent up front to purchase the option. So also with R&D: companies that relate R&D spending to the certainty of a project's financial outcome are not giving due consideration to the danger of foregoing learning about new technologies.

To see how R&D resembles taking an option on the future, consider companies that began to explore automatic and electronically controlled machine tools when that technology first appeared in the mid-1970s.[24] Those companies were well positioned to exploit the microprocessor-based revolution in capabilities—much higher performance at much lower cost—that hit during the early 1980s. Because their operators, maintenance personnel, and process engineers were already comfortable with electronic technology, they found it was relatively simple to retrofit existing machines with powerful microelectronics. Companies that had earlier deferred spending R&D funds on electronically controlled machine tools fell behind: they had acquired no option on these new process technologies.

For actual investment proposals, as distinct from R&D spending, it probably is sufficient to recognize that not all future costs and benefits of today's investments are captured in the money magnitudes customarily tracked by the double-entry accounts. Recognizing that fact, one can then go ahead and reckon the net present value of flows that can be reduced to such money variables. Then, if a project does not have the requisite net present value to warrant going ahead with it, one can consider how much net value would have to exist in the "imponderables" (such as deeper customer relationships, flexibility, etc.) to make it go. Usually managers will know if the unquantified variables are or are not capable of carrying the balance.

In fact, the "hard" numbers in traditional capital budgeting often rest on untenable assumptions that companies are less likely to adopt if they use people-oriented and process-based performance information to evaluate investment proposals. Contrast, for example, how traditional capital budgeting and people-oriented budgeting might treat the cost of training in an investment proposal. Training would presumably have the same importance for the outcome of an investment project no matter how the proposal is evaluated. But the traditional approach, where short-run cost saving carries the day, might consider training expendable if eliminating it makes a difference to the net present value outcome. The newer management approach, however, where cutting lead time might be the primary goal of the investment, would identify training as critical to the outcome and not expendable regardless of cost.

Cost of Quality. For years, quality experts have urged people in companies to estimate the "cost of not taking quality seriously" and to use that number to attract top management's attention to the need for a quality program. The cost of quality generally is defined to include the cost of prevention, inspection, and correction (both inside the company and outside—after customers find something wrong). It takes a little doing on the accountants' part to recast cost numbers according to these categories, which are categories normally not used in keeping the accounts. (This is another good place to use the activity-based costing techniques described in Chapter 8). But it isn't a monumental task, and the results can have a salutary effect. It gets managements' attention to see, for example, that costs associated with correcting what wasn't done right the first time can add up in many cases to 25 percent of revenue! It also is enlightening to see that costs of correction usually exceed costs of inspection and costs of inspection often exceed costs of prevention. Because one dollar spent on prevention can often save at least ten dollars or more on inspection and correction, the cost-of-quality numbers usually reveal a need to shift priorities. Moreover, the attention that cost of quality numbers can focus on quality is magnified even more when someone mentions the cost of lost opportunities—especially lost customers—that result from failure to attend to quality.

What cost-of-quality advocates often do not recognize is that companies' efforts to reduce or eliminate these costs from their systems may impair competitiveness. To most top managers, cost is cost. You tackle unwanted cost in one of two ways—either reduce spending or increase output to "economize" on the constraint that creates the cost. Managers don't automatically leap to the conclusion that "cost of quality" represents a host of problems that are solved not by managing costs, but by empowering the work force to manage processes. Cost of quality, in top-down systems managed by remote control, can become just another excuse for workers to manipulate processes, to cut costs. Cost information will not point people in the right direction they must move to eliminate "cost of quality." Once people know the right directions to move, they don't need cost information to guide them.

Accounting Simplification. Accountants recently have become aware how process improvements that generate simplified work flows should also simplify the flow of transactions and paperwork used to account for work flows.[25] Companies such as Hewlett-Packard and Harley-Davidson are celebrated for making dramatic reductions in effort spent on tracking accounting transactions following their earlier success at simplifying work and reducing resources in production processes. Many businesses have followed their lead in the last year or two.

You know it is time to think about the cost of account keeping when the cost of tracking direct labor hours begins to approach or exceed the amount of the direct labor cost itself; or when the cost of periodic inventory taking exceeds the value of the inventory. In such cases, you are well advised to scrap these systems. And do the same with purchase requisitions, receiving reports, and invoices that relate to supplies vendors now ship "just-in-time" almost without a hitch. Scrap them and consider booking production cost and issuing payments when manufactured products are finished and shipped. In fact, where lead times still are too long to permit such simplified record keeping, an interesting twist would be for the controller's office to track ongoing improvement processes, to determine when lead times will be reduced enough to comfortably eliminate such record keeping.

Someday, when every person in an organization is infused with the "DNA code" of customer service, companies may be able to dispense altogether with using accounting information to keep score of performance. Double-entry accounting embodies the essence of analytical, mechanical systems that are organized around the use of energy—the technological basis of business competition down to the 1950s. In such systems, as Peter Drucker points out, the whole is the sum of the parts and is amenable to interpretation by analysis. The same is true of accounting systems: the integration of all parts with the "bottom line" is the heart of double-entry accounting. Using accounting systems to measure business performance in effect forces a "whole is equal to the sum of its parts" mindset onto an organization. While that may be appropriate in energy-based mechanical systems, it does not seem appropriate in systems where information, not energy, is the technological basis of competition. In an information-based organization, where the whole is not equal to the sum of the parts, you cannot "tie" cause to result in an unambiguous way. Hence, accounting eventually may not be a useful tool for compiling results in an information-based global organization. In any case, it is inconceivable that accounting systems *ever* can help people control operating processes in a customer-focused global enterprise.

WRAP-UP

Coming out of the cave does not mean companies no longer create accounting and financial shadows. Nor does it mean they no longer will develop and use variance tools, activity-based costing, and other techniques to analyze financial and accounting information. Indeed, companies will continue for a long time to compile such information for public reporting and to make decisions. Accounting information has filled those purposes for nearly two centuries of industrial history, and it will continue to do so for many years to come. However, companies that come out of the cave will no longer use accounting and financial information to dictate how people perform processes in the workplace.

Companies that fail to unplug their operating control systems from accounting controls pay an enormous hidden tax in unnecessary costs of doing business. Here are three examples of this "tax":

1. Opportunities often are wasted by basing outsourcing decisions on cost. I once observed a large multidivisional company whose production managers in one plant achieved dramatic improvements in cutting lead times and batch sizes just as top management independently embarked on a major campaign to cut costs by outsourcing component production. It seems top management was oblivious to how this one plant's improvement processes would reduce component-making costs. Now, with the decision to outsource a fait accompli, the plant has lost opportunities for learning and for redeploying redundant workers and is stuck with added problems caused by outside vendors' poor quality.

2. Opportunities for continuous improvement often are passed over out of fear they will cut inventory. There are two sides to this problem—a tax side and a net income side. The tax side shows how insidiously accounting considerations can pervert business decision making. There still are manufacturing companies that resist cutting lead times and batch sizes because reducing inventory will eliminate LIFO layers and increase tax payments. Overlooked is the magnitude of

ongoing savings and benefits from reduced lead times and batch sizes, as opposed to the one-time expenditure for additional taxes. The net income side of this issue shows managers resisting improvement projects that reduce inventory because they are afraid to take the one-time hit on reported net income caused by deferred inventory burden. This attitude shows up every year in stories of companies that boost reported earnings by overproducing at year-end.

3. Opportunities to cut lot sizes are sometimes passed over for fear they will increase costs. Traditional cost information does not apprise managers of the competitive advantages that accrue from faster changeovers and smaller lot sizes. American managers, seeing two plants with identical total setup costs or identical purchasing costs, seldom understand why performance probably is superior in the plant with faster setups or in the plant with more frequent deliveries from vendors. The usual reaction to more frequent setups or purchases is "it costs too much."

Capturing these opportunities by removing constraints and eliminating work is a strategy not supported by traditional management accounting information. Support for that strategy requires new management information that is real-time and problem-solving-oriented. Having workers control process and customer information—seeking out problems, solving problems, and removing constraints—is not inconsistent with achieving increased profits in the short term. Eventually, companies that become good at competitive excellence will have their cake and eat it too: by doing the things that make them competitive in the global marketplace, they also can achieve attractive quarterly returns. But first they must become good at executing the steps to global competitive excellence. A program for implementing those steps is outlined in Chapter 9.

CHAPTER 8

ACTIVITY-BASED COST MANAGEMENT: RELEVANCE LOST *DÉJÀ VU*

No amount of low-cost production or high-yield selling is good enough in the service of what is not itself good enough. Nothing is more wasteful than doing with great efficiency that which should not be done.

—Theodore Levitt[1]

If we keep doing what we've always done, we'll get what we always got.

—Ralph C. Stayer[2]

The recent plethora of articles, books, software, and seminars on activity-based cost management suggests that a juggernaut is loose in the business world. New activity-based cost tools have generated enormous interest and excitement among business people, especially among accountants and company controllers. Why all the excitement? It is not just that these tools have the power to greatly increase the quality of cost accounting information. The excitement arises also because people believe that this increased quality transforms accounting information into a powerful tool to improve the competitiveness of business operations.

The belief that activity-based cost management tools will improve

131

business competitiveness is a dangerous delusion! *No accounting information, not even activity-based cost management information, can help companies achieve competitive excellence.* Still, that has not kept armies of consultants, software designers, and companies from trying to make gold out of dross. Americans, especially, are big believers in the power of innovative breakthroughs and "quick fixes." The widespread belief that activity-based cost management offers a magic "solution" to American business's flagging competitiveness is no exception.

The enormous attention given to activity-based cost management in recent years makes it necessary to explain the activity-based cost concept (often known by the acronym ABC) and to evaluate its utility in the light of the message delivered in this book. It's time to set the record straight by explaining just what activity-based costing is and is not. As a tool to improve cost accounting information it is impeccable. But as a tool to improve the competitiveness of a business it is pure snake oil. Any claims that activity-based cost management helps businesses become more competitive rest upon a poor understanding of what competitiveness means in the global economy.

This chapter describes and evaluates the two primary roots of current activity-based cost management practice. The older root originated at General Electric in the early 1960s as a result of efforts by finance and accounting people to develop better information for managing indirect costs. GE thirty years ago was probably the first place where people used the term "activity" to describe, and analyze, work that causes costs. The other root of current activity-based cost management, usually referred to by the acronym ABC (activity-based costing), developed in the early 1980s, quite independently of GE's development of activity cost analysis. ABC was the result of many companies' efforts to improve the quality of product cost accounting information.

Seen in retrospect, these two developments were attempts to resolve the problems companies created after 1950 when they extended their management uses of accounting information from just *planning their extent and financing* to also *controlling their operations* and *guiding their marketing decisions* (see Figure 2–1). Activity cost analysis at GE dealt with problems caused by using accounting information to control operating costs. ABC efforts in the early 1980s dealt with problems caused by using accounting information to make marketing decisions. Both activity cost analysis and ABC have merit in certain applications. But neither provides the information companies now require to empower personnel continuously to improve processes with an eye to satisfying customer wants.

ACTIVITY COST ANALYSIS AT GENERAL ELECTRIC: "MANAGE ACTIVITIES, NOT COSTS"

In 1963 indirect costs absorbed about 52 percent of every sales dollar at General Electric. A team appointed that year to study indirect costs noted that cost improvement efforts always focused on direct material and labor costs, yet those direct costs consumed only about 38 percent of every GE sales dollar. The team also noted that most indirect costs are triggered by "upstream" decisions made long before the cost is incurred. For example, engineering decisions made during the design of a product ultimately trigger myriad indirect costs for parts ordering, machine changeovers, parts stocking, and customer service calls. However, those "downstream" costs, when incurred, are never traced back to engineering decisions. Nor are engineers ever informed about the downstream cost consequences of their decisions. The company's accounting and budgeting systems focused attention primarily on the costs incurred in each department, not on decisions in other departments that caused the costs.

To get better control of indirect costs, GE's 1963 study team proposed a novel technique to control the *activities* that cause those costs.[3] The technique traces each indirect activity in the company to one output of an upstream department, such as engineering, marketing, or manufacturing engineering. The engineering department, for example, produces outputs such as "new drawings," "old drawings," "requisitions to make components," "requisitions to buy components," "parts list items for products," and "manufacturing change orders." Those outputs cause downstream departments to engage in activities such as parts ordering, production standards setting, tooling, receiving, stockkeeping, quality control, and internal transportation. To identify linkages between engineering's outputs and other departments' activities, you interview supervisors and workers in the other departments to find out just what it is they do that is triggered by output of the engineering department. Interviewing the supervisor of the manufacturing department may reveal, for instance, that a high percentage of his or her department's activity is tooling, triggered by manufacturing change orders that come from the engineering department.

The goal of this analysis is to determine the approximate percentage of time each employee spends in a month or a year on indirect activities such as tooling or parts ordering (or whatever), and to trace the cause of each activity to one output of an upstream department. For example, after interviewing all supervisors to determine the percentage of company time spent on tooling (not all tooling may be done just in the manufacturing department), it may be decided that "manufacturing change orders" from the engineering department is the single most important cause of tooling. GE in the 1960s referred to causes of activities as "key controlling parameters." "Cost driver" or "activity driver" would be terms people are more likely to use today in similar contexts.

GE introduced cost information into this activity analysis by tallying costs of each activity in every department of the business for an interval of time, such as a month or a year. Costs were estimated by multiplying the time devoted to each activity by an appropriate average rate for labor or machines, and adding estimates of related costs for resources other than labor and machinery. These other costs would include utilities, rents, and any other costs deemed appropriate. Then they collected information about the quantity or count of each activity driver, or "key controlling parameter," such as the number of new drawings, number of old drawings, number of purchase orders, number of manufacturing operations, and so forth. These counts were estimates that covered the same time interval as that used to compile costs of activities.

With the information about activity costs and "driver" counts one can estimate the activity cost per unit of each driver. Thus, if one year sees the engineering department generate 10,000 "new drawings" (an activity driver) when the cost of "drafting" (an activity triggered by new drawings) is $950,000, then the average cost generated in the drafting activity by each new drawing is $95.00. To estimate the *total* cost generated by a new drawing, add in the other costs of *all* activities that are caused (driven) primarily by "new drawings." The activities caused by "new drawings" are, of course, not just those located in drafting or engineering. They include activities such as data processing, inspection, quality control, stockkeeping, and parts ordering.

Thus, GE's activity analysis measured cost on two dimensions. First, it measured the *cost of a single activity* in terms of that activity's primary driver—say the cost of inspection (activity) at $15 per new drawing (activity driver) or the cost of drafting at $95 per new drawing. Secondly, it measured the *cost of an activity driver* in terms of the costs of each activity that the driver triggers—say, $275 per new drawing as the total cost per drawing of all activities that new drawings trigger (see Figure 8–1). These data provide two messages to cost managers: one is to manage activity costs by controlling activity drivers; the other message is to manage the cost of a driver by controlling the costs of the activities the driver triggers.

With such information, product design people in the Engineering Department ostensibly can judge more effectively the impact of decisions to initiate "new drawings," as opposed to using existing "old drawings." Design engineers presumably can make better decisions about their own work if they know that the total downstream cost of

Figure 8–1
Activity-Based Cost Analysis at GE, Circa 1963

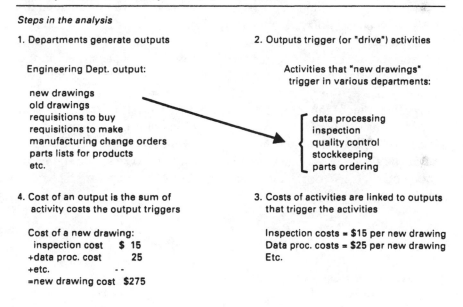

Steps in the analysis

1. Departments generate outputs

   Engineering Dept. output:

   new drawings
   old drawings
   requisitions to buy
   requisitions to make
   manufacturing change orders
   parts lists for products
   etc.

2. Outputs trigger (or "drive") activities

   Activities that "new drawings"
   trigger in various departments:

   data processing
   inspection
   quality control
   stockkeeping
   parts ordering

4. Cost of an output is the sum of
   activity costs the output triggers

   Cost of a new drawing:
     inspection cost $ 15
   +data proc. cost   25
   +etc.   - -
   =new drawing cost $275

3. Costs of activities are linked to outputs
   that trigger the activities

   Inspection costs = $15 per new drawing
   Data proc. costs = $25 per new drawing
   Etc.

Implications for accounting control systems

• Accounting budgets only classify costs by departments, according to categories of spending, e.g., salaries, maintenance, supplies, depreciation, utilities, etc.

• Managing costs reported in departmental accounting budgets means cutting spending on accounting categories, such as salaries reported in the inspection department budget. In the long run, cutting spending usually does not cut costs. Why? Because it doesn't change the work, such as "new drawings," that triggers salaries in the inspection department.

• Activity cost information, by classifying costs by type of work, gives cost managers better direction for managing costs than accounting information does.

introducing a new product with a new drawing is, for example, $275 and the cost of introducing the same product by modifying an old drawing is $60—because of less inspection, less new parts ordering, less drafting, less production engineering, and so forth. Moreover, information on costs of activity drivers presumably gives supervisors of indirect activities a better understanding of the forces that cause their costs. Supervisors in charge of parts ordering or inspection, for example, can point to the impact of engineers' new drawings on costs in their own departments.

GE modified and perfected this activity-based cost management technique over the years by developing standardized lists of activities known as "activity dictionaries" and by creating efficient interviewing techniques for collecting activity and activity driver information. However, the principle always remained the same: costs reported in accounting-based budget reports are too aggregated to be managed directly, only causes (drivers or activities) of resource consumption can be managed.

A succinct description of this activity-based cost analysis technique comes from a promotional brochure published in 1981 by Arthur Andersen & Co., an organization that licensed GE's activity-based cost management techniques and has led in developing those techniques in its own consulting practice since the 1970s. The only change from GE's early 1960s' description of the technique is Arthur Andersen's use of the term "cross-functional cost analysis" to describe the technique and their use of the term "cost generator" instead of "key controlling parameter."

Activities, decisions or policies in one department often generate costs in other parts of an organization. For example, a customer order generates costs across several functions in the organization: in the sales area, the costs to acquire the order; in the operations area, the cost to check stock availability, pick and deliver the order; in the finance area, the cost to invoice, record and collect payment.

Traditional cost analysis does not sufficiently relate costs to their causes or generators across departmental boundaries. The technique of cross-functional cost analysis overcomes this problem. For example, the total cost in many departments is affected by the number of customer orders processed. Thus, the number of orders is a cost generator. Costs can be controlled by controlling the volume of cost generators, such as the number of orders, rather than by trying to control cost in each department affected.

The cross-functional technique is applied in two phases. In the first phase, each major business activity is defined. Activities are discrete actions performed by the various departments [e.g., sales, operations, accounting, purchasing, information systems]. Many activities take place in more than one function or department. Examples of business activities which take place in a number of departments are [order acquisition, stock checking, order picking, delivering, and invoicing]. The cost of each activity in each department is determined using work measurement techniques among other approaches.

In the second phase of cross-functional cost analysis, the generators for the costs of each of the business activities are identified. The costs that each generator produces are estimated by adding the costs of the various activities which each generator drives. Actions which will reduce the number of generators which cause activity costs then are explored. In the example of the generator "sales orders" an organization can reduce costs by reducing the number of sales orders. Usually, the goal would not be to reduce total sales volume but to increase the average order size.

Thus, in cross-functional cost analysis the various business activities are identified and costed, and their costs generators are determined. An analysis is then made of the ways to reduce activity costs by reducing the number of generators.[4]

An interesting twist that GE (and others) might have added to this technique is to use cost generator information to estimate product costs. If one knows the annual count of cost generators in a product line, one can add the total costs of each generator to get the cost of the product line. This is exactly the procedure followed by architects of ABC product costing systems after the early 1980s. The considerable information processing required by this procedure for costing products was scarcely feasible, however, before the advent of modern PC-based spreadsheet software. GE seems never to have taken the additional steps to compile product cost information from their activity-based cost management information.

The issue of product costing aside, GE's technique for activity-based cost analysis anticipates virtually everything that is claimed for present-day activity cost management systems. Today literally hundreds of annual cost management seminars around the world highlight presentations by consultants or company personnel who breathlessly describe the features and benefits of activity-based cost generator (or "driver") information, as though they were being discovered for the first time.

Undoubtedly activity cost analysis thrived and received wide use in GE during the 1970s and 1980s.[5] That fact should cause present-day advocates of activity-based costing to temper their claims that activity cost management will reverse declining competitiveness in American companies. General Electric certainly ranks among America's best-managed companies in any era. Yet that company, like so many others, faced severe problems coping with Japanese import competition in the 1970s and early 1980s. Widespread application of modern activity-based cost management tools, from as far back as the early 1960s, certainly did not avert declining competitiveness at GE during and after the 1970s. Nor, one supposes, did it avert declining competitiveness in countless clients of consulting firms that licensed and used GE's activity cost analysis techniques after the mid-1970s.

There is no reason, however, why activity cost analysis tools would have led GE or any other American company down the path they had to follow after 1975 to compete with Japanese competitors such as Toshiba, Toyota, Hitachi, and so forth. *These activity-based cost management tools did not generate process maps, had no customer focus, and did not lead to bottom-up ideas for generating continuous process improvement.* Their activity-based information identified causes of costs far better than traditional cost accounting and budget tools did (cf. Figure 8–1). For that reason, this activity information undoubtedly improved many companies' efforts to cut costs. But never could it have prompted actions that improve competitiveness by increasing customer responsiveness and flexibility.

Activity analysis of the type espoused by GE in the 1960s, and manifest in virtually all modes of activity cost management promoted today, focuses attention on changing the amount of activity (or work) a company does for a given amount of revenue. It does not focus people's attention on changing how work is done, nor does it explicitly and systematically link activity with satisfaction of customer wants. It simply links activity with activity drivers and says: reduce the amount of activity (hence, cost) for a given amount of revenue by reducing or "economizing" on activity drivers. As the example in the above quotation from Arthur Andersen & Co. points out, sales orders drive countless activities throughout a company. So, to reduce costs, reduce the activity (and cost) that goes with handling sales orders by reducing the number of orders—presumably by eliminating orders that generate far below average revenue.

The logic in this strategy is impeccable, if cutting costs and raising margins is your main objective. But the strategy may be a road to disaster if customers really want frequent delivery of small lots, not large shipments at infrequent intervals. If customers really want frequent delivery of small lots, and someone else can meet their needs at an acceptable price that is below your costs, then you might want to ask if activity analysis is really pointing you in the direction you should be moving to be competitive. To satisfy customers, you probably should change the way you do work so that you can efficiently handle *more* activity drivers (e.g., sales orders) per dollar of revenue, not less. But to compete on smaller-sized and customized orders means you probably must reduce the lead time of processes involved in major activities such as order processing, parts ordering, stocking, and component assembly. No activity analysis I know will point you in that direction.

Instead of activity analysis, companies seeking the pathway to competitiveness need to map and improve customer-focused processes. Indeed, there is almost no similarity between the process analysis discussed today by quality management experts and the activity analysis discussed by cost management authorities. Process information identifies a customer, a supplier, and a mechanism to transform a supplier's inputs into customer-directed output. Cross-functional activity information simply shows where and how much time (or cost) a company devotes to a broad class of work, such as engineering, maintenance, order acquisition, or budgeting. While that information can be revealing, and usually is not available from cost accounting information (cf. Figure 8–1), it does not show how work (i.e., activity) is done or how well it contributes to customer satisfaction. Like the management accounting information it is designed to supplant, cross-functional activity cost information tracks results, not processes. It is a tool that greatly improves cost-focused management practices of the past, but it is not a tool for managing competitive operations in the global economy.

Indeed, activity-based analysis does not create an environment for learning about problems, nor does it invite people to identify and remove constraints that create delay, excess, and variation. Unlike process information, activity information usually is compiled and monitored by central staff personnel or outside consultants, not by company personnel who actually do the work. Whereas process information is compiled and monitored by the people in the process, cross-functional modes of activity analysis tend to be top-down and not customer oriented. They do not reveal how the work of an individual or the work of a team of people contributes to customer satisfaction. Hence, activity analysis data do not motivate continuous process improvement.

Cross-functional activity analysis and process analysis are deceptively similar in that both provide a horizontal, not a vertical, view of work and cost. Cross-functional activity analysis aggregates data from many different functions in the horizontal "chain of value," from design and manufacture to delivery and payment. It certainly does not compile data solely by function, and therefore is quite unlike accounting data that typically are compiled according to the vertical functional hierarchy of the company's organization chart. Because of this cross-functional orientation of their data, activity analysts often articulate their results in terms of a "horizontal pipeline" or "value chain." However, this abstract view of work is at a level of aggregation that does not identify internal customers and workers. The horizontal value chain depicts disembodied and inanimate macroeconomic flows in an enterprise and focuses attention on financial aggregates such as cost and revenue. In contrast, the "horizontal" that Deming and other quality experts talk about when they discuss "process maps" refers to specific work that links actual customers and suppliers. A horizontal process map depicts the work of every person in an organization in terms that focus attention on continually improving the capacity of people in each process to satisfy customer wants.

Thus, despite its apparent "horizontal" orientation, cross-functional activity analysis—and virtually all of modern activity-based cost management that it has spawned—becomes just another type of top-down command tool if it is used to control work and processes. Indeed, the growing popularity of cross-functional "activity-based management" tools reflects the long-standing proclivity of American managers to substitute top-down decision-making systems for human judgment. These tools presuppose that outside consultants or a sophisticated staff of overhead personnel observing a system of macro-financial relationships can employ abstract rules (often embedded in computer software) to generate better decisions than the decisions that would be made by workers who learn by directly observing and participating in processes and work.

This may explain why the Japanese, so far, have shown little interest in American cross-functional activity management tools (as opposed to activity-based *costing* tools). As Boston University accounting professor Alfred Nanni observes, "the control approach which seems to be favored by the Japanese relies less on the system and more on the employee's ability to learn about the process and to make decisions about process improvement based on direct observation."[6] Smart American companies already have discovered the same thing. For example, as we show in the next chapter, General Electric itself apparently has subordinated its activity-based management tools to a process-oriented approach to continual improvement through worker empowerment. GE's experience suggests that companies will not find the path to global competitiveness by pursuing activity-based management, even though they find cross-functional activity cost analysis a useful accounting tool.

ACTIVITY-BASED PRODUCT COSTS (ABC)

The other root of activity-based cost management grew out of concerns about the quality of product cost information. Peter Drucker in the early 1960s had articulated the dangers in using product cost accounting information to guide marketing decisions.[7] This was a problem many people noticed and spoke about, but no one did much about it until the early 1980s. Today's best known "solution" to the problem, cost-driver activity-based costing (ABC), was eventually codified by Harvard Business School professor Robin Cooper. Cost-driver ABC, as Cooper articulated it, had developed during the early 1980s in a few companies such as Schrader Bellows, John Deere, Union Pacific, and—if we stretch the definitions a bit—perhaps at Caterpillar and Hewlett-Packard. The chief impetus driving the development of ABC in those companies was the search for better product cost information to guide pricing and product mix decisions.

Product cost accounting is the only one of the new managerial uses of accounting information since the 1950s that can be enhanced by improving the quality of accounting information itself (see Figure 2–1). As I have said several times already, the other new managerial use of accounting information—using accounting information to control business operations—is inherently wrong and can not be made right by improving the quality of accounting information. It is quite proper, however, to use cost accounting information to plan and to guide marketing decisions. The current attention many businesses pay to activity-based costing reflects a legitimate desire to improve the cost information they use to evaluate and plan either pricing strategies or product and customer mix decisions. ABC tools, by improving on accountants' traditional overhead cost allocation techniques, reduce distortions in this very important type of accounting information businesses use to plan and make marketing decisions. Let's examine this use of activity-based costing more closely.

Distorted Overhead Allocations Disguise the Cost of Complexity

As a guide for planning, and to choose among alternatives, businesses need information about the financial consequences of intended actions. They especially need reliable cost information. Cost information serves in many planning and decision-support roles, such as estimating profit margins of products and product lines, preparing departmental cost budgets, and charging administrative services to production departments.

An important source of management cost information in American business since the 1950s has been the cost accounting system. Cost accounting systems were designed in the early 1900s to attach production costs to manufactured goods in order to divide an accounting period's total production costs between products sold and products still unfinished or unsold at the end of the period. These systems were designed to facilitate preparation of financial reports required by regulators, tax authorities, and participants in capital markets. They were not intended to provide information about costs of individual products. Moreover, companies rarely used accounting information to gauge individual products' costs before World War II. In the late nineteenth and early twentieth centuries, companies often managed complex multiproduct strategies with nonaccounting cost information or by creating focused organizational profit centers.[8] But American companies generally used accounting information to evaluate costs of products after the 1950s.

Accounting systems provide poor information to evaluate modern manufacturers' product costs.[9] Manufacturing cost accountants traditionally allocate overhead to products more or less in proportion to output volume, using cost drivers (i.e., allocation denominators) such as direct labor hours, machine hours, or material dollars. Using these so-called "volume-sensitive" (i.e., they vary more or less proportionately with output volume) drivers to attach overhead costs to products is a convenient and economical way to insure that production costs are properly matched against revenues at a macro level in financial statements. But this exclusive reliance on volume-sensitive drivers systematically distorts costs at the micro level of individual products.

Allocating overhead with volume-sensitive drivers provides reliable product cost information only if we assume all overhead costs are triggered by or vary in proportion to units of output. However, the fastest growing overhead costs in American manufacturing companies after the 1950s were caused by drivers that are triggered by batches put into production and by number of product lines, not by units of output.[10] Setting-up and material handling, for example, are drivers of overhead cost that are triggered by *batches* of output, regardless the number of units in a batch. A setup costs just as much for a batch with one unit as for a batch with one hundred units. Engineering change notices and the number of part numbers in stock also drive overhead costs, but both are triggered by *introducing new product lines*, not by the number of batches or number of units produced.

By using drivers triggered by units of output (e.g., direct labor hours or machine hours) to allocate overhead triggered by batches and product lines, companies systematically *undercost* the low-volume products that have tended to cause most overhead growth in recent years, and they systematically *overcost* high-volume products that tend not to cause overhead to grow. For example, they undercost capital-intensive products that are custom-made in small batches with newer, less familiar, and more expensive materials and equipment; as well as rapidly proliferating varieties of new products that demand expensive design, scheduling, and rework time—all sources of overhead cost. Moreover, they overcost established lines of commodity-type products that are mass-produced in long runs and large batches with older labor-intensive technologies.

These systematic distortions tend to cancel out at the macro level and therefore do not affect income and asset totals reported in financial statements. But they give a misleading picture of an individual product's margins, as many American and European manufacturers discovered in the 1970s and 1980s when, using financial cost accounting information to measure product costs, they erroneously assumed they could improve their company's profitability by abandoning *overcosted* commodity-type product lines and by proliferating *undercosted* varieties of newer "high-tech" lines. In fact, that strategy usually depressed earnings and, in several cases, generated a "death spiral" that led companies to the edge of bankruptcy.[11]

An example of the unfortunate effects of using financial product cost information to judge products' costs comes from the semiconductor industry.[12] In the early days of the industry, plants made low-density chips—say, 16K capacity—that did not incur nearly the overhead plants would later incur to make high-density chips, say in the 256K range. Processes to make low-density chips are more labor-intensive and require less sophisticated clean rooms or assembly machines than processes to make high-density chips.

Accounting procedures to allocate those overhead costs came to haunt many plants that eventually built high-density chip lines along-side existing low-density lines. The usual cost accounting system, by distributing overhead on direct labor hours with a single plantwide rate, charged proportionately more of those overhead costs to the low-density, direct-labor-intensive chips. The high-density chips that caused the overhead didn't bear their full share of the cost.

Competitive market prices, however, tend to follow actual cost, not accounting cost. Hence, prices of low-density "commodity" chips eventually fell relative to prices of the newer, more sophisticated high-density chips. Companies that relied on their cost accounting systems for product cost information perceived declining margins (falling prices and rapidly rising costs) for the "commodity" chips and rising margins (rapidly rising prices and steady costs) for the new high-density items. In the late 1970s and early 1980s, many large semiconductor manufacturers with diverse product lines (hence more distorted product costs) surrendered what they thought were unprofitable commodity lines to focused, often foreign, competitors who were not misled by distorted cost signals.

Recognition of problems with traditional product cost accounting grew during the late 1970s. Activity-based costing began to appear in the early 1980s as a solution to the distortions inherent in product cost accounting information.[13] Advocates of ABC tell companies, in effect, to cost products differently for financial reporting information than for planning and decision-support information. For financial reporting they recommend companies continue allocating overhead using the volume-sensitive drivers they have used since the early years of this century. For more reliable planning and decision-support information, however, proponents of ABC tell companies to trace costs to both volume-sensitive and nonvolume-sensitive driver pools. ABC estimates costs of products by adding up costs of the actual drivers that each product consumes.

Table 8–1 compares the difference in a product's cost when a batch-triggered overhead cost, setup cost, is allocated using direct labor hours, a traditional volume-sensitive driver, and when it is allocated using setups. As the example shows, product overhead cost varies by a factor of 10 ($100 versus $1,000) when setup costs are allocated with direct labor hours and by a factor of 50 ($50 versus $2,500) when the same setup costs are allocated using number of setups. The variation shown here for one overhead cost item will, of course, be different when the costs of *all* nonvolume-triggered overhead items are traced properly.

Simple in concept, ABC was a practical impossibility until the ad-

Table 8–1
Traditional Product Costing versus ABC

	Product A	Product B	Amounts
Annual production volume	100	1,000	
Number of setups (SU)	1	50	
Direct labor hours (DLH)	10	100	
Setup costs (plant-wide total)			$50,000
Number of setups (plant-wide total)			1,000
Direct labor hours (plant-wide total)			5,000
Setup cost allocated to products —			
Traditional (DLH as driver)	$100	$1,000	
ABC ($ / SU as driver	$50	$2,500	

vent of low-cost microchip technologies in the 1970s made it economic to collect and compile large amounts of nonvolume-sensitive
cost driver information. In principle, a two-stage approach is used to
conduct an ABC analysis. The thrust of the design, as codified originally by Robin Cooper, is to identify a relatively small set of both
volume-sensitive and nonvolume-sensitive overhead cost drivers (say
six to twelve) in stage one and to trace indirect costs to each driver. In
stage two, the company determines the percentage of the drivers consumed by each product or service. The result is an estimate of the indirect costs of each product based on nonvolume-sensitive drivers such
as engineering change notices (ECNs), setups, and inspections, as well
as the traditional volume-sensitive drivers such as direct labor hours
and material dollars.

The "drivers" referred to here resemble both the "activity drivers"
(or cost generators) and the "activities" found in GE's early cross-
functional activity cost analysis. In the ABC literature, the word "activity" often is used synonymously with "driver," although activity is
the word that has stuck to describe the nonvolume-sensitive driver-
based product costing technique. While there is confusion in the literature as to the meaning of the terms activity and driver, neither term is
synonymous with "process." Most often "activity" and "driver" refer
to nouns; for example, setups, purchase orders, change notices, part

count, and so forth. Less frequently does "activity" refer to an action—a noun and a verb—such as move a cart, verify a price, make a call, and so forth. Never does activity refer to a customer-focused process. As we will show in a moment, most proposals that use activity-based cost management information to "improve operations" invariably fulfill financial imperatives of remote-control management, not the customer-focused imperatives of global management. These proposals usually recommend building to scale or working for speed, to cut costs by producing output. Too often, activity-based cost recommendations aim at economizing on an "activity driver" by producing output customers probably don't want in the first place.

Nevertheless, activity-based cost-driver information is appropriate for marketing decisions. In pricing, for instance, it helps marketing managers confirm their suspicions that a company has been overestimating the cost of standard products. It also helps in evaluating the profitability of product mix. With this kind of information, managers in tough competitive situations can "know when to hold and know when to fold." Products with lower margins will be an easier discard. Those with higher margins will be easier to defend. Whenever a company turns out a wide array of products that consume resources in diverse ways, multiple-driver ABC analysis costs products more reliably than does traditional cost accounting information. Moreover, information about costs of drivers, such as the cost of a purchase order, can be an efficient and very effective way of differentiating unit, batch, and product-level costs among products. This can provide useful information for preparing income statements.[14]

Manufacturers often have easily available driver information in production control and materials requirements planning systems. MRP production control data are not useful input for process mapping, but they are satisfactory to make the allocations that ABC product costing requires. Bills of material and product routing data give counts by product of the number of setups, the number of material moves, the number of part numbers, and so forth. Most companies that have implemented activity-based costing systems to date seem to sort costs into pools defined by drivers already present and accounted for in an MRP system. With MRP data in place, it is an easy matter to count the drivers incurred during a production interval, and to count the drivers in each product line during the same interval. (Companies without MRP systems incur much higher costs, of course, to accumulate driver information for an ABC system.) In concept, at least, it is a simple matter to trace indirect costs to products using the average cost per driver in each product. While not perfectly accurate,[15] it is widely believed that this technique provides a better "rack and stack" of indirect costs than traditional systems that allocate all indirect costs with one or a few volume-sensitive drivers.

Returning to our earlier reference to Plato's Allegory of the Cave, consider once more how driver-based activity costing helps managers progress from appearances—shadows on the wall of the cave—to understanding reality. Sorting and tracing costs by volume-sensitive and nonvolume-sensitive drivers helps managers look "behind the barrier" and clarify the different costs of the resources a company consumes to design, make, and deliver diverse products or services. Although ABC product costs and driver costs do not provide information about processes or customer wants "outside the cave," American manufacturers who were decoupling their processes in the 1960s and 1970s still might have benefited, at least in the short run, if such cost information had been at their disposal. It is reasonable to assume that ABC information would have tempered their belief that better profits result from proliferating varieties of products. Undoubtedly, such information would have enabled many companies to generate higher profits, at least in the short run, and not have to capitulate as soon as they did to focused competitors.

Indeed, a Swedish consulting firm that specializes in activity-based costing uses the term "hidden profits" to describe the profits a company foregoes by selling what traditional accounting costs show is the most profitable product mix rather than selling what ABC accounting costs would show is the most profitable mix.[16] In particular, companies that use traditional accounting costs to measure product profitability will believe it is quite profitable to set up frequently and sell products in small batches, when in fact ABC costs will show that more profit is to be earned by producing in long runs and selling large batches, to economize on setup and order costs.

But is that really the approach companies should take to improve performance in the global economy? What if customers don't want to purchase in large quantities at infrequent intervals? Do you tell them they must pay more for frequent delivery of small lots, or that perhaps they should take their business elsewhere? Certainly not if you want to survive in a customer-controlled economy!

I believe this notion of "hidden profit" ignores another much more important sort of "hidden profit"—call it "hidden profit number two." This is the long-term profit you forego by failing to change the way you do business so that you can efficiently supply what customers want, as they want it, when they want it. ABC product cost information will not show you the changes you must make to become a truly flexible producer. We have already discussed those changes in Chapters 3 and 6. It is sufficient to say at this point that if "hidden profit number two" is what you are after—and it *must be* the goal of any company intending to compete in the global economy—then you only waste time by implementing an ABC system in order to capture "hidden profit number one." Investing in an ABC system simply to discover that units produced in large batches cost less than units produced in small batches is as futile as arranging the proverbial deck chairs on the Titanic. Instead, you should be investing in customer-focused problem-solving efforts to remove constraints that cause variation, delay, and excess in processes.

Ironically, companies that continually improve customer-focused processes will discover, probably fairly soon, that their process improvements eliminate much, if not most, of the "overhead activity" causing the distortions in product costs that gave rise to the development of ABC tools in the first place! Many cost management authorities describe this "overhead activity" by referring to the "Pareto relationship," named for the relationship between population and income discovered in the late-nineteenth century by economist Vilfredo Pareto. These cost management experts say that ABC usually helps managers discover that 20 or so percent of a company's products, or revenue, generates 80 or so percent of their overhead activity—the Pareto 80:20 relationship. While I don't dispute the existence of this skewed relationship between work and results in most American businesses today, I would challenge the suggestion that ABC cost information is the proper way to achieve a more balanced relationship. ABC advocates tell companies, in effect, not to change the way they orchestrate work—just create better information to identify products that require a lot of work for little revenue and shift production away from those dogs and cats toward more "big hitters." However, we have already seen several cases (and will discuss more in the next section) where this short-term cost-cutting or margin-enhancing strategy leads to decisions that impair competitiveness in the long term. Instead of wasting time designing ABC systems to locate "hidden profits" on products that customers probably don't want anyway, companies should begin taking steps to eliminate delay, excess, and variation from processes. Soon they will discover, I believe, that better orchestration of work will lead to closer correlation between effort and results *everywhere*. At the limit, one percent of effort will always generate one percent of results, and so on. In that world, only two forces drive product costs—time (and the price of time) and material. In that world you don't need ABC or any other system to cost products—you just need to know the time it takes to do something, the price of that time and the price of any material consumed to get the job done.

ABC Costs Merely Change Decisions, Not Management Thinking

Better marketing and sourcing decisions based on ABC cost information are not what companies with systems of decoupled processes need to improve their long-term performance in the global economy. In the long run competitive businesses must change completely the way they organize people and work—to become responsive and flexible. Until a company changes the way it thinks about customers, people, and work, it undoubtedly will use ABC product cost information simply to improve how it does business as usual—that is, seeking economies of scale and speed in decoupled processes. *The pathway to global competitive excellence is not reached by doing better what should not be done at all.*

Many people will disagree with the statement that ABC information does not open doorways to competitiveness. They will argue that the new activity-based costing tools do in fact go beyond shadows and enable operating managers to control the determinants of competitiveness better than they could with traditional standard cost information. In fact, ABC costs, by focusing on resources, do yield better understanding of costs than one gets merely by studying traditional accounting shadows. But I firmly believe that the use of activity-based cost driver information to control operating activities—not just to reconfigure costs of products and other objects—leads companies to make decisions every bit as damaging to their long-term competitiveness as traditional standard cost information did in the last thirty years. Such uses of activity-based cost information commit "relevance lost" all over again!

My main point is that activity-based cost driver information in itself will not cause managers to change the way people work—from cost-oriented practices associated with remote control to time- and people-oriented practices associated with global competitive excellence—and it often will prompt actions that impede responsiveness and flexibility.

Indeed, published studies of activity-based costing systems implemented to date demonstrate an overwhelming tendency for companies to use cost-driver information to do efficiently what they should not be doing in the first place. As the following two examples will show, problems result when activity-based cost driver information is used to make operating decisions:[17]

1. An auto components manufacturer called in outside experts to advise them on product costing. With ABC information, they found that the company was abandoning its most profitable product lines and replacing them with lines that barely broke even, if at all. This disclosure by ABC information was eye-opening for the company: they found that product costs varied by as much as 300 percent from what they had thought.

Then they started to manage the driver costs. One insight the new ABC data revealed was how much it really cost to set up machines every time an order for a batch of components was released to the shop floor. The old cost accounting system pooled setup costs with all other indirect factory costs and spread them over components in proportion to direct labor hours. Components ordered in large lots that kept machines running steadily for long periods of time absorbed the same overhead cost per unit (including setup costs) as components ordered in small lots that required more frequent and costlier setting-up. Obviously, the old costing system did not reveal the true cost of handling small lots produced in short runs. The ABC analysis, however, by pooling setup costs separately from other indirect costs and applying them to components in relation to their demands for setup time, eliminated that distortion and put the costs where they belonged—on the small lots.

The new ABC information prompted management to alter its pricing and operations practices. They cut prices of components produced in large lots and charged a premium to buyers ordering small lots. They also discouraged the sales staff from taking orders from buyers who insisted on frequent delivery of small quantities.

2. A manufacturer of personal computers and electronic measurement equipment followed a similar path in applying ABC information to operations. Management always had costed products by pooling all factory overhead and allocating it over direct labor hours. Thus, the cost accounting system did not reliably differentiate between costs of printed circuit boards that were fabricated through very different processes, such as three different types of component insertion (dip, axial, and manual) and two types of soldering (wave and manual). Consequently, costs of boards with substantial numbers of manually inserted components were not significantly different from costs of boards with components inserted automatically. This was counter intuitive to what

every design engineer believed to be the true costs of printed circuit boards.

The company performed an ABC analysis to give product design engineers more reliable information about the cost of design decisions. In this analysis, indirect costs (essentially all costs except materials and purchased components) were pooled separately for automatic and manual insertion. ABC confirmed that manual insertion procedures cost several times as much as auto-insertion.

However, auto-insertion machines could not operate reliably in spaces as small as human hands could. Therefore, designs for products made on auto-insertion machines had to space components further apart and further from the edge of a board. That meant trading off lower auto-insertion costs for somewhat larger boards. Nevertheless, design engineers proceeded to design manually inserted boards out of existence.

In both of these cases, the ABC information prompted managers to reduce costs and improve short-term profits by altering product mix or process mix, not by altering the way work is performed or customers are served. They improved the bottom line either by moving out of products that consumed a disproportionately high share of costly drivers, such as setups, or by designing products to use processes that consume less costly drivers, such as auto-insertion. But in the long term, both companies made choices that were likely to impair their competitiveness and profitability.

To achieve competitive and profitable operations in a customer-driven global economy, companies must give customers what they want, not *persuade* them to purchase what the company now produces at lowest cost. If customers favor frequent delivery of small lots or if they favor smaller-sized products, then companies must respond accordingly—*even when it initially costs more.* The long-run global imperative, of course, is to find ways to reduce costs (primarily by removing constraints that cause delay, excess, and variation) of producing what the customer wants, in the form the customer wants it.

In each of the cases just cited, management failed to ask two crucial questions:

1. Do consumers really want the product that the ABC analysis says is the most profitable?
2. If not, what type of analysis can help us identify changes in the way we work so we can produce the product customers want efficiently and effectively?

To compete well today, companies need information about the work people do and the time they take to do it—process information. Achieving competitiveness, identified with total customer satisfaction, means finding and removing constraints that impair the company's ability to respond flexibly to customer needs. To accomplish that goal, companies must really understand how work taking place in their organizations is leading to customer satisfaction. As the experience of the companies described above shows, it's easy to get the cart before the horse when using driver-oriented ABC information to manage operating costs. To improve operations, companies should assess processes first, *in terms of satisfying customer wants*. Only then should they invest in efforts to compile better cost information concerning products, customers, channels, etc. Companies need to do both, but in the right order.

If the auto components manufacturer mentioned above had mapped its processes and tracked lead times, it might well have discovered opportunities to reduce batch sizes. Similarly, customer focus groups or other customer inquiries might have led the computer manufacturer to assess the trade-off between automatic and manual insertion of circuit boards in terms of customer satisfaction, not cost. Competitiveness in the global economy really requires companies to focus on changing processes, not on managing drivers of cost.

All the ABC analysis in the world isn't going to help in the long run if companies mindlessly seek scale economies with high utilization rates and high output. Indeed, with remote-control thinking at work, managers looking at the costs of "drivers" will tend to economize on drivers by using them sparingly in hopes of cutting costs as such. In other words, don't set up so often (it costs too much) or don't design for manual insertion (automatic is cheaper). The results, as we have seen, often diverge greatly from what customers find satisfactory. On the other hand, if a company gauges its actions according to the earmarks of global competitiveness (cf. Table 4–1), then it will take steps to achieve small lots, short lead times, and defect-free output. It follows that those steps probably will lead to faster changeover, less work, and—incidentally—lower costs.

Activity-based cost driver information—ABC—overcomes distortions inherent in traditional cost accounting information. Driver-based ABC tools—especially those pioneered in companies such as John Deere and Kanthal and described in the writings of Robin Cooper and Robert S. Kaplan[18]—restore relevance to product cost information and thereby help companies avoid costly marketing blunders in the short term. However, ABC information does not necessarily help companies achieve continuous improvement of globally competitive operations. I do not believe better product cost information itself could have prevented most American manufacturers from losing long-term market share and profitability in the 1970s and 1980s. It might have been enough to sustain market share and profitability if competitors, especially from Japan, had not changed fundamental assumptions about how to organize work to satisfy customers. That is the point—how to discover and adopt competitive ways of organizing work, not how to be more profitable by shifting product mix in companies that continue to follow traditional remote-control management practices. While ABC gives companies a better "rack and stack" of their overhead costs, it does not drive them to change their fundamental views about how to organize work to efficiently satisfy customers.

WRAP-UP

Activity-based prescriptions for improved competitiveness usually entail steps that reduce costs or raise margins while doing "business as usual." At best, these steps usually lead to selling more or doing less of what should not be sold or done in the first place. Indeed, activity-based cost information does nothing to change old remote-control, top-down management behavior. Simply because improved cost information becomes available, a company does not change its commitment to mass-produce output at high speed, to control costs by encouraging people to manipulate processes, and to persuade customers to buy output the company has produced to cover its costs. American businesses will not become long-term global competitors until they change the way managers think. No cost information, not even activity-based cost management information, will do that.

Moreover, the answer to competitiveness is not to do the activity analysis that leads up to calculating ABC product costs. I have heard some companies say that going through the activity analysis it takes to calculate activity-based driver costs has helped them improve their operations. I have no doubt this is true, especially given the chaotic state of decoupled operations in most American companies when they first wake up to the need to improve. One-time savings—sometimes referred to as "low hanging fruit"—await any rational attempt to analyze work. But something more is needed to continuously improve the output of customer-focused processes.

Instead of beginning with ABC, begin at the beginning by articulating a customer-focused mission statement and then encourage everyone to help map and systematically improve the processes in which they work. If your goal is competitive operations, don't waste time gathering data and compiling information in order to cost work you shouldn't be doing anyway. Focus on reducing variation and lead time in the work itself and costs will take care of themselves. Do ABC if you think you must. But don't fool yourself into thinking that ABC will help you become a global competitor. For that, get busy with the improvement process!

CHAPTER 9

PUTTING AN IMPROVEMENT PROCESS IN PLACE

▼

Every company can buy the same technologies and tools, but not the same people power. That you must create inside. That is the ultimate source of competitiveness.

— Robert W. Hall[1]

Despite the great number of improvement programs they pursued in the 1970s and 1980s, America's businesses have not restored their lost competitive edge. Scarcely any company's recent performance prompts one to say, "They, at last, have the answer." The preceding chapters in this book explain why that is the case. American companies have not driven out and replaced management information and management philosophies that view business as a deterministic financial machine in which people—customers, workers, suppliers, and society—merely act as passive gears and cogs.

It is time to eliminate and replace all vestiges of remote-control information and thinking. They impair competitiveness by impeding change. The most pervasive feature of competition in the global economy is the need for continuous change. The power that information technology gives a customer to scan, to evaluate, and to choose requires companies continually to monitor and respond to change in customers' opportunities, wherever those opportunities appear in the world.

Adapting quickly and efficaciously to continuous change requires continuous learning by every member of the organization. Learning implies that every person in every process must have the freedom to observe and identify change and have the power to recommend opportunities for improvement. That freedom and power—hallmarks of process ownership—require that all workers have command of all the information from their own processes. This is the key to organizational learning. Ownership and learning—bottom-up empowerment—enable an organization to be responsive and flexible—to meet the two imperatives of competition in the global economy (see Table 9–1).

The absence of bottom-up ownership and learning is what stops most American businesses from making the final leap to competitive excellence. Bottom-up empowerment is virtually inconceivable in organizations that are dominated by top-down control systems. Top-down systems give ownership of information and decision making to top management. They give top management all the power, but they do not insure that top management exercises this power with any sense of responsibility for what occurs in processes. Unfortunately, no one

Table 9–1
Bottom-Up Empowerment versus Top-Down Control

Bottom-Up	Top-Down
Information technology empowers the customer and gives the customer CHOICE.	Companies learn and change in "big steps" that draw on knowledge from the outside.
The customer's power of choice makes it necessary for companies to quickly CHANGE.	Information is owned by top management who PLAN AND DECIDE.
To change quickly, everyone in a company must continually LEARN.	Top management passes down INSTRUCTIONS to subordinates and workers who
Constant learning and adaptation to change require the work force to have OWNERSHIP	MANAGE RESULTS by manipulating processes
of information from processes. That ownership of information generates worker EMPOWERMENT.	

really owns or controls processes in organizations run by top-down remote control. Process management under those conditions degenerates into what Dr. Deming refers to as "tampering," or what I have referred to in this book as manipulation.

If this tampering and manipulation is to cease, top managers must demonstrate a new spirit both by committing to a convincing customer-focused mission statement and by committing to bottom-up process management. The beginning of empowerment and the dawn of competitive excellence is a commitment by top management to give everyone in the organization ownership of the information that comes from inside their processes. Without that commitment there can be no genuine process improvement; hence, no meaningful adaptation to change.

Evidence that top managers of leading businesses are beginning to question their past commitment to remote financial controls is found in the attention companies give to financial information in periodic top-level performance reviews.[2] Robert Galvin, CEO of Motorola when the company received the Malcolm Baldrige Award, originally announced his commitment to the quality improvement process by telling his operating chiefs he would no longer sit in on the portion of monthly and quarterly performance review meetings devoted to discussions of financial plans and results. He stayed through discussions of nonfinancial matters, especially those pertaining to quality initiatives, knowing that when those matters were attended to properly, the financial results would take care of themselves. A similar remark was made by the CEO of Westinghouse Commercial Nuclear Fuel, John Marous, when he accepted the Baldrige Award for his company. He is so confident that quality improvement leads to positive financial outcomes that he no longer asks people for financial review. Instead, he focuses attention on quality "pulse points." Moreover, Chris Fosse, the Vice President of Quality at Blount, Inc., a holding company whose Oregon Cutting Systems Division (formerly Omark Industries, Inc.) is known around the world for its quality improvement process, reports that financial matters, until two years ago, were the first item at monthly senior management meetings. Now they are last. Whereas discussions of financial matters formerly consumed up to half or three-quarters of these one-day meetings, they took up just ninety seconds at the meeting in August 1991!

In the global economy, process improvement is a competitive organization's main task. Process improvement is achieved by everyone finding and removing constraints—the causes of variation, excess, and delay that impede timely and efficient satisfaction of customer expectations. Using the improvement process to remove constraints is the alternative to the practice of optimizing within constraints that remote-control managers have followed for the past forty years. How to launch a company on the path to process improvement is the subject of this chapter.

DISCOVERING THE CONTINUOUS IMPROVEMENT PROCESS

Virtually all business improvement programs of the past two decades will have a place in well-managed global enterprises. There will be a place for both JIT-style programs that focus on better ways to organize work and TQM-style programs that focus on better ways to tap the power of people's minds. But companies no longer can afford to view these various programs as independent pieces of a puzzle that, when enough are located and assembled, will miraculously form a picture of global competitiveness. Something more is needed, as the paucity of overwhelmingly successful American business turnaround stories in recent years indicates.

Indeed, conditions arise from time to time to suggest that something more is needed even in the most celebrated success stories. Harley-Davidson is certainly one of the great turnaround success stories of the 1980s. Their share of the domestic U.S. market for heavy motorcycles recently hit the 60 percent range, rebounding from a trough in the low 20 percent range in the early 1980s. At the same time, Honda's share slipped from around 50 percent to about half that amount. Harley's turnaround was built upon thoroughgoing implementation of customer-oriented, JIT-style changes in the way they organize work. Yet mid-1991 saw the company experience labor walkouts that slowed production and curtailed dealers' already short supplies of their much-admired bikes. The walkouts, associated by some observers with "JIT stress," suggest that something still is missing on the "people management" side of the business.

The missing element in most cases, I believe, is an understanding of improvement as a continuous *process of discovery,* not an intermittent series of "solutions" to overwhelming problems. The latter view says "fix it only when it's broke," whereas the former view says "never stop looking for better ways to do it." A clear sign that competitive excellence has arrived will be when companies automatically view improvement as *opportunities* created continuously by a permanent process designed to increase customer loyalty and to improve workers' abilities. The cost-focused, adversarial spirit of remote-control management that has dominated American business practice for at least thirty years causes most business leaders to view improvement programs of any stripe—JIT, TQM, or whatever—as one-shot efforts to fix problems by cutting cost. They view improvement as cutting cost, not as continuously discovering and creating opportunities.

To recap what was said in earlier chapters, the practice of controlling operations with accounting targets since the 1950s steadily eroded most managers' understanding of work, processes, and customer satisfaction. In most American businesses, management's job became less concerned with people than with manipulating resources and products according to rules of managerial economics and financial management. Preoccupied after 1970 with pursuing the sterile imperatives of finance and economics, American businesses in the next two decades unwittingly passed the torch of industrial leadership to overseas businesses that were responding to imperatives of the information-driven global economy. In the transition, American managers increasingly saw customers, workers, and suppliers as price-driven robots, while overseas managers increasingly understood and appreciated the implications of *customers having the power to choose* and *workers and suppliers having the ability to contribute ideas.*

Belated recognition of these implications of information technology fuels much of the current enthusiasm for "quality improvement processes" in the United States. The concept is not new. Its proximate origins are in writings from the 1950s and 1960s by W. Edwards Deming, Joseph Juran, Armand Feigenbaum, Kaoru Ishikawa, and others—and the sources of their ideas probably antedate World War II. But the remote-control financial management practices that have dominated American business thinking for so long are totally different than the quality improvement process. Hence, most people today see the concept of an improvement process as a radical new idea that will be difficult, if not impossible, to implement. Some even see it as an untested fad that may disappear, and not disturb our pursuit of business as usual, if we just wait.

More companies might embrace the concept of a permanent improvement process if the idea seemed less radical, and less like a fad. It will help advance understanding of the concept, and help affirm its permanence, to show how such a process can cure deficiencies in our more familiar remote-control approach to management.

People today respond eagerly to customer-focused, problem-solving improvement processes because these offer the promise of restoring communication that American businesses lost in the last few decades by decoupling processes in the name of financial optimization. As I said before, decoupling of processes should not be equated with Adam Smithian specialization and division of labor. The workers in a Smith-type pin factory specialize and divide tasks in order to increase productivity. They don't necessarily stop communicating with each other. Indeed, they can work in a "cell" and pass parts from process to process in "lot sizes of one" with little loss of output. Typically, that is not what American businesses do in the name of decoupling. They tend to *isolate* people in separate processes, to achieve economies of scale and speed, and rely on centralized top-down systems to communicate information about processes. The resulting "silos" or "chimneys," referring to the physical form of these decoupled units on organization charts, become fortresses where communication occurs among specialists, not across specialties. The sense of group "mission" in such entities focuses inward on centrally defined (but not jointly achieved) financial goals. It should be no surprise if people in companies organized this way do not view themselves as members of teams whose talents are joined to solve customer problems. They view themselves as distinct groups of specialists who compete to satisfy central management financial targets, not as people who cooperate to satisfy customers.

I am not surprised when I see the enthusiasm American workers and managers show for the team building, problem solving, and group dynamics that discussions of the quality improvement process bring to the table. Humans are gregarious animals. Left to themselves, people naturally seek out other people, to communicate and share ideas. And I believe they dedicate themselves more strenuously to goals that speak of serving customers than they do to goals that speak of serving shareholders. For over thirty years American businesses have wasted incalculable reserves of human energy and initiative by forcing people to manipulate processes in decoupled systems in the name of remote financial controls. The enthusiasm people show for the quality improvement process is a long overdue reaction to our long-standing remote-control methods of management.

Not every program designed to link workers across functions, to "remove chimneys," to remove buffers, or to build teams deserves to be classified as an "improvement process." Bad consequences of remote-control management can be eliminated without eliminating remote-control thinking. For example, consultants may perform "cross-functional work analysis" as a means of identifying so-called nonvalue work—repetitious or redundant work caused by years of poor communication across decoupled processes and functions. Usually such analysis is requested by top management and is performed by the consultant, not by people in the processes. The underlying objective is, of course, to cut costs, not to address the imperatives of global excellence. The result all too often is fewer people working much the same way as they did before. Customer responsiveness and flexibility may be better or worse, no one really knows because no one asks.

Other examples abound of companies pursuing programs labeled as JIT or TQM where the objective is to cut costs, not improve competitiveness. Such programs remove buffers, lead time, or redundancies but pay no attention to the added flexibility that shorter lead times offer, or the opportunity to improve responsiveness by assigning redundant workers to the field, to meet customers. No one asks. Top management, seeking lower costs, doesn't get the point. Business continues as usual, with less cost in the short run, but probably with fewer long-run opportunities to improve competitive advantage.

Genuine improvement processes begin by focusing on the customer, not on costs. And they draw information for improving processes primarily from customers and from the people who work in processes. The objective is to improve the company's long-term ability to fulfill imperatives of competitiveness—the ultimate source of profitability. Many excellent books on total quality management (TQM) provide useful, detailed directions to follow to implement and sustain a continuous quality improvement process in almost any type of business. *Assuming top management commits to bottom-up process management, renounces top-down remote control, and affirms the primacy of satisfying customer expectations,* the steps outlined in these books should be enough to lead any company along the path to global excellence.

Here is a list of observations synthesized from many published sources and from personally observing efforts to implement improvement processes in many organizations. This list merely recounts some of my personal observations—it does not purport to map the steps you follow to systematically implement a quality improvement process.

1. The concepts of competitive excellence and bottom-up improvement owe their existence to the power information technology gives customers (to choose) and employees (to contribute ideas). The imperatives to be responsive and to be flexible derive from that power.

2. Competitive excellence in the information-based global economy requires continuous learning and adapting to change. (Continuous monitoring of change is the essence of benchmarking.)

3. An improvement process that focuses on defining customer expectations and removing constraints is the primary instrument for learning and making change.

4. Continuously increasing customer loyalty and continuously improving workers' and suppliers' abilities to serve are the main goals of an improvement process.

5. An improvement process will not improve long-term competitiveness until top management renounces all remote-control systems and practices that motivate people to manipulate processes.

6. The main opportunity to improve satisfaction of customer wants is by removing constraints that cause variation, delay, and excess. Identifying and removing constraints distinguishes the globally competitive organization's improvement process from the remote-control organization's efforts to optimize within constraints. Removing constraints eliminates cost trade-offs.

7. Although the ultimate consumer who finally pays all the bills is the focus of an organization's existence, the combined efforts of the organization's "internal customers" create the final consumer's satisfaction. An improvement process must concentrate equally on the final consumer's wants and the internal customers' efforts.

8. An early step in any improvement process is to map the processes (and estimate their lead times) by which internal customers satisfy the final consumer's wants. Mapping links downstream customer wants with upstream opportunities to improve satisfaction of those wants. Mapping helps identify sources of variation, delay, and excess. Mapping helps reverse decoupling—the enemy of cross-functional communication.

EXAMPLES OF IMPROVEMENT PROCESSES AT WORK

The quality literature provides numerous examples of improvement processes at work in actual companies. Many American companies, notably those that have won the Malcolm Baldrige National Quality

Award, now provide excellent examples of quality management principles in practice. Of those, perhaps the two best known are Motorola's "Six Steps to Six Sigma" and Xerox's "Nine-Step Quality Improvement Process." However, no company embarked on quality improvement that I know has renounced the trappings of remote-control management as completely as I advocate here, although many, such as Motorola, Westinghouse Commercial Nuclear Fuels, and Blount, have begun to emphasize the primacy of quality indicators over financial indicators in measuring and controlling operational performance. The following sections describe efforts to create continuous improvement processes in three companies whose experiences parallel many of the points I have made in the preceding chapters.

General Electric: Keeping Ideas Coming[3]

General Electric, by all measures one of the largest industrial businesses in the world, also stands as one of the major contributors of new management ideas in this century. Although not one of the early diversified industrial companies to articulate a multidivisional form of organization before World War II, they may have been the first large diversified company to seriously question some of the remote-control financial practices being espoused in multidivisional firms after the 1950s. As I indicated already in Chapter 8, finance people at GE began in the early 1960s to improve budgeting processes with information about activities and activity drivers. Those GE finance people probably invented the expression "you can only manage activities, not costs." No doubt these people were influenced by developments in value engineering that have roots at GE at least as far back as the 1940s. GE people always have been in the vanguard of new management practice, with concepts such as cross-functional activity analysis, cost driver analysis, activity dictionaries, nonvalue activity analysis, and much more.

It may be no surprise, then, to learn that GE is once again breaking new ground, this time by developing a novel approach to a bottom-up continuous improvement process. Largely the brainchild of CEO John L. Welch, the new approach emphasizes winning "on our ideas, not by whips and chains." It seems that Welch intends to replace much of the old top-down style of management with newer approaches that involve employees, expressly to generate more new ideas and thereby increase productivity. In Welch's terms, "The only ideas that count are the A ideas. There is no second place. That means we have to get everybody in the organization involved. If you do that right, the best ideas will rise to the top."

Welch's new approach comprises three techniques. Each stresses employee involvement. The first technique, known as Work-Out, "jimmies the locks that keep employees out of the decision-making process." The second, called Best Practices, seeks to spread good practices quickly throughout the company. The third technique is Process Mapping.

By themselves, each of the three techniques reflects old familiar ideas. At Work-Outs, so far at least, personnel from all ranks and functions in a plant, shop, or department meet to discuss and seek solutions to common problems in the workplace. Sometimes customers and suppliers attend. Work-Outs are informal three day meetings where teams form to work on agenda items prepared ahead of time. They utilize the skills of trained meeting facilitators and scribes. Nothing new. Except that open exchange of ideas across ranks and functions is new at GE.

Work-Outs have been designed to break the ice on decades of fairly formal, cold internal relationships that typify large hierarchies in general, not just GE. They are orchestrated expressly to maximize employee involvement and to minimize intimidation and second-guessing by bosses. At Work-Out sessions, bosses are obligated to accept or reject proposals for change on the spot—or ask for more information by an agreed-on date. Senior management can not overrule subordinate managers' Work-Out decisions.

Eventually, say within ten years, GE hopes to move Work-Outs from off-site locations ("unnatural places for unnatural acts") into the day-to-day workplace. In other words, behavior that now is limited to rarified Work-Out sessions will become the company's modus operandi. The cultural change this presupposes is perhaps the most radical aspect of Welch's new program. Welch hopes it will give GE, with over 300,000 employees, the capacity for bottom-up process ownership and learning that one might ordinarily associate with a company of 100 people. Strong stuff!

Best Practices is a program that focuses people's attention on the way processes are managed, rather than on results. It views improvement as I described it above: as a *continuous process of discovery,* not an intermittent series of "solutions" to overwhelming problems. It also embodies the idea of benchmarking as a means of learning what the customer will find that is best, wherever it is, before the customer finds it. In short, Best Practices has teams visiting companies (or other units in GE) to learn their secrets of success.

Last is Process Mapping, which is just what you think it is. It is a team-oriented, group problem-solving tool, the object of which is, of course, to feed information into Best Practices and Work-Outs. You don't really know what to study and what to improve until you've mapped it.[4]

Smaller companies that are intimidated by the thought of empowering workers to engage in a continuous process of discovery will do well to study and keep up to date on the status of GE's new improvement process program. No business in the world was more steeped in remote-control management than GE in the 1970s and early 1980s. If Jack Welch and his colleagues successfully renounce that concept in favor of continuous bottom-up constraint busting, there is no question that American business can restore its lost competitive edge—perhaps even by the end of this decade.

Weyerhaeuser: Quality Licks Administrative Overhead

The Weyerhaeuser Company, a forest products giant based in Tacoma, Washington, has struggled for the past decade to cope with corporate-level administrative "overhead creep." Their object of concern was the perennially rising cost of the myriad services that headquarters staff provide to the diverse marketing and producing units of a large-scale industrial organization. The services include everything from legal, to engineering, to central accounting, to applied R&D, to computer services, and telecommunications. Like most large American companies of the 1970s and 1980s, Weyerhaeuser discovered that the costs of such central overhead services tended to "creep" steadily upward as a percentage of gross revenue, even though accountants tended to classify them as "fixed" costs. But Weyerhaeuser is now different than most other companies—they seem to have found a long-term solution. The answer to controlling "overhead creep," they recently discovered, is a quality improvement process.

Weyerhaeuser's corporate overhead managers went through three stages on the road to discovering the quality improvement process.[5] I have talked to scores of companies who see containment of corporate overhead costs as one of their most acute problems. Usually these companies are at the first stage that Weyerhaeuser passed through on their migration to an improvement process. When I mention the Weyerhaeuser Company's experience, they always perk up and say "that's exactly our problem—how did they solve it?" In the first two stages the company went from managing overhead costs as such to managing underlying activities that cause the costs. In a sense these two stages are analogous to the transition many companies go through when they discover activity-based costing.

In the first stage, lasting from the early 1970s to 1985, Weyerhaeuser used classic budgeting procedures to make costs visible, ostensibly to stimulate efficiency, by allocating corporate overhead costs to product departments. Previously such costs never were allocated below the corporate level. Now corporate overhead costs were allocated to departments in proportion to gross revenues. However, control over spending amounted to little more than the usual first-of-year budget reviews and exhortations to be frugal. Occasional grumbling arose over cross-subsidies caused by allocating costs over gross sales. Light consumers of corporate services, such as a newsprint mill that used minimal invoicing services because it sold millions of dollars of merchandise to a small handful of metropolitan daily newspapers, complained about subsidizing heavy consumers of invoicing services, such as lumber mills that sold many small orders to thousands of retail establishments. Both departments sold about the same amount of stuff, but lumber sales obviously caused much more invoicing cost than did newsprint sales. Those being subsidized, of course, never complained and those being overcharged never raised any fundamental question about the service or its cost. Life went on and corporate overhead continued to creep.

The second stage began in 1985 with a restructuring of the company that created semi-autonomous product-line divisions. A decision was made to charge divisions for the corporate overhead services they used—not to continue allocating costs over gross revenue and hoping for the best. The vehicle selected for charging costs to divisions was the unit of service, or activity, performed. For billing services that unit was an invoice—for standard accounts—or number of invoice lines for more complex accounts. For handling accounts receivable the unit was a customer or an invoice. For computer services the units were CPU units of mainframe time or hours of programmer time. For legal services the unit was hours of lawyer's time. And so forth. For each type of service, users were charged estimated costs per unit of service for every unit of service used. No more cross-subsidies, no more free rides. Now users thought twice about demanding services from headquarters staff.

A twist Weyerhaeuser gave these "chargebacks" was to allow users to buy services on the outside if they could be had at the same quality for less than headquarters charged. At the same time, headquarters suppliers were allowed to sell on the outside if they felt the price they were asking was competitive and inside users weren't calling for all their capacity. These steps added an entrepreneurial spirit to the management of overhead costs. After its first year of operation, in 1986, the company estimated that its freewheeling entrepreneurial chargeback system had resulted in savings of $250,000 on a budget of $11 million. Not a lot of savings, but a savings nevertheless. "Overhead creep" seemed to be over, and that was just the first year.

A few years later, while gathering material to update my file on Weyerhaeuser Company's activity-based chargeback initiative, I learned that the company had adopted a new approach to controlling corporate overhead cost in 1989 and 1990. Activity-based chargeback information was still being compiled and was still used by the accounting department to budget and keep track of overhead costs. But control now was achieved by a quality improvement process that went into operation in 1990. The company discovered that activity-based chargeback costs, like activity-based product costs generally, removed distortions from vital information that was used for decision making. That was good. But the improved cost-driver information used to calculate chargebacks did little to enhance people's understanding of processes and work. The cost-driver information, by still focusing people's attention on a result, not on a process, did nothing to replace the traditional top-down culture of fear with true bottom-up search for opportunities to improve.

Indeed, activity-based chargebacks do not address the fundamental difficulty posed by corporate overhead—the decoupling of processes over many years, in the name of centralized scale economies, that finally makes it almost impossible to connect upstream causes with downstream effects. Chargebacks attempt to restore lost cause-effect linkages with market-based incentives and distortion-free cost information. But that really doesn't get at the underlying processes, it only sharpens the definition and allocation of financial results. For example, Weyerhaeuser's corporate finance group, one of the service providers, spent time before 1990 improving the cost drivers used to charge back accounts receivable claims and collection costs. This helped reduce cross-subsidies and assigned the costs to those units whose billings caused the most problems. But that simply threw the problem over the wall to the proper user of the finance department's services. It invited the using department to cut costs, either by hammering their customers, or by getting rid of the ones whose bills cause high claims and collection costs. It also invited the supplying department to cut costs by striving to handle claims and collections "more efficiently."

With a quality improvement process put in place in 1990 Weyerhaeuser found a better answer. Instead of internal units working "to save costs" in isolation from each other, teams made up of internal and external customers and suppliers now work to identify customer wants and to solve the problems (constraints) that cause delay, excess, and variation. The result is more satisfaction for much less work.

In the case of claims and collections, for example, the improvement process strives to eliminate claims and collections, not to cut their costs either by devoting time and money to figuring out how to handle them more efficiently or by getting rid of drivers (i.e., dissatisfied customers). Now both internal and external customers are happier (many of the claims and overdue payments were Weyerhaeuser's fault, for shipping the wrong thing or charging the wrong price). And internal suppliers, especially those who supply corporate overhead services, feel a stronger sense of ownership in the process *and* the results.

Here's a brief summary of their results as of early 1991. Working as teams, corporate groups employing about 1,500 people in the third quarter of 1990 submitted about 5,000 (mostly small) ideas for improvement. Approximately 1,600 of those ideas have been chosen for implementation in 1991 and the first half of 1992. The expected cost savings (including resource redundancies) will amount to about *25 percent* of Weyerhaeuser's entire 1990 administrative overhead budget. That's not an insignificant chunk of the company's expected net income. Quite a difference from the $250,000 of savings identified in 1986, the first year of the activity-based cost chargeback initiative. As someone once said, quality pays!

Connor Formed Metal Products: Giving Employees Ownership of Information

Connor Formed Metal Products, a small job-shop manufacturer of custom metal springs headquartered in Los Angeles, seems to be giving its employees the ownership of information that I associate with bottom-up empowerment.[6] Moreover, the company turned to empowerment in 1990 to boost sagging profits, after the high costs of several improvement plans implemented during the previous three or four years left the company in the red in 1989 for the first time in over twenty years. The company's previous improvement efforts—radical decentralization of power to the heads of the company's four plants, an employee stock ownership plan, quarterly cash bonuses based on profits at the plant level, company-wide statistical process control—had not hurt by any means. Connor's sales rose from $12.4 million in 1985 to $16.4 million in 1989 and employee morale was high. The company became a certified vendor to Hewlett-Packard and Xerox and was being approached by Japanese transplants looking for U.S. vendors. The problem was poor profit performance.

The answer was to develop an information system that gave every employee in the company access to everyday nuts-and-bolts information about operating details that affect customers and profitability. This entailed more than just computerizing information flows—it meant making information about everything and anything available to everyone, and "sharing the power all that knowledge carries with it." To accomplish this revolution in ownership of information the company hired a full-time programmer to design PC-based information processing and networking software. By mid-1990 every employee had instant access to full information about every job in the plant: full history of the job; special notes and instructions from engineering or customer service; full data on price and margin; and real-time instructions or information about the job emanating from anyone connected with the work or the customer.

With this information, problems could be dealt with as they occurred. More important, access to this information enabled employees to come up with far more ideas for improvement than anyone ever could have anticipated. For example, two employees in customer service who always spent large chunks of their time handling change orders on jobs queried the system to learn more about the sources of these changes. They discovered that a large share of the 20 percent of all orders generated internally were caused by errors that occurred when customer orders were first entered. They designed a customer purchase-order checklist that now eliminates most change orders emanating from that source. Other examples: the employee in charge of raw-material purchasing now tracks the status of vendors' shipments and rates vendors' performance; and an outside sales manager uses a laptop to communicate customer needs directly with the shop floor and to keep posted on the current status of customer orders.

The actions employees now take to spot and solve problems has dramatically reduced defects, credits issued to customers, and late shipments. Connor now receives near-perfect annual quality ratings from several customers. One customer hired Connor as a sole source despite Connor's generally higher prices! And once again the company is reporting profits, with the price of its stock rising 35 percent in 1990. After putting the power of information in every employee's hands, the company is confident it can take on all competitors. CEO Bob Sloss says, "We're competing with the best house in Japan, and the best in Germany, and the best in Korea, and we're still in the game."[7]

None of these companies has adopted completely the continuous improvement process as I have defined it. In particular, they have not unequivocally renounced the use of remote-control management information that motivates people to manipulate processes. However, each company provides powerful examples of what I call bottom-up empowerment. They are taking seriously the idea of giving employees ownership of processes in order to motivate continuous learning. And top managers of these companies have committed to customer-focused missions. They are not unique. Undoubtedly there are hundreds, perhaps thousands of companies in the United States that have advanced as far as GE, Weyerhaeuser, and Connor have on the road to achieving a continuous improvement process. The direction they are moving in and the progress they have made convinces me there is light at the end of the proverbial tunnel. The decade of the 1990s may at last be the decade when American business recovers its lost competitive edge.

WRAP-UP

Here are five important points about the concept of an improvement process:

1. People sometimes forget that an improvement process should not operate in a vacuum. It must start with a vision of *where you want to be* when you improve. You can improve short-run costs and profit in a remote-control setting and do nothing to improve long-term competitiveness in the global economy. I believe that is how we must judge most attempts companies have made to date to improve "competitiveness" with activity-based cost information. To improve at fulfilling the imperatives of global competitiveness you must know the *earmarks* of globally competitive behavior, as those were defined in Table 4–1. Beware the possibility of embarking on a "TQM" improvement campaign that focuses on improving processes without any sense of where

you are headed. Earmarks, as I have defined them, address, I believe, Deming's "constancy of purpose." Don't use team-oriented problem solving to improve what you should not be doing in the first place!

2. As Edwards Deming often says, managing processes, not results, means you reward people for effort (as long as they follow the process), not just for results. Getting results ever closer to a desired mean requires group effort to improve the process, not forcing individuals to excel. With that in mind, most companies must rethink their incentive compensation schemes. Although the jury is still out on how to solve this problem, it seems likely that motivating individuals to excel does impair long-term performance of the group.[8]

3. A variation of the improvement process is the self-assessment quality audit, of which the Malcolm Baldrige Award criteria in America and the ISO 9000 series quality standards in Europe are probably the best known examples. Quality audits may well become one of the most pervasive institutions of business, worldwide, by the end of this decade. It behooves everyone to become familiar with these audit processes and to *be aware of differences* between the demands of a quality audit and the demands of an improvement process, as I have defined improvement process here. In light of the increasing worldwide attention being paid to quality audits, accountants and financial auditors should assess the role they can play filling the coming demand for quality auditors.

4. The quote from Robert Hall at the head of this chapter emphasizes the importance of people power—the main product of a quality improvement process—as a source of competitive advantage. This can't be overemphasized. Competitiveness in the global economy is going to mean much, much more than just designing better products or running processes more efficiently than the next guy. If that were all it took to be competitive, then everyone could learn the secrets with a little reverse engineering and a few plant tours. Unfortunately it isn't so easy. Such steps will not reveal the secrets of "people power" any more than cutting open the goose revealed the source of the golden eggs.

5. The global competitor's view of learning and change should avert the short-term focus that usually is blamed on Wall Street's obsession with quarterly earnings figures. I believe

Wall Street is blamed unfairly for causing the managerial myopia that sacrifices long-term competitiveness for short-term financial results. Indeed, companies can improve quarterly earnings if empowered employees continuously improve the business's system and build stronger customer relationships. There need be no conflict between competitive excellence and positive short-term financial performance. Conflict between short-term and long-term performance occurs when managers and employees view themselves as powerless to change the system, see change coming only from outside, and do not seek out opportunities to remove constraints or build stronger relationships. People who in such cases attempt to influence financial results by changing the rate at which the system operates will fail to satisfy customers or to improve the way people work in the company. Even if there were no Wall Street, short-term behavior generated by the business as usual mindset would still impair long-term competitiveness and profitability. On the other hand, steps to empower people to manage activities with a customer focus need not be in conflict with satisfying Wall Street's demands for short-term financial performance.

PART III

INFORMATION, EMPOWERMENT, AND SOCIETY

The power that new information technologies give people to learn and to choose has ramifications extending far beyond the need for businesses to meet new imperatives of competition. The last two chapters of this book address some of these ramifications.

Chapter 10 discusses the implications for university business schools of addressing these imperatives in a global economy. Business schools must rethink everything they do in teaching, research, and management. Because most business schools view editors of academic journals, not corporations, as their primary customer, they face the need to make monumental changes in their thinking and in their practices.

The final chapter of the book compares the impact that information technology and empowerment have on top-down business systems to the impact that those same forces have had recently on the centrallly planned dictatorships of Eastern Europe and the Soviet Union. Business leaders must not lose the opportunity the information revolution gives them to build their organizations upon a foundation of democratic principles and dignified human goals.

CHAPTER 10

NEW FRONTIERS
FOR BUSINESS EDUCATION

Between 1963 and 1987 the annual number of M.B.A. graduates rose from 5,787 to 67,496. There are now more than a million M.B.A.s. If they were improving the quality of U.S. management, the results ought to be obvious by now. They aren't. Indeed, the M.B.A. explosion has coincided with a deterioration in the performance and stature of corporate America.

—Robert J. Samuelson[1]

[B]usiness schools still have as their major philosophical set, their paradigm, something articulated in the fifties. That's going to have to change.

—James E. Howell[2]

If [business] schools don't respond to the nation's problems in competitiveness, the schools themselves will become irrelevant.

—Robert H. Hayes[3]

It would be fair for business people outside universities to assume that teaching and research in American business schools focus primarily on problems facing business organizations. This is not to deny, of course, that "pure" academic research by business school faculty might deal with certain issues long before businesses face them. But lay persons naturally would assume that business school professors and business practitioners concentrate on similar phenomena and speak similar languages—no less than, say, medical school professors and physicians, law school professors and attorneys, or professors of design and architects.

In fact, nothing could be farther from the truth. Professors in American business schools—especially in the so-called "leading" graduate schools—tend, on the whole, to focus on issues and phenomena that have no bearing on what business people must know to run a competitive and profitable organization in the global economy. Professors who specialize in accounting and finance do focus on issues germane to, sometimes in advance of, the concerns of their nonacademic practitioner peers. But that may not be saying much when one considers how divorced most professional accountants and finance professionals are from understanding the demands of competition in the global economy. Indeed, the concerns of their professional nonacademic peers suggest that accounting and finance professors may belong partly in law schools and partly in economics departments. Very few people teaching in American business schools today are concerned with problems that face managers of businesses in the global economy.

Since the early 1960s, virtually all business school teaching and research in the United States have been firmly grounded in principles of "remote-control" management. Graduate schools train aspiring business PhDs to espouse the "hard" quantitative-analytical principles of top-down control, and to spurn the "soft" verbal-inductive principles of bottom-up empowerment. Editors of the "leading" academic research journals usually tell faculty not to submit manuscripts that don't feature "hard" empirical testing of "scientific" hypotheses. Moreover, this attitude has been embedded in teaching and research by the business school accreditation standards enforced since the 1950s by the American Assembly of Collegiate Schools of Business.

Robert S. Kaplan, former Dean of Carnegie-Mellon's business school and now professor at Harvard Business School, recently compiled convincing evidence that American business school research and teaching have been firmly shuttered against the winds of one of the most dramatic changes to affect the business world in this century—the quality revolution.[4] Kaplan surveyed research published in recent years by leading academic journals in operations management and he reviewed the research and teaching at America's top schools of business. He concluded that perhaps only 1 or 2 percent of American business schools "have truly been affected, as of early 1991, by the TQM revolution that has been creating radical change in many U.S. and worldwide businesses." Despite the business schools' frequent claim that "their enormous commitment to research is necessary to keep abreast or ahead of business developments," Kaplan notes that business schools, in fact, "completely missed the quality revolution in management." Although his research focused only on quality, Kaplan believes his conclusion applies equally to any subject that is germane to competitiveness in the global economy. In general, American business schools have completely missed the information-based management revolution.

Business schools can not be blamed for the failure of American business to remain competitive in the last few decades. Obviously, the convergence of many political, international, historical, and social forces has contributed to the current plight of American business. Recent competitive reversals in the business world are not of the business schools' making. However, business schools can be blamed for rationalizing and sanctioning management practices that exacerbated the impact of those reversals.

Moreover, business schools, unlike businesses, have failed to acknowledge or even recognize that business reversals of the past two decades are due to shifts in the competitive environment that have changed forever the terms of business competition. Indeed, many business school leaders don't even believe that fundamentally new terms of competition exist in quality, time-based competition, information technology, or concurrent product-process design. Businesses around the world have mobilized on quality, for example. Nevertheless, as Kaplan points out, "business school professors are still wondering whether quality improvement creates value to organizations, whether research on quality is legitimate for them to do, and whether they will get recognition and be rewarded for performing such research."

This attitude of people in business schools reflects the ostrich head-in-the-sand mentality one often sees in companies whose products or services have yet to face the new global competitive challenge. These companies see the plight of embattled auto makers or manufacturers of consumer electronic products, but they do nothing to change their own way of doing business until they suffer similar pain themselves. Most business schools have not felt the pain of lost markets—*yet*. But competitive threats forming on at least two fronts may shock business schools out of their complacency.

One threat is posed by American businesses themselves. Fed up with business schools that don't respond to their needs, and tired of paying premium salaries for graduates who don't understand the new competitive environment, many businesses, such as General Electric, Westinghouse, Motorola, and IBM, are expanding the scope and depth of in-house education programs.[5] Although designed originally to upgrade the skills of existing employees, someday these in-house "schools" may cater to students who are not employees.[6] The threat to the MBA is obvious.

Another threat comes from European business schools that are responding more creatively than American schools to the need business people have for continuous, lifetime training, as opposed to one-shot intensive degree programs at the start of one's career. Europe's graduate business schools, generally much younger than American business schools, typically have very small MBA programs that are overshadowed by much, much larger executive "short-course" programs. The European schools feature more on-the-job training, more teachers with executive experience, and more training similar to what companies themselves provide in their own in-house schools. While geography may prevent these schools from drawing large numbers of American students, their popularity among European businesses (in contrast to the lukewarm reception American business schools now receive from U.S. businesses) suggests American business schools should study their methods very carefully.

Why are American business schools so isolated from businesses, and apparently unaware of recent trends in the global marketplace? I believe the chief reason for business schools' neglect of the global competitive situation is their decision some forty years ago to focus attention on the wrong customer. They do not see business as their customer. They focus inward and serve academic customers. This must change before schools can begin to help businesses spot and adapt to change in the marketplace. To appreciate better the importance of this problem, examine briefly the history of business education in the United States since World War II.

WHY BUSINESS SCHOOLS FOCUS ON THE WRONG CUSTOMER

In the 1950s, veterans of World War II and the Korean War, taking advantage of their GI Bill rights pushed university enrollments into the stratosphere, especially in state-supported institutions. In contrast to prewar college students, this postwar college generation expressed a strong preference to major in business, not in traditional liberal arts subjects. However, these burgeoning enrollments in business courses created a "crisis of legitimacy" in American business schools. Their efforts to meet this crisis caused business schools to adopt other academics, not businesses, as their primary customer.

People who were then in control of university affairs—typically nonbusiness professors with PhD degrees in the arts and sciences—expressed concerns about the credentials of business faculty. Business professors tended not to have the PhD credentials of other faculty. For years, most courses in business subjects such as accounting, advertising, commercial law, and production management had been taught by people with experience and credentials in business—CPAs, lawyers, production engineers, or retired executives—not by people with traditional academic training in PhD programs. University leaders in the early 1950s believed that this condition should change. The message to business schools was clear: professors of business increasingly would have to earn PhDs if business schools were to hold their own as peers among the other university departments.

However, there were virtually no PhD programs in "business" before World War II. Of the few PhDs who taught business subjects before the 1940s, probably most had received their doctoral degrees from programs in economics, a few in psychology. When large numbers of business schools began cranking up their own new PhD programs after the early 1950s, most piggybacked on existing doctoral programs in economics and psychology. Probably the politics of university communities made it wise to pattern business PhD training after already established doctoral programs in the social sciences. However, this decision had an insidious long-term effect.

The decision to cast doctoral business training in the molds of the social sciences pointed academic research and teaching in business schools away from consideration of business problems, toward consideration of problems that vexed academicians in economics, psychology, and other social sciences. It didn't have to be that way. Indeed, the great philosopher-mathematician Alfred North Whitehead, speaking at Harvard Business School in the late 1920s, had said that the mission of a university business school should be to put the power of academic inquiry—the university's traditional strength—to the service of a business profession. As it turned out by the 1960s, however, business schools lost sight of the professional "forest" by focusing too intently on the academic "trees."

This focus on the social sciences as an academic model widened the gap between business and business education after the mid-1960s as the social scientists themselves accelerated their own efforts to mimic what they defined as research paradigms of the physical sciences. The "scientific" tone of much of the research published in academic business journals by the late 1970s bore an eerie resemblance to research published in economics and psychology journals a decade earlier. Many people in business were aware by the 1980s that most published research from business schools was irrelevant to their own problems.

Ironically, it was the quest for "academic rigor" that caused business school research to become increasingly irrelevant to businesses after the 1950s. Rigor was defined in terms set by the social scientists, especially the economists, whose departments were the home for most early business PhD training. The two most frequently cited features of academic rigor were the reduction of "real world" complexity to terms expressed in mathematical models of economic theory and the use of large-sample statistical data to test hypotheses suggested by such theory. However, the rigor of mathematics and "scientific" hypothesis testing had two unfortunate side effects.

First, the models of theoretical economics attempt to portray formal and contractual behavior of "economic man"—the self-aggrandizing creature of neoclassical economic price theory. Nowhere do those models attempt to capture the dynamics of the communal, essentially self-effacing, behavior that drives competitive business organizations. Secondly, the emphasis on large-sample statistical hypothesis testing caused business school scholars to question the legitimacy of field-based research. Business schools considered it appropriate to study macro-financial data compiled from the records of 1,000 companies, but not to study intensely the activities of one real company. Hence, the emphasis on mathematical modeling and large-sample statistics drove business school research farther and farther away from studying the problems of real business organizations and real business people.

One consequence of business school scholars borrowing the theories and research paradigms of social scientists in other disciplines was their failure to develop an indigenous theory of business practice. They applied to business questions a theory that caricatured (badly) the dynamics of businesses. The alternative, to go into the field where one might observe and measure actual business behavior, seemed too messy, too "unscientific" to be legitimate. Harvard Business School, with its emphasis on case teaching and case-oriented field research, stood virtually alone among American business schools by defining real businesses, not the editors of "rigorous" academic journals, as their primary customer.

Eventually, sound field research might suggest generalizations that could lead to genuine theories of business. Johannes Kepler and Isaac

Newton, in the seventeenth century, surmised a powerful theory of motion to explain measurements taken in the field by earlier astronomers such as Copernicus and Brahe. Kepler and Newton didn't work from large-sample statistics drawn from the universe as a whole. They used data from a sample of one—our solar system.[7] Oblivious to the example of Renaissance European scientific developments (or perhaps never understanding the history of science in the first place), today's business school academics in the United States debate what purport to be business issues, using economic theories that have no grounding in the study of management problems.

Writing in the late 1970s, the great Harvard marketing maven Theodore Levitt pilloried the pretentiousness of this business school research:

> New tools of management, new concepts, special "advanced" ways of analyzing and simulating markets, customers, investments, balance sheets, distribution systems, and organizations—all these, with unctuous promises of mathematical and behavioral precision, tumble out from numerous graduate business schools in rising abundance. Increasingly, scholasticism replaces common sense, formalism supersedes dexterity, organizational routines become more tortuous, and the staff dominates the line. "Methods" rivet the attention as much as results. Entropy threatens energy.[8]

As someone once said, the problem in American business schools is "too many second-rate economists chasing third-rate questions."

Actually, the irrelevance of published business school research to business practice is just the tip of the iceberg. Business people seldom perceive how the social science paradigms underlying that research also shape what business schools teach, and how that teaching reinforces practices that are antithetical to competitiveness in the global economy. Indeed, most business people by the 1970s who had university degrees in business were themselves victims of training that focused on social science paradigms, not on the problems of businesses striving to be competitive.

Public criticism of the training received by business students in the late 1980s does not reflect a recent change in what business schools teach. Rather, it reflects a growing awareness by American businesses of what is required of workers and managers if companies are to compete in the global marketplace. Mindful of these new requirements, businesses are suddenly aware that business school graduates lack the same understanding. These graduates seem to lack the training required to work in the new world that businesses are awakening to. This criticism is being heard especially from companies that have "discovered" quality.

One often hears from business people today that business students are not taught what they must know to work effectively in quality-oriented organizations. Students, they say, learn solutions to textbook problems, not problem-solving techniques to apply in real-life situations. They learn how to compete as individuals, not how to cooperate in teams. They learn almost nothing about improvement processes, even less about performing as facilitators or team leaders. Businesses that practice TQM find they must teach recent business graduates about continuous improvement processes from the ground up. Understandably, they ask why business schools do not equip students with the tools of modern quality management.

The point is they never have equipped students with relevant business tools. At least not since the 1950s. That is why business schools are so slow in responding to these criticisms. They don't know what businesses are talking about when they preach quality. A few schools have responded to businesses' alarms by adding a small number of quality management courses to the existing curriculum. That's not a bad start. Students who take such courses can graduate with at least a rudimentary understanding of the quality improvement process. And a small handful of business schools are beginning to offer courses that give students firsthand experience working on company problem-solving teams. Employers undoubtedly bring such graduates up to speed a lot faster, at less cost, than graduates who must start from ground zero.

But I don't believe adding a few quality courses to the existing business curriculum is enough. Business schools should push further and consider how the entire curriculum would look had it been built from the start to teach imperatives of competition pertinent to today's economy, where the customer is in charge of the marketplace and workers are in control of processes. Business schools must examine assumptions underlying their traditional core courses. For the most part, those courses indoctrinate students with the principles of remote-control management, not the principles of empowerment and customer satisfaction. Adding a few "quality" courses onto this core is not enough to answer business's current needs.

Consider, for example, core courses in subjects such as management accounting, financial management, and operations management. Usually, they teach "solutions" that would have businesses adopt practices such as: push output to cut costs; minimize cost by specializing resources in large units; use standard cost variances to achieve financial targets; "tamper" with a process to manage bottom-line financial results; and so forth. If those courses were geared to teaching how to manage in the global economy, they would have students learn, instead, how to focus on customer satisfaction; how to continuously improve through ownership of processes; and how to ensure that a process is in statistical control and capable.

Underlying the "solutions" business schools teach in existing courses is, of course, the social-science model of business behavior that is quite at variance with the behavior of businesses that compete effectively in today's customer-driven global economy. The reason for that model's dominance, as I said before, is the decision business schools made forty years ago to clone social science research paradigms, not to study businesses that operate in the real world. Business schools that genuinely want to respond to the call for global management education must acknowledge their long-standing failure to recognize their real customers, society's business organizations and the graduates they hire—not other academics, such as editors of major academic journals. Business schools must examine the consequences of focusing their teaching and research on subjects considered important by the arbiters of academic legitimacy, not on subjects considered important by people in managed organizations. Business schools face an absolutely revolutionary change if they adopt the employers of their graduates as their primary customers. Let's consider the changes that might occur were business schools to build their research and teaching upon the principles of competitive excellence in the global economy.

HOW BUSINESS SCHOOLS CAN RESTORE RELEVANCE TO BUSINESS EDUCATION

The fundamental change in the terms of competitiveness precipitated by new information technologies ultimately should affect business schools in the same way it affects business organizations. Information-age technologies invalidate all the premises and practices of traditional American-style top-down management control. The need to be responsive and flexible requires companies to adopt bottom-up systems that listen to the customer and to the processes that serve customers. These customer-focused organizations will manifest entirely different structures, different atmospheres, and different attitudes than organizations that manage with remote top-down controls. Similar differences must occur in business schools—in modes of research, in what they teach, and in how they teach.

In businesses, merely implementing "improvement programs" associated with concepts such as JIT and TQM will not do the trick if atmosphere and attitudes don't also change. Grafting those concepts onto a company's existing top-down control structure simply wastes good resources in the pursuit of erroneous competitive goals. The same idea applies to business schools.

However, business schools seem impervious to the change in milieu that I associate with information-based competitiveness. This is evident in the way they have tried in recent years to respond to several new developments that reflect the impact of the information revolution on business. Business schools—through their accrediting organization, the American Assembly of Collegiate Schools of Business—have responded (perhaps unwittingly) to the imperatives of global competitiveness by promoting campaigns to enhance teaching and research in subjects such as computer literacy, interpersonal communication, management of technology, and, most recently, quality. These campaigns never challenge the underlying social science foundation on which business education rests. They leave in place the core of research and teaching that focuses on analytical and mathematical top-down models of management control. The recommended changes invariably entail adding new courses or stuffing discrete modules into existing courses. The new material on communication, technology, computers, or quality is simply new icing piled on top of an old cake. Eventually, disinterested professors neglect and ignore the new thrust. The tide washes away the new courses and restores the familiar bedrock of "business as usual."

I once saw this same theme played out in a slightly different context. A major manufacturer of personal computers, to promote the AACSB's campaign to increase the use of computers in business school classes, invited several hundred business school professors to a two-day conference that featured presentations of novel and exciting new software applications that promised to make this company's personal computers a key element in the educational process. It was a brilliantly orchestrated conference, featuring real professors demonstrating classroom uses of leading-edge computer, sound, and video technology. But I was troubled to see that virtually every application of software to classroom teaching involved solving problems of the sort business school professors had taught for decades. There were programs for simulation, queuing, linear programming, forecasting, market analysis, cost variance analysis, and so forth. I recall no one talking about tapping the power of the computer to study processes, to increase workers' ownership of processes, or to communicate with customers and suppliers. No one talked about technology and quality as dimensions of competitiveness that should permeate everything a business school teaches. Technology and quality were simply "topics" added to familiar educational programs. In fact, the conference replayed a theme I had heard many times before: how businesses, and business teachers, can use computers to do faster (and with fantastic multicolored visual effects!) what they should not be doing or teaching in the first place.

The computer manufacturer that hosted this conference can not be faulted, of course, for not introducing business school professors to concepts with which the company itself probably had little or no understanding. This company, as most of its customers I know will attest, is hardly a model of customer attentiveness. Nor do published reports about its own management methods demonstrate a strong sense of what I mean by employee empowerment. I'm not suggesting the company should advocate concepts it does not practice or understand itself. My point is that even well-known, reasonably successful high-tech businesses often miss the mark when they try to help business educators update their teaching and research. Indeed, the reforms needed in business education may be more difficult to articulate and execute than the reforms needed in business.

To make business education more relevant to the concerns of people working in competitive organizations will require more than redesigning courses, although new courses will be required. It will require professors to adopt business as their primary customer and to define the conditions for business success in different terms than they have ever understood before. Let's examine these implications of information-age competitiveness for business education, starting with general changes in the mindset of business faculty and ending with specific changes in business courses.

General Changes in Mindset

The changes discussed here concern professors' attitudes toward constrained optimization, problem-solving processes versus solutions to problems, focusing work on customer-oriented projects instead of on profession-oriented staff activities, team-oriented learning versus mathematical analysis, on-the-job teaching, and field-based research.

Constrained Optimization.   The mathematical-economic models underlying most business school teaching, especially in management accounting and financial management, emphasize profit maximization or cost minimization "subject to constraints." Those models allow one to calculate "optimal" quantities or prices of outputs and inputs *assuming* that no change occurs in a number of stated and unstated conditions, or constraints, such as the layout of a plant, the technology imbedded in production processes, the company's human relations policies, the way products are designed, the way processes are orchestrated (including, among other things, the time to change over processes), the government's tax and spending policies, and so forth. Holding constraints constant recognizes, of course, the impossibility of mathematically finding equilibrium solutions in a system where all things can change at once. There's nothing wrong with using mathematics to make choices where resource scarcities exist. Linear programming is but one example of powerful constrained optimization tools that have extremely valuable applications in business (and elsewhere).

The problem occurs when such tools are used to define a manager's central concern, as has been the case in American business schools for over thirty years. Students seldom are taught to define, much less challenge, the constraints that underlie solutions to optimization problems. Perhaps it is no surprise that managers of American businesses since the 1960s have shown little inclination to remove constraints—rather, they seem to prefer to optimize within them. Earl Cheit, a sage observer of American business education and former business school dean himself, once noted that the root of "short-term thinking" in business is the view "of a manager as someone who works with what is available."[9] According to Cheit, it is customary in business and in business schools to assume that "the manager allocates, or makes decisions about what is given to him. When conditions become more (or less) generous, the manager will respond, but always within the circumstances defined for him." Unfortunately, managers who always work within "a context given to them" will never see when the most important thing they must do is *shape the context* that is given to them.

Earlier I suggested the idea that "short-term" thinking, so often associated with focusing on short-term financial results, is really nothing more than passively accepting constraints as given. Managers can focus on long-term financial results but, if they passively accept constraints as given, may overlook enormous opportunities for gain. On the other hand, managers who continuously remove constraints have no reason not to expect consistently good short-term financial results.

Seeing the difference between working within the context given and shaping that context is one of the most important concepts business schools can teach to students today. That difference is perhaps the main thing separating American-style remote-control management from Japanese-style modes of continuous improvement. The key to success in the global economy will be to remove constraints that cause delay, excess, and variation. Move them slowly, a small bit every day, but never stop. Eliminating constraints must become one of the chief obsessions of teams engaged in daily problem solving. Constrained optimization is still understood and practiced, but it will become a tool, useful in its place, not a spirit that guides all management action.

Problem-solving Processes versus Solutions to Problems.   One of the key features of total quality management is the continuous problem-solving improvement process. The idea originated, perhaps, with the concept of managing variation in processes that is central to statistical process control. Problem solving begins with identifying processes and measuring variation in their output. The process of identifying causes of variation and discovering solutions to those causes is the essence of teamwork aimed at improving customer satisfaction. Many variations of the problem-solving process exist, such as Motorola's Six Steps to Six Sigma or Xerox's Nine-Step Quality Improvement Process. Most of them entail some twist on a Shewhart/Deming Plan-Do-Study-Act (PDSA) cycle.

Instead of teaching problem solving, business schools teach *solutions* to problems. This is wholly antithetical to the concept of continuous improvement aimed at customer satisfaction. The "problems" to which business schools pose solutions almost never involve customer satisfaction. They usually focus on issues raised by the mathematical models professors find useful. Moreover, the solutions invite students to consider the "problem" only in terms the solution addresses. For example, management accounting courses teach students how to "solve" make-buy problems. These solutions invariably couch the problem in terms of cost, never in terms of customer wants or it terms of workers' capabilities to improve a process that is being considered for outsourcing. The solutions are static and are blind to possibilities not considered by the economic model that defines the problem.

When I once asked a quality management spokesman from Xerox what one change he would make in business schools he immediately replied, "stop teaching students solutions to problems; start teaching them about problem-solving processes."

Focus Work on Customer-oriented Projects, Not Profession-oriented Staff Activities.   Empowered global enterprises are not likely to offer MBA graduates many opportunities to ride the "fast track" to a top position inside a specialized department. Success from now on is more likely to be achieved by building lifetime *employability* by working on several different customer-oriented teams that meld talents of many specialists. Business school teaching and research should begin to reflect the shattering of departmental boundaries that already is occurring in leading-edge businesses.

The main work done in an information-age customer-focused business is project-oriented work by cross-functional teams, aimed at satisfying specific customer requirements. Proctor & Gamble, for instance, recently began to assign cross-functional task forces, sometimes as large as two to three hundred people, to major customers such as Wal-Mart and K Mart.[10] These task forces include people from every function and field of specialization that touches upon a customer's needs, and they serve full time at the customer's premises as the voice of P&G. The benefits and savings that flow from the relationships these teams create with a customer are enormous. Business schools should perhaps teach students according to similar arrangements.

The point to all of this is not that specialization is dead. Quite the contrary. Robotics engineers are still needed to design CIM software. That job isn't going to be delegated to someone who is responsible primarily for filing tax returns. Moreover, filing tax returns isn't going to be the task of robotics engineers. Workers still specialize. But specialties increasingly are performed in the service of customer needs, not in the service of professional interest groups called departments. People trained in one special field increasingly will join hands with people trained in other specialties to leverage up opportunities for serving customers—not to build empires inside isolated "silos." Business schools have much to learn from business in this regard.

Team-oriented Learning versus Learning Solutions Individually. American university educators insist on the importance of students doing their own work and being graded for their individual performance. Working together usually is classified as cheating. This attitude fits well, perhaps, with the emphasis business schools place on learning how to apply solutions, especially mathematically articulated solutions, to stylized textbook problems. In learning solutions individually, everyone is supposed to end up knowing the same things and seeing the world through the same lenses. Grades are distributed on the basis of demonstrated ability to memorize and regurgitate the party line.

Traditional business education seldom gives students an opportunity to appreciate the power of problem-solving in a team environment. Business professors who preach the virtues of competition among individuals in the same workplace do not properly serve their customers—businesses or students. Competition among individuals, motivated by personal gain at the group's expense, doesn't work in business, and it should not be expected to work in the classroom.

On-the-job Teaching. Learning by doing is an old adage that seems to be terribly applicable to the customer-focused business of the information age. Universities with co-op learning plans have known for a long time the advantages of mixing classroom and on-site work experience. It's time to make the practice universal and make it a major part of the activity in every subject taught in a business school.

Field-based Research. There is little to add to what I said above on this issue, except to emphasize it one more time. Faculty in American business schools since the 1950s have focused on the wrong customer. The ultimate customer is business—the organizations without which there would be no reason to operate business schools. The most appropriate place to learn about business, and to research and develop theories about business is in places of business. If anyone says it is impossible to make scientific generalizations by studying samples of one, tell them they have much to learn about the concept of "scientific" investigation. Going inside and studying intensely over a long period of time the workings of a real business organization is *certainly* the most important research any business professor can do. A socially responsive and enlightened business school will not keep in its employ any business professor who denies the validity—no, the *primacy*—of field-based research. Businesses should stop funding the research programs and hiring the graduates of business schools that refuse to adopt this policy.

Specific Changes in the Business School Curriculum

Changes to the curriculum can not separate what is taught from how it is taught. The primacy of project-oriented team problem solving in business should influence how business courses are taught. That entails, as well, on-the-job learning. Team-oriented and field-based approaches to teaching are new to business school people, but a few business professors are leading the way, including Scott Dawson and Richard Sapp at Portland State University, Harry Davis and Harry Roberts at the University of Chicago, and Mark Finster at the University of Wisconsin.

Business schools have almost no precedent to follow, however, showing the new content that must be taught. Here I believe business schools face some of the most radical changes they have ever made. The main challenge is to infuse into every subject taught—every single class taught every day—a sense of what matters most in running a business where computer-information technology puts the customer in charge of the market and the worker in control of the process. The curriculum should dwell on the two imperatives of global competitiveness: responsiveness and flexibility.

Responsiveness.   The customer in charge of the market is not an altogether alien concept in business curricula. Marketers for decades have articulated what they call "the marketing concept." The problem is that the concept never affected other disciplines. In fact, it has not been widely accepted as the starting point even with marketers. The Quality Crusade, with its emphasis on satisfying and exceeding customer expectations, gives closet adherents to the marketing concept a reason to come out and speak up. Marketers who believe in the concept should go around to all the faculty and ask "What can we do to help people in your field discover what it takes to make a company more responsive to the customer?" Business school deans must give top priority to infusing the marketing concept, and the related notion of customer relationship building, into everything taught in the business school.

Flexibility.   To think of work in terms of series of linked customer-focused processes and to concentrate on continually reducing the lead times of processes is essential to achieving flexibility. Here we draw a complete blank in the existing business curriculum. Tasks and speed, the old Frederick Taylor concerns, are the closest we come to processes and lead time. As usual, what is being taught is antithetical to what must be taught. Who will lead this change? No doubt the operations management people are best equipped to do it. They certainly know about process mapping and lead time concepts, even if the courses they teach seldom focus on those issues. Some already may be teaching JIT, which is a big step in the right direction. If a school has an operations management professor teaching JIT, draft him or her to lead this charge.

After initiating campaigns to inculcate the spirits of responsiveness and flexibility into every corner of the curriculum, the next logical step is to replace all vestiges of top-down control thinking with an appreciation of bottom-up empowerment. Hardly any subject will escape notice here, but the main impact will be in management accounting and financial management. The changed thinking needed in those two subjects is to a large extent the subject of this book. There is little to say here that does not repeat what I have already said in previous chapters. Table 10–1, based on a graphic I have used in academic presentations for several years, summarizes in the left-hand column key principles taught in traditional remote-control management accounting courses

Table 10–1
How the Terms of Competition Affect Management Accounting

Remote-control	Global	Obsolete
• Products cause cost	• Work causes cost	• Cost is fixed/variable
• Cost varies with volume	• Costs vary with work	• Contribution margin
• Contribution covers fixed cost	• Manage resources consumed by work	• Break-even analysis
• Control operations with accounting targets	• Empower workers to control processes	• Control operations with budget variances
• Optimize resource use within constraints	• Continuously remove constraints	• Constrained optimization

and in the middle column the counter-principles dictated by the imperatives of customer-focused global competition.

The right-hand column then lists the topics in traditional management accounting textbooks that are rendered obsolete by the imperatives of global competitiveness. Anyone who has ever taken or taught a course in management accounting in the last thirty years recognizes the right-hand column as virtually a complete list of everything covered in the course. Moreover, items on the list are widely diffused in non-accounting courses.

Rather than teach students how to use accounting targets to motivate people to manipulate (i.e., tamper with) processes, teach them how people use their brains to control processes and satisfy customers. Indeed, when virtually all costs are viewed as "fixed," as surely they must be viewed in global organizations, what is the role of management except to enhance the intellectual power of the work force? This point was made some time ago by Ramchandran Jaikumar: "When the lion's share of costs are sunk before production starts, the creation and management of intellectual assets becomes the prime task of management."[11] Among other things, this implies the need to eliminate all "break-even" cost-volume-profit thinking from the curriculum.

Undoubtedly business schools should get rid of all courses in management accounting control systems. They are the source from which the financial imperatives of remote-control management emanate and they should be banished from the curriculum forever. A similar fate should befall any finance courses or modules within finance courses that teach people to manipulate processes for the sake of achieving accounting results.

Two qualifications should be made at this point. First, there is a need to continue teaching and supporting research in the areas of finance that have to do with modern capital market theory. Perhaps the best home for this subject is an economics department, not a business school. But a business school should not turn away fine finance scholars who teach and study capital market behavior—one of the most exciting and dynamic fields of economic inquiry in the past thirty years. They only should insist that finance professors draw a clear line between managing portfolios of financial instruments and managing businesses whose cash flows underlie the market value of such financial instruments. I certainly want my pension fund to be managed by people expert in modern capital-asset pricing theory. But I don't want the managers of companies whose securities are in that fund to apply that same theory to their tasks. Companies are people, not portfolios of assets. Companies generate free cash flow by empowering workers to control processes that satisfy customer expectations. Professors of finance (or any other subject) should not teach students otherwise.

Another qualification to what I have said about abolishing management accounting control courses is the need to teach students the art and practice of budgeting—to control cash flows, borrowings, and short-term investments. In most business schools the subject of budgeting fell through the cracks a number of years ago. Hence, what I advocate here will involve bringing something back into the curriculum that once was an important component of accounting and finance education, but was relegated to the trash heap of "unscientific" subjects in the 1970s.

In addition to the changes that I recommend be made in management accounting, other changes should alter the tradition of introducing business majors to business with courses in financial accounting and managerial economics. I don't think it would surprise anyone who has read everything in this book to this point if I said the managerial economics course should be scrapped altogether. At best it belongs only in an economics department, never in a business curriculum. In its place I would introduce business students to the field with a good course in the history of management, preferably one following the lines of Alfred Chandler's timeless classic, *The Visible Hand.* After all, the managed business organization is a relatively recent occurrence in human history, hardly antedating the late eighteenth century. The average American living in New England in 1815 scarcely would have understood the concept of business management. Yet, in less than a century Americans would become accustomed to companies on the scale of Standard Oil, U.S. Steel, and General Motors. What an incredible transformation! But how few business instructors, let alone students, know anything about it. The failure of American business schools to feature core courses on the history of business is one of the most grievous of their many serious flaws.

As with managerial economics, I believe business schools should also abolish the practice of introducing students to business with a course in financial accounting. I already have given many reasons why I believe accounting is no longer the language of business in the information age. The language of business now is the language of processes and customers. We should introduce students to business by teaching them the primary language of processes, statistical process control (SPC)—the language of variation. Business schools should teach students (and themselves!) what variation is, what its consequences are, and how you control and reduce it. No accounting system has ever told anyone if a process is in control or if a customer is satisfied.

That does not mean accounting is banished from the curriculum. Far from it. All business graduates should be familiar with the traditional accounting modes of reporting financial results—balance sheets, income statements, and so forth. That knowledge could be gleaned, however, in one or two courses at the end of a program, not at the start. Accounting majors, of course, will need courses in accounting much earlier in their programs. Perhaps their programs, especially those geared to producing CPAs, should be hived off from business schools and taught in separate departments, like law programs. Indeed, law schools might be a good place to locate schools or departments of accounting, given the highly legalistic concern with accounting regulations that seems to dominate most accounting students' time these days.

One could go on and on articulating ideas for reforming American business school education in the 1990s. Most important is the need for business schools to take action, to begin experiments leading to reform. In that spirit my colleagues and I in the School of Business at Portland State University in Portland, Oregon, are embarked on a far-reaching quality initiative. It is too early to tell where our efforts will lead, but the goal of the initiative is clear: to create undergraduate and graduate business programs that enable students and employers to compete in the global economy. In effect, our goal is to create the customer-focused quality-oriented programs that all American business schools should have built in the last twenty years. I believe this entails a radical overhaul of curriculum—both what is taught and how it is taught—faculty research, and administrative procedures used to run the school.[12]

Quality-focused reform initiatives as broadly conceived as that at Portland State University are also underway at business schools in other universities such as Rochester Institute of Technology, University of Chicago, University of Wisconsin, and University of Tennessee. Like runners carrying the torch at the start of Olympics games, these schools are eager and willing to pass on the flame they have kindled. If you are associated with or know of a business school that desires to play an active part in helping business compete in the global economy, contact the Dean of Business at Portland State University or one of the other schools named here. The combined efforts of scores of business schools can, I believe, restore relevance to American business education.

WRAP-UP

For over thirty years university business schools in the United States have failed to understand or teach the skills and knowledge businesses need to compete in the global economy. Businesses are beginning to realize that customer-focused empowerment of the work force is the key to world-class competitiveness in the information age. It is time for business schools to join the revolution. Those that don't join, soon, will pass from being merely irrelevant to being extinct.

Indeed, business schools are uniquely suited to contribute vital theory and research to the revolution now sweeping the business world. But they cannot make this contribution until they end the tyranny that the economic theory of the firm exercises over their research and teaching. Neoclassical economic theory provides the main rationale for cost-focused, remote-control management by financial results. That theory does not consider people or time as important determinants of competitiveness. Business professors must begin at once to build new theory, based on careful field research in managed organizations. Like Copernicus and Brahe studying the heavens nearly five hundred years ago, business professors today have much to do just to "measure" the phenomenon they purport to study. But the work done so far suggests that JIT and TQM thinking contain elements of a new theory of business, such as time-based management, customer focus, supplier relationship building, and employee empowerment. It is time to combine these elements, and more to come, in a theory that explains how businesses can develop human talents as they efficiently allocate society's resources. Then professors, as good scientists, should articulate and test refutable hypotheses derived from that new business theory. This is an enormous task that business professors should be uniquely equipped to solve.

Businesses must help business schools pursue this task. Businesses should not passively accept what business schools do, mindlessly donate to their faculty development funds, and unquestioningly hire their graduates. They should actively investigate faculty research and teaching. Ask to read copies of faculty research, ask to attend faculty seminars, ask for copies of course syllabuses, and ask to attend classes. Most who do so, I can guarantee, will be shocked at what they see and hear. However, they should not be afraid to speak up if they feel the emperor is not properly attired. And those who feel stunned should vow not to write another check supporting a business school's programs and not to hire another graduate until change occurs. Then get involved in helping that change occur! Business schools that receive such attention, and listen, will be the survivors. The others will continue marching resolutely in the direction virtually all American business schools are now headed, and enjoy a long rest in the tar pits.

CHAPTER 11

THE INFORMATION
REVOLUTION REVISITED

The objective of most corporate leaders is to use people to make a great company. My objective is to use the company to make great people.

— Ralph C. Stayer[1]

By giving the customer power to control markets and the work force power to control processes, new information technologies enable businesses to enhance human potential on a scale never before imagined. To lose that opportunity by failing to change our management thinking and management practices would be a monumental tragedy. Moreover, the forces giving rise to the need for new management thinking have parallel influences that extend far beyond business organizations. The information revolution that makes it imperative to replace top-down control with bottom-up empowerment in businesses is the same force driving the collapse of centrally controlled state economies in Eastern Europe and the Soviet Union. There, too, one sees painfully the need for new thinking and new practices. But underlying the new thinking required by these changes in business and in governments is a pervasive theme in modern history—how to balance the tension between the dignity and rights of the individual and the power of the community.

INFORMATION TRANSFORMS BUSINESSES

As this book shows, the information revolution is beginning to alter profoundly the nature of business. Perhaps the most significant change involves the relationship between managers and workers. In the past managers tended to regard employees as their tools, mere implements to be used and maneuvered to achieve management's goals. The information revolution, however, requires *and enables* managers to empower employees, joining with them in the common venture of interpreting and satisying customer wants and needs. Autocratic, hierarchical control must give way to a cooperative exchange of information and ideas throughout the organization, an exchange involving the insights and perspective of informed workers. A tide of information now allows the work force to assume responsibility for their particular undertakings. They must be empowered now to analyze information, identify problems, and propose solutions.

Bottom-up information systems permit *everyone* in an organization to participate in analysis, planning, and action. Over ten years ago, Peters and Waterman remarked that a "bias for action" distinguished well-managed organizations. They referred primarily to a propensity of managers to act without waiting upon top-down instructions or the results of staff-level analysis. Today it is essential for everyone in an organization—workers and managers—to display a "bias for action." Having detected a customer need or wish, the employee in the well-managed firm must formulate a response and act on it promptly. This rapid response presupposes empowered workers. Unfortunately, few companies evidence this "bias for action." Few companies empower employees to act as responsible, analytical, committed individuals dedicated to the good of the organization.

If companies are to compete in global markets they must abandon the conventional practice of putting exclusively in top management's hands all significant information and authority. Were the world of business today more stable, less changing, and more predictable—in other words, were it more like it was from the 1950s to the 1980s—then autocracy might work. Then top managers could collect and assess accounting information and issue decrees based on their self-contained analysis. But the volatile external environment of the 1990s changes constantly and almost instantaneously, and its prodigious changes compel doing business a new way. Bottom-up information allows workers to appraise their respective processes. Workers for the first time have access to virtually immediate feedback about the nature and implications of their particular tasks. Made recipients of significant knowledge, workers are now in a position to *participate* in important decisions. No longer mute laborers at the bottom quietly awaiting orders from on high, today workers can react intelligently to information about customers and processes, identify the essential response, and act.

Inevitably, contemplating the contemporary business world forces the question: "Why should any worker accept empowerment?" Why should the worker care? Why should even a superbly informed worker assigned tremendous freedom to act care about the good of the organization? The reply to this question is that people care about groups they belong to, groups that exist in part for their own well-being, groups that dignify, honor, and respect individuals. Groups such as these are communities. Communities see each member as unique and valuable. Businesses that value employees will have dedicated employees. However, businesses commonly act as though the worker's value resides entirely and exclusively in his or her performance of a task. Just as nation states which wholly subordinate the person to the state fail to inspire loyalty and dedication, so, too, businesses fail to inspire dedication when they devalue the worker.

To build a sense of community, inspiring workers to seek and accept empowerment, demands creating a strong sense of mission, identifying the company's values, and showing every person how his or her work fulfills that mission. Shared values, a common mission, and awareness of one's role in fulfilling that mission create a harmonious organization with enthusiastic employees. This is a far cry from the commands and controls transmitted to workers by traditional top-down strategic planning and analysis. Indeed, the remote-control managers' bias for strategic financial planning and analysis is the main reason most companies fail to show a "bias for action." Believing that change comes only from the top, and only after careful analysis of the implications of a proposed change, companies assume workers exist only to implement instructions, not to ask questions and initiate changes. In such companies, action is dependent almost entirely on strategic financial planning and analysis, the foundation to top-down command and control. Action is simply programmed response to plan, following analysis. One insidious consequence that results after years of running businesses by the numbers is the widespread belief that the work force lacks the ability to initiate action without instructions. Another result is that top management loses its own willingness to act without the guidance of an analytic model. Everyone is crippled by slavish adherence to the cult of top-down strategic planning and analysis.

Bottom-up empowerment eliminates much of the need for traditional strategic planning, reinforcing Richard Schonberger's view that "the best strategy is doing things better and better in the trenches"[2] and supporting social psychologist Karl Weick's concept of "just-in-time strategies" which, according to Weick, "are distinguished by less investment in front-end loading (try to anticipate everything that will happen or that you will need) and more investment in general knowledge, a large skill repertoire, the ability to do a quick study, trust in intuitions, and sophistication in cutting losses."[3] With just-in-time strategies, learning and choice become part of daily work, not the exclusive domain of planners at the top. Planning and innovation become synonymous with real-time operations. *Operations become strategic.* Strategy, instead of being defined by top-down concerns with financial results, is defined by bottom-up concern with improving processes that satisfy customers' expectations and that fulfill workers' potential. Here, the line between innovation and continuous improvement becomes blurred. The concept known as "strategy deployment" becomes a primary means to bond operations and strategy, making daily improvements a pathway to larger-scale innovation. No longer is the worker viewed as solely responsible for doing well within the process, and management viewed as solely responsible for changing the process. Now everyone does both.

The power of information technology to make operations strategic is articulated by Shoshana Zuboff, who points out that the new silicon-based information technology, unlike earlier generations of machine technology, does not merely help the accomplishment of tasks by imposing information (i.e., programmed instructions) on people; it also translates tasks into information.[4] She equates the use of instructions to accomplish tasks with automation—an extension of the process of substituting machines for human effort that goes back to the nineteenth century. But the capacity of information technology to translate tasks, events, and objects into information—making them visible, knowable, and shareable in ways never before possible—she defines with the word "informate." The new information technology informates as well as automates.

This distinction between the automative and the informative power of information technology is not well understood by most business people today. Too often what is sought is automation—use of information's powers to make existing tasks faster and more reliable

by making them less dependant upon human actions. This uses powerful new information technology to perpetuate the trappings of remote-
control management—a terrible waste of opportunity. Overlooked is
the opportunity to exploit the "informating" possibilities in new information technologies. As Zuboff puts it, "The informating capacity of
the new computer-based technologies . . . poses fundamentally new
choices for organizational futures, and the ways in which labor and
management respond to these new choices will finally determine
whether our era becomes a time for radical change or a return to the
familiar patterns and pitfalls of the traditional workplace."

The choice, whether to use new information technologies to reinforce top-down tendencies of the past or to capture new opportunities
for empowerment that will enhance competitiveness in the future, is
top management's to make. It will take strong leaders, visionary leaders, to make the organizational changes that permit a business to capture the opportunities presented by new information technologies. Ultimately those leaders will create organizations that become competitive
by promoting learning as "the heart of productive activity."[5]

Obviously the change from command-and-control to learning-
based production will not come quickly or easily. Perhaps the toughest
hurdle to cross on the way to this change is the need for companies to
remove old accounting-based management information systems that
drive the work force both to persuade customers and to manipulate
processes. But I believe individual companies will have no other choice
in the long run. The dynamic of global competitiveness makes it necessary for companies to replace top-down control systems with bottom-
up empowerment. Companies that refuse to make the change will fail
to be competitive in the long run.

INFORMATION, CAPITALISM, AND DEMOCRACY

A dramatic analogy to the fate of businesses clinging to obsolete modes
of remote-control management is provided by recent events in Eastern
Europe and the Soviet Union. These events vividly demonstrate the
destructive effects of authoritarian government. Denied freedom,
knowledge, a voice in decision making, coerced into blank submission,
ordered merely to obey orders, the citizen loses heart. These people
have forgotten how to care. Having ignored the talents and wisdom of
its people, the Soviet Union became a maimed giant mired in squalor
of its own making, peopled by helpless robots who have forgotten how
to work or take initiative.

Mismanaged companies stand to fail as dismally as have the Soviet countries. Most American businesses today operate with top-down remote financial controls, keeping information in the hands of top managers, issuing mandates to worker-qua-tool. Such organizations fail, as did the Soviet Union, to empower the individual. They fail to give the individual information and the freedom to act on the basis of that information. But only by making workers into thinkers and doers will firms inspire workers to excel. The top-down managed enterprise deprives itself of the fresh, vital, creative ideas of dedicated, knowledgable employees. Kept in the dark, treated like machines, workers in badly managed firms are as dispirited as citizens in dictatorships.

Differences in performance among companies will result from differences in the quality and dissemination of information. Companies will surely thrive as they use information to empower workers and elicit advice from workers and customers alike. Companies will underperform if they cling to top-down remote controls, soliciting responses neither from workers nor customers. Eventually such ill-managed organizations will collapse or be taken over. The dynamic of the information revolution makes these predictions certain for businesses.

But the message in these events is not that businesses must strengthen free market tendencies inside companies, to make them more productive and competitive. Companies are not served well by being told that employees, and managers, should emulate conditions associated with atomistic free-market competition. Of that American companies already have had enough, to the point where individualistic competitiveness among managers and subunits inside many companies has destroyed any sense of communal goals and social purpose.

Centrally directed American businesses in the past forty years have tended to eschew building strong relationships—social and communal bonds that join company with customer, company with supplier, and company with its work force. Instead, they have moved toward atomistic, individualistic competitiveness. Of course, incentive and reward systems encourage this move. But pressure to compete as individuals surely erodes the capacity of people to build strong, lasting communal relationships. Many times, however, people view this erosion favorably, as a sign of free-market-style forces at work counteracting the evils of centralized bureaucracy. That viewpoint ignores the difference between the arms-length competition among individuals that increases productivity in markets and the cooperative group activity that is needed to improve competitiveness inside companies.

The productivity of companies that empower people is achieved, paradoxically, by cultivating a tension between opposites—the tension that exists between the talents of the individual and the power of teamwork. Obviously, the talents of individuals can be snuffed out by oppressive controls from above, or from the group. What is needed for maximum performance is balance—a mutual surrender of the group and the individual to higher goals and improved results. Companies thrive by cultivating the specialized talents of capable individuals. There are economies to gain from specialization. But there also are gains to be had from coordinated communication and learning among individuals working in customer-focused processes. No matter how talented and smart each individual is, a customer-focused team of individuals is always capable of doing more than all its members working alone.

American business in the last forty years—indeed American society generally—has sacrificed the power of teamwork and community to the quest for individual self-gratification. In the case of companies this development is most evident in the obsessive attention paid to the interests of the stockholder. American companies focus everyone's efforts on the narrow interests of one group—the stockholders—at the expense of the interests of those who serve in and are served by companies. In the end, society and stockholders both have experienced enormous long-term losses of opportunity and wealth.

Indeed, the central institution of our capitalistic system, the privately owned corporation, has failed until very recently to take advantage of the strength inherent in democratic institutions. Most corporations seem intent on combining the free-market model of atomistic competition with militaristic models of command and control hierarchy. Leaders of businesses, especially in the United States, should recognize the importance of patterning their companies on the democratic ideal of prizing the individual's uniqueness while expecting every individual to share responsibility for the commonweal. In the American business system of the last forty years, corporate capitalism has not created a world of action where everyone works to fulfill an edifying mission. Countless businesses do not communicate with, and learn from, an empowered work force. This condition threatens the power of our companies to compete and, ultimately, it jeopardizes their ability to survive. Their demise diminishes opportunities for all Americans to find and enjoy satisfying jobs.

WRAP-UP

Unfortunately, the management themes discussed in this book often tend to be couched in terms of Japan versus The West. That view of these themes will be destructive if self-serving Western business and political leaders use Japan-bashing as an excuse to turn inward and defend the status quo. In fact, the management revolution discussed here has little to do with Japan, the West, or any other group. It reflects enormous opportunity created by profound technological developments. That opportunity is open to any person, company, or nation that is willing to change. The opportunity will be lost to those who refuse to abandon thinking and practices of the past.

APPENDIX: WHERE TO
TURN FOR HELP

Readers of *Relevance Regained* who wish to pursue the development of ideas and practices discussed in this book will not find it easy to locate an association, group, or periodical publication dedicated to the study and practice of bottom-up empowerment. Virtually all professional societies, business groups, and business periodicals promote the interests of specialists who work in one or more of the traditional functional silos, such as production control, inventory management, management accounting, internal auditing, cost management, marketing, quality control, finance, and so forth. The programs of those groups and periodicals evolved in a business world where information and power reside at the top, and actions at the bottom rely on instructions from above. These associations, groups and magazines appeal primarily to specialists in middle management ranks who translate and transmit information and instructions up and down the hierarchy. They pay less attention to the needs of companies and general managers who appreciate the need to adopt entirely new ways of doing business in the 1990s.

However, I see signs of change in the right direction appearing in a few organizations. One example is the Association for Manufacturing Excellence (AME), an organization of companies and individuals dedicated to improving the competitiveness of all businesses in the global economy. The AME offers a wide variety of workshops, company visits, and meetings that keep people abreast of new business practices such as those discussed in *Relevance Regained*. Especially notable is the AME's bimonthly periodical known as *Target*. Referred to by management authority Tom Peters as the "best business periodical published in the United States," *Target* provides a wealth of articles on actual company practices as well as articles on the latest management concepts. In my opinion, the workshops of AME and *Target* provide an excellent source of information about bottom-up management. For further information about membership call AME headquarters at (708) 520-3282 or write AME at 380 West Palatine Road, Wheeling, IL 60090.

A second organization that deserves serious consideration is the American Society for Quality Control. Founded in 1946 to serve quality control and quality assurance specialists, the ASQC in recent years has expanded its menu of interest groups, conferences, and publications devoted to total quality management. Especially useful is the ASQC's monthly publication, *Quality Progress*. Readers interested in learning more about ASQC should call 1-800-248-1946 or write to 611 East Wisconsin Avenue, Milwaukee, Wisconsin, 53202.

Aside from organizations such as AME and ASQC, the best source of help and advice on the issues discussed in *Revelance Regained* is people in your own community who are trying to transform their workplaces, to create opportunities for more customer satisfaction and more fulfilling jobs. "Quality networks" are springing up all over the United States, often patterned after well-established models in cities such as Lawrence (Massachusetts), Philadelphia (Pennsylvania), and Madison (Wisconsin). Join a network if one exists in your area; help start one if your area does not already have a network.

I always am glad to share information with anyone who writes or calls. I also like to hear from companies who are willing to share their experiences with me. Please feel free to contact me at the following address and numbers:

Professor H. Thomas Johnson
School of Business Administration
Portland State University
Portland, OR 97207-0751 USA
phone: (503) 725-4771
fax: (503) 725-4882

NOTES

PREFACE

1. A similar point about results-oriented versus process-oriented management is one of the key themes in Masaaki Imai, *Kaizen: The Key to Japan's Competitive Success* (New York: Random House, 1986), especially pp. 16–21, 46, and 227–228.

CHAPTER 1   INFORMATION, ACTION, AND BUSINESS PERFORMANCE

1. W. Edwards Deming, *Out of the Crisis* (Cambridge, MA: MIT Center for Advanced Engineering Study, 1986), selected sentences from pp. ix–x.
2. Richard S. Teitelbaum, "LBOs Really Didn't Pay, Say the Chiefs," *Fortune* (August 26, 1991), pp. 73–76.
3. H. Thomas Johnson and Robert S. Kaplan, *Relevance Lost: The Rise and Fall of Management Accounting* (Boston: Harvard Business School Press, 1987), p.1.

CHAPTER 2   REMOTE-CONTROL MANAGEMENT IN THE DARK AGE OF RELEVANCE LOST

1. Albert Lee, *Call Me Roger* (Chicago: Contemporary Books, 1988), p. 110.
2. The historical material in this chapter draws extensively on ideas from H. Thomas Johnson, "Managing by Remote Control: Recent Management Accounting Practice in Historical Perspective," in Peter Temin, ed., *Inside the Business Enterprise: Historical Perspectives on the Use of Information* (Chicago: The University of Chicago Press, 1991), pp. 41–66.
3. Daniel M. G. Raff and Peter Temin articulate these levels of decisions in "Business History and Recent Economic Theory: Imperfect Information, Incentives, and the Internal Organization," in Temin, ed., *Inside the Business Enterprise*.
4. This paragraph is based on material from Johnson and Kaplan, *Relevance Lost: The Rise and Fall of Management Accounting* (Boston: Harvard Business School Press, 1987), ch. 4 (esp. p. 85).
5. H. Thomas Johnson, "The Decline of Cost Management: A Reinterpretation of 20th-Century Cost Accounting History," *Journal of Cost Management* (Spring 1987), 5–12.
6. Johnson and Kaplan, *Relevance Lost*
7. Ibid.
8. Ibid.

9. Robert H. Hayes and William J. Abernathy, "Managing Our Way to Economic Decline," *Harvard Business Review* (July-August 1980), pp. 67–77.

10. The following section is adapted from H. Thomas Johnson, "Beyond Product Costing: A Challenge to Cost Management's Conventional Wisdom," *Journal of Cost Management* (Fall 1990), pp. 17–19.

11. *The Republic of Plato,* translated by Francis M. Cornford (New York: Oxford University Press, 1945), pp. 227–229.

12. Alfred D. Chandler, Jr., *Strategy and Structure: Chapters in the History of the American Industrial Enterprise* (Cambridge, MA: The M.I.T. Press, 1962); Oliver E. Williamson, *Markets and Hierarchies:Analysis and Antitrust Implications* (New York: The Free Press, 1975).

13. This quotation and the several that follow are from Hayes and Abernathy, "Managing Our Way to Economic Decline," pp. 67–77.

14. The quotations from Hayes and Abernathey in this paragraph and several that follow are from "Managing Our Way to Economic Decline."

15. Robert H. Hayes, Steven C. Wheelwright, and Kim B. Clark, *Dynamic Manufacturing: Creating the Learning Organization* (New York: The Free Press, 1988), p. 56.

16. Ibid., p. 57.

17. The following paragraphs on Carnegie, Sloan, and portfolio strategy are taken from Johnson, "Managing by Remote Control," pp. 49–50 and 61.

18. Joseph Frazier Wall, *Andrew Carnegie* (New York: Oxford University Press, 1970), p. 337.

19. Ibid., p. 350.

20. Ibid., p. 348.

21. Ibid., p. 352.

22. Henry Ford (in collaboration with Samuel Crowther), *Today and Tomorrow* (Cambridge, MA: Productivity Press, 1988 reprint edition. Original edition by Doubleday, Page & Company, 1926), p. 29.

23. Ibid., p. 44.

24. Statement attributed to Sloan in Lee, *Call Me Roger*, p. 90.

25. Max Holland, *When the Machine Stopped: A Cautionary Tale from Industrial America* (Boston: Harvard Business School Press, 1987).

26. The Mesta story is told in Hayes, Wheelwright, and Clark, *Dynamic Manufacturing*, pp. 33–35. The direct quotations that follow in this paragraph are all from p. 35.

CHAPTER 3 CONSEQUENCES OF REMOTE-CONTROL MANAGEMENT

1. Russell Ackoff, *Creating The Corporate Future* (New York: John Wiley & Sons, 1981), p. 18.

2. Richard J. Schonberger, *Japanese Manufacturing Techniques* (New York: The Free Press, 1982), p. 157.

3. Takao Tanaka, "Two Giants, Mitsubishi and Toyota: A Historical Study of Management Accounting in Japan," unpublished paper delivered to the Annual Meeting of the American Accounting Association (August 1989), esp. pp. 17–18; Alfred J. Nanni, Jr., "Automation and Management Accounting in Japan," *Accounting: A Newsletter for Educators* (New York: John Wiley, 1991); Callie Berliner and James A. Brimson, eds., *Cost Management for Today's Advanced Manufacturing* (Boston: Harvard Business School Press, 1988), ch. 9.

4. Daniel M. G. Raff, "Making Cars and Making Money in the Interwar Automobile Industry: The Manufacturing that Stood Behind the Marketing," unpublished Harvard Business School working paper; David A. Hounshell, *From the American System to Mass Production, 1800–1932: The Development of Manufacturing Technology in the United States* (Baltimore: The Johns Hopkins University Press, 1984), ch. 7.

5. Henry Ford (in collaboration with Samuel Crowther), *Today and Tomorrow* (Cambridge, MA: Productivity Press, 1988 reprint edition. Original edition by Doubleday, Page & Company, 1926).

6. Ibid., p. 107.

7. Ibid., pp. 114, 112, 118.

8. Taiichi Ohno, *Toyota Production System: Beyond Large-Scale Production* (1978; translated and reprinted by Productivity Press, 1988), ch. 5.

9. David Halberstam, *The Reckoning* (New York: William Morrow, 1986), p. 81.

10. On how Ford's system evolved from being completely dedicated to typifying "flexible mass production" see Hounshell, *From the American System to Mass Production,* ch. 7.

11. Two sources that develop several of the ideas I express in the next two sections are: Michael A. Cusumano, *The Japanese Automobile Industry* (Cambridge, MA: Harvard University Press, 1985), ch. 5; James Gooch, Michael George, and Douglas Montgomery, *America Can Compete!* (Dallas, TX: Institute of Business Technology, 1987), passim.

12. A theory of focused operations is set out in Wickham Skinner, *Manufacturing in the Corporate Strategy* (New York: John Wiley, 1978).

13. The Toyota story as told by Taiichi Ohno is found in his *Toyota Production System: Beyond Large-Scale Production* (1978); *Workplace Management* (1982); and *Just-In-Time for Today and Tomorrow* (1986). All three books are translated and reprinted by Productivity Press, Inc. of Cambridge, MA.

14. W. Edwards Deming, "Statistical Techniques and International Trade," *The Journal of Marketing* (October 1952), pp. 428–433.

15. James P. Womack, Daniel T. Jones, and Daniel Roos, *The Machine That Changed The World* (New York: Rawson Associates, 1990), pp. 119–126.

16. John K. Shank's comments on a panel presented to the 1989 Annual Meeting of the American Accounting Association, in "Contribution Margin Analysis," edited by Michael A. Robinson, *Journal of Management Accounting Research* (Fall 1990), pp. 17–19.

17. The remainder of this section is based largely on H. Thomas Johnson, "Using Cost Targets to Control Operating Performance," in Robert W. Hall, H. T. Johnson, and P. Turney, *Measuring Up: Charting Pathways to Manufacturing Excellence* (Homewood, IL: Dow Jones-Irwin, 1990), pp. 61–69. I want to thank Robert Hall and Roy Shapiro for contributing many suggestions to improve this material.

18. Jeffrey G. Miller and Thomas E. Vollmann, "The Hidden Factory," *Harvard Business Review* (September-October 1985), pp. 142–151.

19. The evils of standard cost performance measurement systems are recounted both in H. Thomas Johnson, "Performance Measurement for Competitive Excellence," in Robert S. Kaplan, ed., *Measures for Manufacturing Excellence* (Boston: Harvard Business School Press, 1990), pp. 63–90, and in Robert S. Kaplan,

"Accounting Lag: The Obsolescence of Cost Accounting Systems," in Kim B. Clark, Robert H. Hayes and Christopher Lorenz, eds., *The Uneasy Alliance: Managing the Productivity-Technology Dilemma* (Boston: Harvard Business School Press, 1985), pp. 195–226.

20. Descriptions of these systems are found in most of the popular university cost accounting textbooks.
21. William S. Scherkenbach, *The Deming Route to Quality and Productivity* (Milwaukee, WI: ASQC Quality Press, 1986), pp. 31–34.
22. On GE see H. Thomas Johnson, "Performance Measurement for Competitive Excellence." On Harley-Davidson see William T. Turk, "Management Accounting Revitalized: The Harley-Davidson Experience," *Journal of Cost Management* (Winter 1990), pp. 28–39.
23. I first heard Brian Joiner use this high-jump metaphor.

CHAPTER 4   IMPERATIVES OF COMPETITION—PAST AND PRESENT

1. John Browning, "The Ubiquitous Machine," *The Economist* (June 16, 1990), section on information technology, p. 5
2. Peter F. Drucker, *The New Realities* (New York: Harper & Row, 1989), p. 256.
3. Ibid., p. 262.
4. Ibid., p. 259.
5. Taiichi Ohno, *Toyota Production System: Beyond Large-Scale Production* (Cambridge, MA: Productivity Press, 1988 translation of 1978 Japanese text), pp. 97, 100, 107, 109.
6. David A. Hounshell, *From the American System to Mass Production, 1800–1932* (Baltimore: The Johns Hopkins University Press, 1984), p. 252.
7. Ernest C. Huge (with Alan D. Anderson), *The Spirit of Manufacturing Excellence: An Executive's Guide to the New Mind Set* (Homewood, IL: Dow Jones-Irwin, 1988), p. 108.
8. Drucker, *The New Realities*, p. 256.
9. See both Ramchandran Jaikumar, "An Architecture for a Process Control Costing System," in Robert S. Kaplan, ed., *Measures for Manufacturing Excellence* (Boston: Harvard Business School Press, 1990), pp. 193–222, and Shoshana Zuboff, *In the Age of the Smart Machine* (New York: Basic Books, 1988).
10. Susan Moffat, "Japan's New Personalized Production," *Fortune* (October 22, 1990), pp. 132–135.
11. "King Customer," *Business Week* (March 12, 1990), p. 88.
12. Ibid.
13. Alex Taylor III, "Here Come the New Luxury Cars," *Fortune* (July 2, 1990), pp. 58–65.
14. I first heard this idea expressed by John M. Thompson, Vice Chairman of Index Group Inc. The same idea also is a central theme in Stanley M. Davis, *Future Perfect* (Reading, MA: Addison-Wesley, 1987).

CHAPTER 5   BECOMING RESPONSIVE BY BUILDING LONG-TERM CUSTOMER RELATIONSHIPS

1. Theodore Levitt, *The Marketing Imagination* (New York: The Free Press, 1983), p. 111.

2. Peter F. Drucker, *Management: Tasks, Responsibilities, Practices* (New York: Harper & Row, 1973), p. 61.

3. Levitt, *The Marketing Imagination*, p. 142.

4. A good example of this thinking is in Christopher W. L. Hart, James L. Heskett, and W. Earl Sasser, Jr., "The Profitable Art of Service Recovery," *Harvard Business Review* (July-August 1990), pp. 148–156.

5. The distinction between transactions and relationships discussed in the next three paragraphs was developed in joint work with F. Brown Whittington and Barbara Feinberg done for the Customer-Focused Activity Management (CFAM) project at Arthur Andersen & Co. in 1989–1990, under the direction of Robert J. Berling, Jr. I thank Brown Whittington and Barbara Feinberg for contributing to this concept and to ideas elsewhere in this chapter.

6. I thank Robert J. Berling, Jr. and members of the 1989–1990 Arthur Andersen & Co. CFAM team for this example, the Alpha-Beta example that follows, and other anecdotes that have contributed to this chapter.

7. Geoffrey Colvin, "The Wee Outfit That Decked IBM," *Fortune* (November 19, 1990), pp. 165–168.

8. Levitt, *The Marketing Imagination*, p. 167.

9. The most ambitious research into relationships between customer retention and long-term profitability has been done by the Technical Assistance Research Programs (TARP), located in Washington, D.C.

10. An interesting approach to using customer-level cost and profitability information is found in Randy Myer, "Suppliers—Manage Your Customers," *Harvard Business Review* (November-December 1989), pp. 160 – 168.

11. Levitt, *The Marketing Imagination*, pp. 166–167. Italics added.

12. See Richard J. Schonberger, *Building a Chain of Customers* (New York: The Free Press, 1990) for a practical and comprehensive discussion of steps entailed in focusing an organization on satisfying internal customers.

13. Based on James P. Womack, Daniel T. Jones, and Daniel Roos, *The Machine That Changed The World* (New York: Rawson Associates, 1990), pp. 178–191.

14. Based on Paul B. Brown, "The Real Cost of Customer Service," *Inc.* (September 1990), pp. 49–60.

15. Ibid., p. 58.

16. Ibid., p. 60.

17. A frequently cited source of such studies is TARP (see note 9 above).

18. I first heard Stanley M. Davis present this idea.

19. Levitt, *The Marketing Imagination*, pp. 166–167.

CHAPTER 6 BECOMING FLEXIBLE BY EMPOWERING WORKERS TO REMOVE CONSTRAINTS

1. Ramchandran Jaikumar, "Postindustrial Manufacturing," *Harvard Business Review* (November-December 1986), p. 75.

2. Robert W. Hall and Jinichiro Nakane, *Flexibility: Manufacturing Battlefield of the 90s* (Wheeling, IL: Association for Manufacturing Excellence, 1990).

3. Interview with Ohno quoted in Isao Shinohara, *NPS: New Production System*, English translation edition (Cambridge, MA: Productivity Press, 1988), p. 147.

4. I am grateful to Robert W. Hall for help in formulating this list.

5. Jaikumar, "Postindustrial Manufacturing."

6. Tom Peters, "The retooling of a 'nightmarish' manufacturing process," *The Business Journal* (February 4, 1991), p. 16.

7. This experiment resembles one often suggested by Shigeo Shingo. For example, see " 'Eliminate Waste!' Is a Nonsensical Slogan" in Shigeo Shingo, *The Sayings of Shigeo Shingo: Key Strategies for Plant Improvement,* English translation edition (Cambridge, MA: Productivity Press, 1987), pp. 19–20.

8. On the subject of JIT-induced stress see Janice A. Klein, "The Human Costs of Manufacturing Reform," *Harvard Business Review* (March-April 1989), pp. 60–66.

9. Jaikumar, "Postindustrial Manufacturing," pp. 69–76.

10. Ibid., p. 70.

CHAPTER 7 MANAGEMENT INFORMATION FOR COMPETITIVE EXCELLENCE

1. Steven C. Wheelwright, "Restoring the Competitive Edge in U.S. Manufacturing," in David J. Teece, ed., *The Competitive Challenge: Strategies for Industrial Innovation and Renewal* (New York: Harper & Row, 1987), p. 90.

2. Ralph Stayer, "CEO Opinion: The Flight of the Buffalo," *Target* (Spring 1990), p. 21.

3. Ibid., p. 20.

4. Adapted from Richard J. Schonberger, *World Class Manufacturing Casebook: Implementing JIT and TQC* (New York: The Free Press, 1987), pp. xi —xxiii.

5. Richard J. Schonberger, *Building a Chain of Customers* (New York: The Free Press, 1990), p. 96.

6. The example in this paragraph is taken from H. Thomas Johnson, "Managing by Remote Control: Recent Management Accounting Practice in Historical Perspective," in Peter Temin, ed., *Inside the Business Enterprise: Historical Perspectives on the Use of Information* (Chicago: The University of Chicago Press, 1991), p. 59.

7. The remainder of this paragraph and the next two paragraphs are taken from Johnson, "Managing by Remote Control," p. 61.

8. David Allen, "Strategic Financial Management," in Michael Bromwich and Anthony G. Hopwood, eds., *Research and Current Issues in Management Accounting* (London: Pitman Publishing, 1986), pp. 48–49.

9. T. C. Davis, "How the Du Pont Organization Appraises its Performance," *AMA Financial Management Series No. 94* (New York: American Management Association, 1950).

10. J. Shank and N. Churchill, "Variance Analysis: A Management-Oriented Approach," *Accounting Review* (October 1977), pp. 950–57.

11. Alfred Rappaport, *Creating Shareholder Value* (New York: The Free Press, 1986).

12. The Gordian Knot analogy is discussed in J. Robb Dixon, Alfred J. Nanni, and Thomas E. Vollmann, *The New Performance Challenge: Measuring Operations for World-Class Competition* (Homewood, IL: Dow Jones-Irwin, 1990), pp. 21–22 and 32–36.

13. Ibid., p. 22.

14. Schonberger, *Building a Chain of Customers,* p. 187.
15. Robert W. Hall, "Measuring Progress: Manufacturing Essential," *Target* (Summer 1987), p. 7.
16. This account of Company J is based on correspondence and interviews with Kenneth J. McGuire, President of Manufacturing Excellence Action Coalition in Simsbury, Connecticut.
17. Schonberger, *Building a Chain of Customer,* pp. 194–198.
18. Ramchandran Jaikumar, "An Architecture for a Process Control Costing System," in Robert S. Kaplan, ed., *Measures for Manufacturing Excellence* (Boston: Harvard Business School Press, 1990), pp. 193–222.
19. Ibid., p. 217.
20. Robert S. Kaplan, "Texas Eastman Company," Harvard Business School case 190–039 (1989).
21. See comments regarding Daihatsu Motor Company in Toshiro Hiromoto, "Another Hidden Edge—Japanese Management Accounting," *Harvard Business Review* (July-August 1988), pp. 23–24.
22. This section is taken from H. Thomas Johnson, "Using Cost Targets to Control Operating Performance," in Robert W. Hall, H. Thomas Johnson, and P. Turney, *Measuring Up: Charting Pathways to Manufacturing Excellence* (Homewood, IL: Richard D. Irwin, 1990), pp. 79–81.
23. Graham R. Mitchell and William F. Hamilton, "Managing R&D as a Strategic Option," *Research: Technology and Management* (May-June 1988), pp. 15–22.
24. Robert S. Kaplan, "Must CIM Be Justified by Faith Alone?" *Harvard Business Review* (March-April 1986), pp. 87–95.
25. William T. Turk, "Management Accounting Revitalized: The Harley-Davidson Experience," *The Journal of Cost Management* (Winter 1990), pp. 28–39.

CHAPTER 8 ACTIVITY-BASED COST MANAGEMENT: RELEVANCE LOST *DÉJÀ VU*

1. Theodore Levitt, "From The Editor," *Harvard Business Review* (November-December 1989), p. 8.
2. Ralph C. Stayer, "CEO Opinion: The Flight of the Buffalo," *Target* (Spring 1990), p. 18.
3. General Electric, "Lower Business Costs: A Method for Evaluating Indirect Effort" (ENS-A-179A, July 1964).
4. Arthur Andersen & Co., "Guide to Profit Improvement" (Subject File AD 1545, Item 7, 1981), pp. 6–7.
5. Thomas M. O'Brien, "Improving Performance Through Activity Analysis," in *Performance Excellence in Manufacturing and Service Organizations,* Proceedings of the Third Annual Management Accounting Symposium (Sarasota, FL: American Accounting Association, 1990), pp. 21–31.
6. Alfred J. Nanni, Jr., "Automation and Management Accounting in Japan," *Accounting: A Newsletter for Educators* (John Wiley, 1991), p. 5.
7. Peter F. Drucker, "Managing for Business Effectiveness," *Harvard Business Review* (May-June 1963), pp. 59–62.
8. H. Thomas Johnson and Robert S. Kaplan, *Relevance Lost: The Rise and Fall of Management Accounting* (Boston: Harvard Business School Press, 1987), ch. 6.

9. Johnson and Kaplan, *Relevance Lost,* ch. 8; Robin Cooper and Robert S. Kaplan, "Measure Costs Right: Make the Right Decisions," *Harvard Business Review* (September-October 1988), pp. 96–103.

10. The distinction between unit, batch, and product-level cost drivers, articulated originally by Robin Cooper of Harvard Business School, is the conceptual foundation that supports modern activity-based product costing. The definitive statement of this distinction is found in Robin Cooper, "Cost Classification in Unit-Based and Activity-Based Manufacturing Cost Systems," *Journal of Cost Management* (Fall 1990), pp. 4–14.

11. For a detailed example, see the story of "margin retreat" by SKF Bearings in George Stalk, "Time-The Next Source of Competitive Advantage," *Harvard Business Review* (July-August 1988), p. 43; also see Robin Cooper, "Schrader Bellows," Harvard Business School Case, numbers 6–186–050 et al. (1985).

12. This example comes from H. Thomas Johnson, "Managing Costs: An Outmoded Philosophy," *Manufacturing Engineering* (May 1989), p. 44.

13. Robin Cooper, "The Two-Stage Procedure in Cost Accounting: Part One," *Journal of Cost Management* (Summer 1987), pp. 43–51; Johnson and Kaplan, *Relevance Lost,* ch. 10.

14. Robin Cooper and Robert S. Kaplan, "Profit Priorities from Activity-Based Costing," *Harvard Business Review* (May-June 1991), pp. 130–135.

15. For an interesting perspective on the accuracy of ABC product cost information see Eric Noreen, "Are Costs Strictly Proportional to Their Cost Drivers?" Unpublished working paper (October 1990).

16. Samarbetande Konsulter AB, *Competitive Cost Management: How Companies Are Using New Costing Methods to Uncover Hidden Profits* (London: Business International Ltd Research Report No. 2054, 1990), passim.

17. Both examples and several paragraphs that follow are from H. Thomas Johnson, Thomas P. Vance, and R. Steven Player, "Pitfalls in Using ABC Cost-Driver Information to Manage Operating Costs," *Corporate Controller* (January-February 1991), pp. 26–32. Reprinted with permission of Faulkner & Gray, New York.

18. A. March and Robert S. Kaplan, "John Deere Components Work," Harvard Business School Case, number 91-87-107 (1987); Robert S. Kaplan, "Kanthal," Harvard Business School Case, number 9-190-002 (1989); Robin Cooper, *Journal of Cost Management,* four part series on "The Rise of Activity-Based Costing," Part One (Summer 1988), Part Two (Fall 1988), Part Three (Winter 1989), Part Four (Spring 1989) and "Cost Classification in Unit-Based and Activity-Based Manufacturing Cost Systems," (Fall 1990).

CHAPTER 9   PUTTING AN IMPROVEMENT PROCESS IN PLACE

1. Phone conversation with the author, May 2, 1991.

2. The following comments by Galvin of Motorola and Marous of Westinghouse Nuclear Fuel are from the official 1988 Malcolm Baldrige National Quality Award videotape interviews. The comment by Chris J. Fosse, Vice President of Quality at Blount, Inc., was made in a conference presentation given on October 4, 1991 in Portland, Oregon.

3. This section is based primarily on Thomas A. Stewart, "GE Keeps Those Ideas Coming," *Fortune* (August 12, 1991), pp. 41–49. Also see Noel Tichy and Ram

Charan, "Speed, Simplicity, Self-Confidence: An Interview with Jack Welch," *Harvard Business Review* (September-October 1989), pp. 112–120.

4. For an extended discussion of process mapping at GE see George D. Robson, *Continuous Process Improvement: Simplifying Work Flow Systems* (New York: The Free Press, 1991). A discussion of process mapping as it developed at IBM is found in H. James Harrington, *Business Process Improvement* (New York: Mc-Graw Hill, 1991).

5. The first two stages are discussed in H. Thomas Johnson, "Organizational Design versus Strategic Information Procedures for Managing Corporate Overhead Cost: Weyerhaeuser Company, 1972–1986," in William J. Bruns, Jr. and Robert S. Kaplan, eds., *Accounting and Management: Field Study Perspectives* (Boston: Harvard Business School Press, 1987), pp. 49–72. Also see H. Thomas Johnson and Dennis A. Loewe, "How Weyerhaeuser Manages Corporate Overhead Costs," *Management Accounting* (August 1987), pp. 20–26. Preliminary steps leading up to the third stage were described in Dennis A. Loewe, "Quality Management at Weyerhaeuser," *Management Accounting* (August 1989), pp. 36–41. Detailed information on the third stage is taken from an interview by the author with Dennis A. Loewe at Federal Way, Washington on March 29, 1991.

6. This section is based on John Case, "The Knowledge Factory," *INC.* (October 1991), pp. 54–59.

7. Ibid., p. 59.

8. M. Scott Myers, "Rethinking Your Reward System," *Target* (Special Issue 1991), pp. 25–33; Mary Walton, *Deming Management at Work* (New York: Perigee Books, 1991), pp. 219–231.

CHAPTER 10 NEW FRONTIERS FOR BUSINESS EDUCATION

1. Robert J. Samuelson, "What Good Are B-Schools?" *Newsweek* (May 14, 1990), p. 49.

2. "An Interview with Professor James E. Howell," by James W. Schmotter, in *Selections* (American Assembly of Collegiate Schools of Business, 1984). An interview with the co-author on the 25th anniversary of the publication of "The Gordon-Howell Report on Higher Education in Business," first published in 1959.

3. Robert H. Hayes, "Can Business Schools Help America Compete?" *Newsline* (American Assembly of Collegiate Schools of Business, December 1985), p. 5.

4. Robert S. Kaplan, "Quality in Business School Education and Research," presentation to Annual Meeting of American Assembly of Collegiate Schools of Business, St. Louis, MO, April 22, 1991.

5. Alan Deutschman, "The Trouble With MBAs," *Fortune* (July 29, 1991), pp. 67–78.

6. "Management Education: Passport to Prosperity," special supplement to *The Economist* (March 2, 1991).

7. I am indebted to Chuck Christenson of Harvard Business School for this anecdote on Kepler and Newton.

8. Theodore Levitt, "A Heretical View of Management 'Science,'" *Fortune* (December 18, 1978), p. 50.

9. Earl F. Cheit, "Business Schools and Their Critics," *California Management Review* (Spring 1985), p. 59.

10. See Barnaby J. Feder, "Moving the Pampers Faster Cuts Everyone's Costs" and "Partnering That Touched a Nerve," *New York Times* (July 14, 1991).
11. Ramchandran Jaikumar, "Postindustrial Manufacturing," *Harvard Business Review* (November-December 1986), p. 74.
12. H. Thomas Johnson, "Relevance Lost After Five Years," presentation to the Corporate Associates of the School of Business Administration at Portland State University, delivered April 24, 1991.

CHAPTER 11 THE INFORMATION REVOLUTION REVISITED

1. Ralph C. Stayer, "CEO Opinion: The Flight of the Buffalo," *Target* (Spring 1990), p. 18.
2. Richard J. Schonberger, *World Class Manufacturing: The Lessons of Simplicity Applied* (New York: The Free Press, 1986), p. 222; also see his *Building a Chain of Customers* (New York: The Free Press, 1990), ch. 2.
3. Karl E. Weick, "Substitutes for Strategy," in David J. Teece, ed., *The Competitive Edge* (New York: Harper & Row, 1987), p. 229.
4. Shoshana Zuboff, *In the Age of the Smart Machine* (New York: Basic Books, 1988). This paragraph and the next are drawn from pp. 9–12.
5. Ibid., p. 395.

ACKNOWLEDGMENTS

This book builds upon research into management methods and management accounting that I have conducted since 1969. Although my previous books acknowledge many of the debts I incurred in doing that research, I want to thank once again, if not name, the vast number of people and institutions who have assisted and encouraged my study of past and present uses of information in managed organizations. That research divides into three phases, and three books. The first phase focused on the evolution of management information in American industrial corporations during the nineteenth and early-twentieth centuries, when America's industrial system and management practices led the world. My research on that period culminated in *A New Approach to Management Accounting History* (New York: Garland Publishing, 1986), a collection of articles published during the 1970s and early 1980s. The second phase of my research compared the management information that companies used in the dynamic century of American industrial development before World War II with the management accounting practices observed in companies during the uncertain decades from the 1950s to the 1980s. In that work I collaborated with Robert S. Kaplan, with whom I coauthored *Relevance Lost: The Rise and Fall of Management Accounting* (Boston: Harvard Business School Press, 1987). The third phase of my research into management information is the subject of this book: the information businesses must have to compete in the global economy of the 1990s and beyond.

I developed ideas for this book between 1987 and 1991 in over a hundred presentations and more than twenty-five articles that dealt with questions not answered to my satisfaction in *Relevance Lost: The Rise and Fall of Management Accounting,* the precursor to this book that I co-authored with Robert S. Kaplan. Bob Kaplan participated with me in several of the early presentations and he reviewed and critiqued preliminary versions of most of those articles. Although our

217

ideas and interests have moved in quite different directions since we collaborated on *Relevance Lost,* Bob continues to give generous encouragement and assistance, for which I am enormously grateful.

An important new influence on my thinking after 1987 came from the field of operations management. I have benefited especially from ideas and encouragement received from Robert W. Hall (Indiana University), Peter C. Lamb (Andersen Consulting), Kenneth J. McGuire (Manufacturing Excellence Action Coalition), and Richard J. Schonberger (Schonberger & Associates). My collaboration on a book with Bob Hall in 1989 and 1990 helped sharpen many ideas used in this book.

Working as an advisor to the Operations Consulting practice of Arthur Andersen & Co. in 1989 and 1990 helped me explore and extend ideas first presented in *Relevance Lost.* I am especially grateful to Robert J. Berling, Jr., the partner in charge of Operations Consulting at that time, who enthusiastically and energetically led our team that developed a new consulting paradigm in Arthur Andersen known as "customer-focused activity management" (CFAM). For many ideas and insights from the field I thank the scores of Arthur Andersen partners, managers, and staff who participated in the CFAM design project, especially Greg Gleason, Jim Garman, Dan St. Peter, Tom Vance, Steve Player, Raul Mora, Ruben Montefalcone, Hector Estruga, Heinz-Jurgen Weiss, John Kerr, Eric Edelstein, John Teegarden, and Larry Wright. Other outside advisors to the CFAM project whose ideas and assistance were especially important to me include F. Brown Whittington (Emory University) and Barbara Feinberg, both of whom contributed significantly to my appreciation of customer relationship building, and Roy Shapiro (Harvard Business School), who added much to my understanding of factory management.

A major influence on this book was an invitation from the economic historian Peter Temin (Massachusetts Institute of Technology) to write a paper on management accounting history for a National Bureau of Economic Research project he directed in 1990. In that paper I articulated the idea of "management by remote control" that is a major theme in this book. I am grateful to Peter Temin for his invaluable help with shaping the content of that paper.

In the past year I have participated in a major initiative to introduce total quality management (TQM) into the School of Business at Portland State University. That experience advanced my appreciation of modern management practices more than any single event in the past five years. For increasing my awareness of the quality improvement process I am enormously grateful to my colleagues in Portland State's School of Business and to numerous quality-minded businesses in the Portland metropolitan area. In particular I want to thank my university colleagues Richard Sapp, Scott Dawson, Jerry Murphy, Ed Grubb, John Oh, Sully Taylor, Bill Manning, Jack Taylor, and Alan Raedels. Portland-area companies I want to thank for assisting me include Tektronix, Northwest Natural Gas, and the Oregon Cutting Systems Division of Blount, Inc.

I want to express my appreciation to the following people who read and provided written comments on manuscript versions of the book: Anthony Atkinson (University of Waterloo), Scott Dawson, William A. Golomski (W.A. Golomski & Associates and University of Chicago), Robert W. Hall, Kenneth J. McGuire, Thomas M. O'Brien (General Electric Company, retired), Harry V. Roberts (University of Chicago), Richard Sapp, and Richard J. Schonberger.

All writers owe a special acknowledgment to their editors who coax a manuscript along and then turn it into a finished book. I am no exception. I owe a very special thank you to Robert Wallace of The Free Press for his encouragement and continuing support of this project and to Lisa Cuff and Edith Lewis for shepherding the manuscript through myriad steps.

Finally, I thank my wife Elaine and my son Thom for unselfishly giving me the freedom to concentrate on writing about the world's businesses as they concentrated on the business of managing our household affairs while pursuing their own careers. Elaine also applied her considerable editing skills to the material presented here, as she has done with almost everything I have written in the last twenty years.

INDEX